REA

✓

The Eclipse of the State Mental Hospital

SUNY Series in the Sociology of Work
Richard Hall, Editor

The Eclipse of the State Mental Hospital

Policy, Stigma, and Organization

George W. Dowdall

STATE UNIVERSITY OF NEW YORK PRESS

Published by
State University of New York Press, Albany

©1996 State University of New York

Consolidated Standards Manual for Child, Adolescent, and Adult Psychiatric, Alcoholism, and Drug Abuse Facilities. Oakbrook Terrace, IL: Joint Commission on Accreditation of Healthcare Organizations, 1981, contents page. Reprinted with permission. "Standardization of Hospitals," American Journal of Psychiatry (October 1924): 399–402. Reprinted with permission. "Standards for Psychiatric Hospitals and Out-patient Clinics Approved by the American Psychiatric Association (1945–46)," American Journal of Psychiatry (September 1945): 264–269. Reprinted with permission. George W. Dowdall and Janet Golden, "Photographs as Data: An Analysis of Images from a Mental Hospital," Qualitative Sociology 12/2 (summer 1989): 183–213. Reprinted with permission. Material from the 1984, 1985, and 1986 editions of the Buffalo News are reprinted with permission of The Buffalo News. Selected passages from Chapter 4 of Care of the Seriously Mentally Ill: A Rating of State Programs, 3rd ed. (1990), Torrey, Erdman, Wolfe, and Flynn. Reprinted with permission of the National Alliance for the Mentally Ill.

For information, address State University of New York Press,
State University Plaza, Albany, NY 12246

Production by Laura Starrett
Marketing by Bernadette LaManna

Library of Congress Cataloging-in-Publication Data

Dowdall, George W.
    The eclipse of the state mental hospital / George W. Dowdall.
        p.   cm. — (SUNY series in sociology of work)
    Includes bibliographical references and index.
    ISBN 0-7914-2895-8 (hc). — ISBN 0-7914-2896-6 (pbk)
        1. State hospitals—United States—History .2. Buffalo State
Hospital—History.   3. Buffalo Psychiatric Center—History.
    4. Psychiatric hospital care—Government policy—United States.
    I. Title. II. Series.
    RC443.D68 1996
    362.2' 1 ' 0973—dc20   94-12517
                                                                          CIP

10 9 8 7 6 5 4 3 2 1

Contents

List of Figures

4

List of Tables

Acknowledgments

This research began while I was on a National Institute of Mental Health Postdoctoral Traineeship in "Epidemiology and Evaluation Methods in Mental Health" at the UCLA School of Public Health. Much of the research was done while I was a recipient of a "Fellowship for College Teachers" from the National Endowment for the Humanities, which also provided a "Travel to Collections" grant that supported gathering the data described in Appendix A. St. Joseph's University generously provided a leave of absence, a grant in aid, a summer research fellowship, a sabbatical year, and extensive computer and library facilities. The American Philosophical Society gave a grant to Janet Golden and me to analyze photographs of the Buffalo State Hospital. I wish to thank the American Psychiatric Association, the *Buffalo News*, Human Sciences Press, the Joint Commission on Accreditation of Healthcare Organizations, and the National Alliance for the Mentally Ill for permission to reproduce text and materials in Appendix B and elsewhere in the book. The map of Buffalo is used courtesy of the National Park Service, Frederick Law Olmsted National Historic Site. All other photographs appear courtesy of the Buffalo Psychiatric Center; the photographs were reproduced by Paul Pasquarella.

The three years I spent in the administration of the institution were invaluable to me and to this project, and have been followed by many visits and calls. It is a pleasure to thank the patients and staff of the Buffalo Psychiatric Center for their help in completing this research, but special thanks go to my colleagues in Program Evaluation (Elaine Hlastala, Rita Kirshstein, the late Joan Phillips, and Joe Stryjewski) and my other colleagues (Eileen Oviedo and Rich Panell); Sue Joffe was extremely helpful in answering my many questions and requests. The Buffalo-area research benefitted from the help of Shonnie Finnegan, David Gerber, Mark Goldman, Michael Katz, Gretchen Knapp, Frank Kowsky, Sister Mary Paul, Jean Richardson, Lily Sentz, and Mark Stern. Archivists and librarians at the College of Physicians of Philadelphia, Harvard University, St. Joseph's University, and the University of Pennsylvania were helpful. My colleagues at Buffalo State (especially Herb Aurbach, Vern Bullough, the late Doris Goggins, Bruce Johnstone, and Ray Waxmonsky); St. Joseph's University (especially Marybeth Ayella, Raquel Kennedy Bergen, Sylvia Clavan, Dan

Curran, Joanne Devlin, Paul Eisenhauer, Barbara Lang, Sally Milliken, Rob Moore, Joe Petragnani, and Claire Renzetti); Brown (Lois Monteiro) and Harvard (especially Henry Wechsler and Marianne Lee) have been very supportive. Several scholars offered advice at various points, especially Paul Allison, Ellen Dwyer, Bill Gronfein, Gerald Grob, Michael Hannan, Charles Rosenberg, Andrew Scull, John Sutton, and Nancy Tomes. Helpful editorial suggestions also came from Sue Baker, Paul Betz, Richard Koffler, Laura Starrett, Gladys Topkis, and Marlie Wasserman.

Several of the chapters were read closely by the Chester Avenue Seminar, with special thanks to David Allmendinger, Len Braitman, Cindy Little, Randall Miller, and Marion Roydhouse. Parts of the research were developed in papers I wrote with Janet Golden, Rita Kirshstein, James Marshall, Wayne Morra, and Diane Pinchoff. Joe Morrissey played a major role in setting the direction of this book. Peter Donaldson and Michael Goldstein were always available with advice, encouragement, support, and friendship. Janet Golden has been a superb friend and collaborator on this project from its beginning, and is the coauthor of the paper that is the basis for the beginning of chapter 6. Diane Pinchoff and Eric Schneider read the complete manuscript and offered invaluable advice. Chris Worden has been a very supportive editor. With all this help and advice, I am still solely responsible for any errors in the book.

Special thanks go to my friends who were particularly close to this project—Mary Crawford and Roger Chaffin, Judy and Alan Duchan, Larry Flood and Caroline Morell, Laura Geller, Alan Harler and Chuck Kalick, Sid and Michelle Harring, Ross and Meg Koppel, Marianna and Pat Luck, Matthew McClain and Doug Hamby, and Linda Wantman—all of whom played important roles in this and many other parts of my life.

And finally, I thank my entire family, especially my daughter Nina. But most of all I thank my wife Jean, to whom this is dedicated, with all my love.

Preface

I first saw the Buffalo State Hospital on a typical Buffalo day in 1971, with a heavy snowstorm driven by high winds off Lake Erie. My wife and I had come from Indiana to interview for sociology teaching jobs at Buffalo State College, and had been given a room in a high-rise dorm. I looked out the window, and saw, through the storm, an immense dark structure with two soaring towers. Like other viewers of Henry Hobson Richardson's master-piece of public architecture, I was stunned not just by its size, which appeared almost a half mile in length, but by its very presence. I certainly had no idea that much of the next period of my life would become enmeshed in that institution, or that I would join its staff, becoming one of the more than 100,000 people who have worked inside its walls or lived out their days in its wards since its opening in 1880. Our move to Buffalo in 1973 merely catalyzed my initially casual interest in this institution.

Books are often public answers to private questions, and this volume has more than its share of both. I want to answer the questions that would have occurred to you if you had been standing with me that day looking through the storm at the giant structure. What is that building? Who could have conceived such a plan, or convinced a state government to launch such an enterprise? What did its founders hope to achieve? Did they suc-ceed or fail? What was life like within its walls? Is it the same today at the Buffalo Psychiatric Center, the name that appears on the tall iron fences that surround its campus?

Some of the questions I will answer are historical, and so some of this book presents a social history of the founding and development of a single institution in Buffalo. Other questions are more sociological, asking about its organizational life. Why did New York commit its wealth so generously to the building of this asylum, and to the others that would make it the national leader in the care of the mentally ill during the late nineteenth and twentieth centuries? Why did an institution that at its founding was called "a most noble charity" end up as the object of public scorn and stig-matization? Was this Buffalo institution unique, or merely one of several hundred remarkably similar state institutions? Did it cure the insane, or merely provide custody to its inmates? Did the Asylum, like many reforms, initially meet the lofty goals of its founders, but then decline into a period of inertia and stagnation? Were the changes in its name—from "asylum" in 1880 to "hospital" in 1890 to "psychiatric center" in 1974—merely cosmetic, or indicative of deeper transformations? Finally, what difference did this institution make in the lives of its patients and its staff?

Although I first saw the state hospital buildings in 1971, the object of study of this book (the state hospital as an organizational form) emerged only after several more years had passed. My wife Jean and I accepted faculty positions at Buffalo State College, living with our daughter Nina a few blocks south of the big state hospital and walking, running, bicycling, driving, and, in the Blizzard of 1977, skiing through its grounds virtually every day for nine years. Through events having nothing to do with the hospital itself, I spent a year as a postdoctoral fellow at the UCLA School of Public Health in 1978–1979, and came back to Buffalo to begin my second career, now as a mental health researcher. Working with several collaborators, I used data from the state hospital to examine the long-term relationship between unemployment and mental hospitalization. I learned of an opening in the state hospital's program evaluation department, and joined that department for three years, serving as director for two years (see Dowdall and Pinchoff 1994). I became intrigued by how state hospitals functioned, and decided to study this issue in more depth and breadth. After moving in 1982 to St. Joseph's University in Philadelphia, I received a fellowship from the National Endowment for the Humanities. This allowed me to collect most of the data during 1986 for what I had assumed would be a short historical essay about just this one hospital. While on a research trip to Albany, I talked with Joe Morrissey, an expert on mental health policy, who first suggested I look at the hospital's history through the lens of the new organizational theory then being published. This suggestion led to the reorientation described in the introduction, and to a much broader project in which the Buffalo institution is compared with the whole population of state psychiatric hospitals to produce a comparative case study of an organizational form. Thus I present both a case study of one institution and a comparative examination of all—a comparative case study. I also argue that state hospitals can be understood as maximalist organizations, and the organizational theory that suggests this category helps in understanding the common elements that make the nineteenth-century asylum, the early- and mid–twentieth-century state hospital, and the late-twentieth-century public psychiatric center into developmental stages of the same organizational form. This organization is the pivot around which care for the seriously mentally ill revolves.

Chapter 1

State Mental Hospitals as the Organizational Pivot of Policy

For more than a century, state mental hospitals have served as the central organization for the care of the mentally ill, the pivot around which public policy has turned. But in the past few decades state hospitals have been eclipsed, by other organizations dealing with mental illness, by the stigma generated by mental illness, and by the spoiled image of institutional failure. The result is that even though state hospitals were, are, and will be centrally important to dealing with mental illness, we know little about this organizational form. The goal of this book is to shed light on the state mental hospital, for without understanding its history, present status, and future, we cannot hope to create effective social policy for the seriously mentally ill. And so this book is about the eclipse of the state hospital: how it came into being, and then how it managed to get lost in the shadows of public policy even when it remained central to that policy. The book is also about stigma: how the state hospital was brought into being to improve the care of the most stigmatized in society, those the nineteenth-century reformer Dorothea Dix might have called the insane poor, and how the state hospital unwittingly may have deepened their stigmatization. Finally, the book is about organization, in that it uses recent organizational studies to better understand what I will call a "maximalist organization," a class of organizations that live very long lives while being unusually resistant to change.

Making better and more effective policy about a complex issue like mental illness requires insight into the core organization that for many years was virtually the sole public policy response to this social issue. Even today, decades after the beginning of its eclipse by mental health organizations in the community, the state mental hospital receives more state funds for treating mental illness than any other public organization. But it is a measure of how deeply the eclipse has proceeded that few professionals in mental health care have spent much time at a state hospital and know little about the history of this organizational form.

This book is analytic and historical, not primarily prescriptive. It will meet its goal if its readers come to understand the historical and organizational forces that brought into being the center of today's mental health care system. But this understanding is crucial to improving that system of care, and so the book's goal is to illuminate public policy about the seriously mentally ill.

SERIOUS MENTAL ILLNESS

Serious mental illness is among the most widespread problems of our society, directly affecting two million Americans and indirectly touching the lives of all. A recent national study (Torrey, Wolfe, and Flynn 1988) concluded that "the lack of adequate services for the seriously mentally ill is *the* major failure of American medicine and social services." Like so many statements about serious mental illness, this statement is controversial. Because "mentally ill" is a term with no precise boundaries and encompassing many diverse subgroups, it is almost impossible to figure a way to test the veracity of the statement. But many advocates for the mentally ill insist it captures the exasperation that they feel about what they perceive as a major policy failure. If it is indeed failure, the failure comes with a very high price, a minimum of roughly eight cents of every dollar spent in the American health care system. Even that number is suspect, since the mental health portion of the cost of many programs such as housing or general health care, which provide some support to mentally ill people but which are not, strictly speaking, mental health programs, cannot easily be established.

Images of the problem of care for the seriously mentally ill sporadically capture public attention, but rarely engage sustained discussion. Paradoxically, the seriously mentally ill are perhaps more visible in the everyday world of American life today than they have been in a century, yet remarkably little is read or even written about them or about ways of addressing their problems. The situation of the homeless (a third or more of whom appear to experience serious mental illness) would seem to contradict this, but the tendency is to discuss their plight almost without any discussion of the social history of the treatment of the indigent mentally ill. It is as if what we call "homelessness" were a brand new problem, never before encountered by Americans. Almost nothing is said about how previous generations confronted the problem of mental illness. This silence is all the more true about the state mental hospital, which for over a century was the primary public policy response to serious mental illness. To understand our present crisis in providing care to the seriously mentally ill requires an understanding of the rise and transformation of the state mental hospital.

I argue in this book that state mental hospitals are the pivot around which public policy concerning the care of the seriously mentally ill has revolved for two hundred years. The state hospital is at the center of care in several senses: its emergence in the last century structured the entire institutional response to serious mental illness. For several generations the state hospital was the primary response, and for the past several decades its decline has been at the center of attempts to redirect public policy. The state hospital remains at the center, but it has become largely invisible. This book is written to shed light on its history, present, and future.

Historians have produced superb studies of colonial and nineteenth-century American mental health institutions, but few have examined the late nineteenth and current centuries, when modern mental health care institutions came into existence. By contrast, social scientists, particularly from World War II to the late 1960s, produced considerable research about the state hospitals of their day, but few today examine the state mental hospital or write about how public policy should be fashioned with regard to its existence. Thus the editor (Gallagher 1987) of the most important journal in medical sociology observed that one might think the mental hospital had simply disappeared from society, judging by how few papers about it were submitted (let alone published). In fact, the present mental health care system (whether for good or ill) remains anchored to the state mental hospital, and cannot be understood without appreciating its role, however changed or diminished.

Part of the problem is semantic, in that what was once called the state mental hospital has persisted, with major changes, under new names. For present purposes, the phrase *state mental hospital* will be used to discuss an organizational form which provides, primarily at public expense, inpatient care or custody of the seriously mentally ill drawn from the civilian population. This definition excludes public hospitals with specialized populations (for example, the VA system or federal hospitals for Indian nations), but includes institutions that for part of their history were controlled by other levels of government (for example, city or county units or a federal hospital such as St. Elizabeth's in the District of Columbia), whose organizational features make them similar to state hospitals. The definition also includes organizations that now bear names such as "Psychiatric Centers" but which in fact continue to focus on the inpatient care of patients with serious mental illness.

This book examines the evolution of the American state mental hospital, concentrating on the period from the Civil War to the present. The book is concerned with making generalizations about public policy, and so it is historical and comparative. But it also balances the 'thick description' of one prototypical state hospital against a comparative analysis of the national experience, thereby blending historical and sociological modes of understanding. The book bases some of its conclusions on an organization that for most of its life bore the name "The Buffalo State Hospital." Like most organizations, it is both unique in the facts of its founding, location, and the men and women who were its patients and staff, and indistinguishable in many basic ways from the several hundred state hospitals that made up American mental health care for so much of the past century. Just as C. Wright Mills once claimed about individual people, the biography of this one hospital cannot be understood without examining the larger history of American mental health care. And for most of its history, American mental health care was largely composed of huge enterprises like the Buffalo State Hospital.

To introduce the subject of the book and its main themes, we can look at two ceremonies that took place more than a century apart, both of which presented the institution to its public.

TWO CEREMONIES: 1872 AND 1980

Had it not been for the weather, the ceremony on September 18, 1872 would have been the grandest in Buffalo's history. Ex-President Millard Fillmore (now Chancellor of the University of Buffalo), Governor John T. Hoffman, and Buffalo's medical, business, and civic elites watched military bands and detachments of brightly uniformed troops perform their drill on the cleared field near the northern edge of the thriving city. After each notable in attendance bested the previous one in calling down divine blessings on the new enterprise and noting how splendidly it reflected the values of its founders and leaders, the Grand Mason set in place the cornerstone of the Buffalo State Asylum for the Insane. A copper box containing a history of the Asylum, United States' coins, the New York "civil list" for 1872, the latest annual reports of the other asylums of the state, and "copies of the latest issue of the several daily and weekly newspapers published in the City of Buffalo" was placed inside the cornerstone. The ceremony made the Asylum once again the leading subject of the city's many newspapers, which commented frequently and favorably on its development. The official account of the ceremony noted, "Thus has been inaugurated an institution which will be a monument to commemorate the founding of a most noble charity, creditable (sic) alike to the city and the State."

Over a century later, on November 18, 1980, a smaller audience sat inside the red brick auditorium of the Buffalo Psychiatric Center's modern, low-slung Rehabilitation Building to attend the 100th Anniversary of the admission of patients to the same institution. Its fourteenth director, Dr. Mahmud Mirza, shared the stage with Erie County executive Edward J. Rutkowski and read a telegram from the Governor of New York congratulating the institution on the centennial. (Mirza would soon leave his post amid rumors of scandal). In the eyes of several audience members, the ceremony was marred by the unwillingness of the president of the union representing its nonprofessional clinical staff to allow his union's lapel pin to be placed among the objects to be added to the time capsule. In a separate ceremony, the capsule was returned to the cornerstone of the immense nineteenth-century structure that served as the institution's administration building but no longer housed patients. Among the objects was a typed list of the 1,000 men and women who served in 1980 as its staff (one percent of those 100,000 persons who had lived or worked inside its walls during the past century). The ceremony was covered by Buffalo's two surviving daily newspapers, with stories far inside each paper's pages. Frontpage coverage of the institution was rare, and usually limited to the occasional scandal about bad treatment or poor management. National attention to its operation was virtually nonexistent and inevitably negative; a few years after the ceremony, a national survey of care for the mentally ill (Torrey, Wolfe, and Flynn 1988: 58) would label the institution "terrible."

These two ceremonies frame the subject of this book, the founding and first 110 years of operation of a large state institution known by three different names: the Buffalo State Asylum for the Insane (1869–1890), the Buffalo State Hospital (1890–1974), and the Buffalo Psychiatric Center (1974 to the present). My primary subject is not the care of the insane or the mentally ill, the practice of institutional psychiatry, or the social control of deviant and dependent populations, though these issues have been the subject of extensive writings by historians and sociologists concerned with similar institutions and will be discussed to the extent that they relate to my primary subject. Rather, this book examines an organization at the center of public policy and its persistence or change over a century.

A comparison of the two ceremonies helps introduce the book's major themes. Whatever else was celebrated at the centennial, certainly foremost was the continued existence of what I will later define more formally as a 'maximalist' organization. The second ceremony took place just yards away from the immense structure that opened in 1880, and that still stands today as the most visible reminder of the typical state mental hospital. Founded to bring about the most dramatic change in human behavior—to cure a malady thought by previous generations to be incurable by human effort—the institution soon became one of the most unchanging of organizations.

In part, this book is a narrative of how this institution came into being and persisted over time. But it is a narrative of an organization, not of an individual, and so its biography uses a framework developed largely from organizational studies to examine continuity and change. I will present some of this framework's main ideas later in this chapter. When the thematic issues of theory or method threaten to overwhelm the historical narrative, I have forced them into notes or appendices in favor of letting the story of the institution play through the text. While my focus is an institution largely shaped by social forces, I specify the men and women whose actions determined its structure and performance. My conception of the 'maximalist organization' includes the assumption that these individuals were constrained, perhaps as much as men and women ever can be, by the organization within which they worked. While the maximalist organizational character of the American mental hospital precluded change from occurring easily or frequently, it is equally true that the organization changed, not merely in name, but in some very basic if often not fully intended or understood ways. One of the central themes of the book, then, is how little or much an organization can change over time, and the degree to which this change is brought about through internal reorganization as opposed to externally induced adaptation. This focus makes the conclusions of this study directly applicable to discussion of mental health care policy, and each chapter addresses how the state hospital is the pivot around which mental health care policy revolves. A concluding chapter examines how the future of public mental health care will be shaped by the role the state hospital has played historically and will play in the coming years. It is my intention that this book not just be a case study of an organization, no matter how fascinating, but a comparative assessment of how that organization has shaped public policy.

Two distinct approaches are used to assess the outcome of care at the institution. First, contemporary mental health program evaluation techniques that employ social science measures and quantitative models are used retrospectively to evaluate the historical performance of the institution over its first century. In addition, more qualitative and critical methods are used. One of the most important consequences of the rise of mental hospitals has been a change in how Americans think about insanity or mental illness. The disappointingly low cure rates of the asylum are perhaps less important than the fact that generations of Americans began to see mental illness as curable, and then preventable, and began to think of organizations as producing or at least facilitating cures. Paradoxically, very low cure rates helped to legitimate the care received by the overwhelming majority of the not-yet-cured. Therefore, much of this book turns away from a quantitative analysis of outcome toward a more qualitative understanding of the organizational context in which "outcome," "care," and "cure" become products of a bureaucratic organization. Assessing the impact and quality of care are among the most important questions for the management of mental health care, and the concluding chapter will discuss these issues. Among the most important questions is an apparent paradox: the more money that is spent on the state mental hospital, the more the state hospital gets criticized for providing poor care.

Another major theme is the journey from the nineteenth-century origins of the state mental hospital, "a most noble charity," to its present state. Although the hospital's survival makes it among the most stable of institutions, it is among the most stigmatized as well. One of the goals of this study is to assess the persistence of an organization that failed almost immediately to meet the goals set for it by its founders and sponsors, yet continued to expand and even thrive after its so-called "failure." More broadly, this book will discuss in detail the evaluation of the mental hospital's record of care across its long history.

Finally, the book rests on a combination of methods. Historical documents and newspaper accounts permit the reconstruction of the two ceremonies, but I sat in the audience of the second one, and my name is on the list of the staff who were then working at BPC. While I played a modest role in its administration, my role in it introduces some potential problems of involvement and bias. With good reason, those who write about the history of organizations usually end their narratives well before the present day, allowing a period of time to elapse so that a somewhat more objective, disinterested assessment of the past can be made. I violate this norm by writing about how the past blends into the present, and by writing about a period of time in which I was a participant. If my participation implies a bias, it is almost certainly a unique one in the literature, for my familiarity is with the world of the nonmedical administration, not with that of the patient or the clinical staff. Moreover, my job was to try to evaluate the effectiveness of the clinical programs, using social science methods and frameworks to measure the outputs of this organization. But I have tried to reduce whatever purely personal point of view I might bring by employing standard scholarly methods for evaluating arguments.

Writing about a highly stigmatized subject like a mental hospital inevitably involves an evaluation of its role. That I worked for several years in its administration makes me much more reluctant to join fellow social scientists whose writings usually have taken a highly critical and often condemnatory stand when writing about mental hospitals (for example, Goffman 1961; Rothman 1971; Scull 1977). But my own research and experience hardly leave me uncritical. Some of the stigma attaching to mental hospitals is richly deserved. The use of the word "asylum" in the early parts of the book emphasizes the humanitarian goals that I believe were a genuine part of the founding of these institutions, but the pages that follow document how, just as with most human action, complex and often contradictory values and interests shaped the origins and development of the state hospital. At its lowest point, the institution fully deserved the epithet "snakepit." How the same very stable organization could wear both titles teaches an important lesson about the social construction of organizational images.

I argue here (and later chapters provide considerable evidence for this argument) that the Buffalo Asylum is a representative case we can use to study much more general trends at work in the entire population of state hospitals. This argument is all the stronger given the special importance that national standards have played in shaping the state hospital. Because these standards are so crucial to my argument, and because they have never been collected and published in one place, I have assembled them in Appendix B.

The historical narrative that makes up some of this book describes the unique events in the Buffalo State Hospital's history. For reasons explained later in this chapter, I compare its history with the entire population of American mental hospitals. I accomplished this by coding and analyzing data from national surveys (undertaken originally by reformers both inside and outside government) of mental institutions at several points in time to present a 'comparative case study' of the Buffalo State Hospital. I attempt to make clear the ways that the Buffalo hospital differed from its sister institutions across the United States, and I present a reconstruction of the loose set of organizations that provided Americans with mental health care in the late nineteenth and twentieth centuries.

This study is socio-historical, blending historical and sociological styles of evidence and analysis. Its conclusions are based on both primary and secondary historical evidence, including the rich archival records found in the institution's medical and administrative departments and in its published annual reports and those of its oversight and management agencies. Other forms of evidence range from the more than 800 photographs that documented daily life at the hospital to the hundreds of local newspaper stories written about the hospital. But the historical narrative answers questions shaped not only by previous historical research but also by sociological theory. Sociological sources include the coding of detailed data on over four thousand individual patients, surveys of U.S. mental hospitals at various points in time, and statistical time series constructed about important measures of the institution's history. For the most part the analysis is historical; the book is an essay that interprets events in the changing context of local and state care for the insane. When possible, I have employed statistical analyses to assess quantitative information, but I confine much of these analyses, along with detailed discussions of the historical evidence, to appendices and footnotes. Quantitative evidence is presented primarily in graphs, which allow a much broader audience to examine these data than would be possible with just statistical discourse. Brief explanations of these statistical issues for the benefit of readers who wish to assess how statistical techniques such as time-series analysis and event-history analysis can help illuminate the study of historical and social change. These discussions too are separated from the main text.

CONTRIBUTION OF THIS BOOK

Why do contemporary mental health reformers and policy makers almost inevitably ignore the state hospital, a central and even pivotal institution in public mental health care? The goal of this book is to help inform public policy discussions by shedding light on an organization largely eclipsed by the rise of other and more recently founded organizations. Some of the light is provided by fusing organizational perspectives with both a view back at history and a glimpse into the future.

This book goes beyond the 'focal organization' approach previously used to study individual mental hospitals by applying several contemporary approaches to organizations of this type. While mental hospitals have been examined by sociologists from Goffman, Belknap, and Parsons to Perrow, Scott, and Scull, no previous study has applied these several approaches to these institutions. I will blend organizational and historical perspectives to examine an entire organizational form from its infancy to the present. First, I will present a detailed overview of how religious, political, class, and medical motivations combined to make the drive to build asylums for the insane a major part of the growth of the institutional state during the last century. The book will account for the rise of the asylum, drawing on the literature of the population ecology of organizations to build and test several models about their founding and failure and to test those models against data on the entire population of American state mental institutions. But I will also offer a detailed case study of the founding and development of the Buffalo Asylum, viewed as an example of a maximalist organization. I will discuss how the struggle for the professionalization of medicine, combined with the movement for Buffalo civic reform and conflict among the city's emerging upper class, led to its founding. While eventually the asylum would come under state control, its early years were shaped by unique local forces. Its immense building wedded the psychiatric orthodoxy of the day with remarkable innovations in architecture and urban design. Once it opened, Judson B. Andrews, the Asylum's first superintendent, created an organization and crafted the one major innovation the Buffalo Asylum contributed to American mental health care, namely, a training school for nurses. This unwittingly contributed toward the transformation of the asylum into a custodial state hospital. Using unpublished records on thousands of patients admitted in its first decade, I will evaluate the care given the insane by the state asylum, a county poorhouse it competed with, and a small private institution run by a religious order. I examine as well the very low rates of recovery produced by the asylum, and explore reasons why the largely stagnant support provided by the public led to an inert institution for much of the present century. The American state mental hospital represents a prototypical example of, in the words of Meyer and Zucker (1989), a "permanently failing organization."

To many contemporary observers, some of them critics of these huge institutions, the state hospital of the early and mid–twentieth century seemed inert, perhaps hopelessly so. But I will trace the increasingly dynamic changes that transformed the institution since the 1940s and resulted in a very different, albeit very troubled, organization. A major force in these changes were the efforts, successful and otherwise, to meet the increasingly elaborate standards imposed from without on the state mental hospital. I will examine the proposition, implicit but untested in much writing about the mental hospital, that the entire set of institutions became remarkably similar in everyday operation, offering an example of 'institutional isomorphism' powerfully shaped by public policy initiatives. Since funding is assumed to be crucial in setting the quality of care, I will review recent empirical research about funding and also about variation in quality among contemporary American state hospitals. The book's focus on policy will lead to a concluding discussion of the implications of the study for both mental health care policy and for the management of mental health care institutions, as well as for the further study of the mental health care system and its component organizations. Given its continued persistence even after "deinstitutionalization," what role does the state mental hospital play in the current system of care for the seriously mentally ill? What role should it play?

Appendix B presents the national standards for state mental hospitals from the 1840s to the present, though the length of recent standards precludes presenting more than informative summaries. This appendix allows inspection of an absolutely central institutional force in shaping the state mental hospital as an organizational form. Though the standards are discussed in detail in the body of the text, I felt Appendix B was essential, in that it provides a unique window through which we can view the norms against which state hospitals were judged. Placing these standards together allows comparison across the entire history of the organizational form. (This is particularly valuable for organizational analysis, where few instances come to mind of attempts at mapping out standards so clearly.)

This study builds on previous historical research on the mental hospital as well as on theories, models, and methods for the study of complex organizations. When organizational theory and historical research converge, we begin to understand the state mental hospital as an organization whose early years decisively shaped its history. The book does not offer the usual narrative of an organizational history, because it looks more closely at turning points than at periods of relative stability. The book examines in detail the founding and early years of the organization. The period from the beginning of the twentieth century to the end of World War II is treated more briefly, since I establish that, aside from population-driven growth, relatively little changed in the organization's structure and function during that period. By contrast, I look in detail at the dramatic changes that emerged when both funding and standards changed beginning in the late 1940s, and at how the last few decades have witnessed the transformation of what had been considered an utterly unchanging and unchangeable organization (Goffman 1961).

Finally, the book does not try to dictate prescriptions for how to change mental health care, but it does explain how a seemingly unchangeable central institution in that system of care has been transformed over the past decades. I believe that state hospitals (or something very much like them) will be a necessary component for public psychiatry for the foreseeable future. This study attempts to explain how state hospitals as maximalist organizations have both survived into the present, but also how they have been changed in important ways. Understanding that even these organizations can change (and understanding how to change them) will be of value in changing care for the seriously mentally ill, of more value than merely advocating a set of abstractly sketched changes might be.

STATE MENTAL HOSPITALS AS MAXIMALIST ORGANIZATIONS

In examining the rise and development of the state mental hospital, it is critical to keep in mind that the type of organization the American mental hospital was at its founding would shape much of its later history. Simply stated, the decisions made by the founders and sponsors in the early and mid-nineteenth century made certain outcomes likely, perhaps even inevitable. In seeking to apply lessons learned from an historical examination of state mental hospitals, it is also critical to understand that these decisions were determined by unique historical factors, and that understanding these factors can help to make the decisions we now face somewhat wiser ones.

Both historical and organizational understandings of the state mental hospital push toward a new model of understanding them as "maximalist organizations." This chapter reviews both the historical and organizational arguments, and then presents a portrait of state hospitals as maximalist organizations. The chapter helps connect this book to the efforts to understand state hospitals not only as historically unique institutions, but also as instances of more general organizational patterns.

HISTORICAL PERSPECTIVES

Because it represents a unique type of organization, the American mental hospital has been the object of considerable historical study. Rather than trying to summarize or duplicate the rich and extensive literature in this area, I will try to indicate how this book's role is different from other contributions. Citations to other work will guide the reader interested in a fuller discussion of the literature to several excellent but lengthy critical reviews, as well as to the extensive earlier literature by other scholars.

Over two decades ago, Rothman (1971: 306) claimed, "There are very few histories of state or private mental hospitals . . . We stand in clear need of research that will carefully and imaginatively relate the histories of these structures to the general society." Citing a collection of almost 170 studies, most published since Rothman's comment, Dwyer (1988: 156) characterized the literature on 'the modern history of madness' as revolving around several basic themes: "troubled domestic relationships, inadequate nosologies and unreliable diagnoses, [and] institutional conflicts between therapeutic and custodial goals. Despite the proliferation of detailed studies of individual mental hospitals . . . scholars have neither been able to resolve these problems nor produce a consensus on their relationship to macro-level social and economic changes." Commenting on psychiatric sociology, the primary field of research about the contemporary mental health system, Brown (1985: 230) notes that this field will have to catch up with medical sociology in recognizing the inseparability of the health care system from the rest of society.

In this respect, historians and sociologists have produced research about the care of the seriously mentally ill that looks at different time periods but shares the same basic weakness: a failure to examine interconnections within the broader social and economic environment of whatever period they are considering. This study of the state mental hospital, which views these institutions in the light of recent organizational thinking, will help explain those interconnections, particularly by taking into account the behavior of the mental hospital as a "maximalist organization."

The first historical assessment of the rise of mental hospitals (Deutsch 1949) saw great progress in the first quarter of the nineteenth century: new institutions were established for the first time in eight different states, and Virginia added its second. The culmination of this progress was the introduction of state care for the insane of New York State, a "great milestone" in the history of the treatment of mental illness in this country. The creation of the several hundred state mental hospitals that eventually followed this early wave was, according to Deutsch, the manifestation of humanitarian reform.

By contrast, other literature takes almost the opposite viewpoint. Contemporary mental institutions were examples of total institutions, organizations oppressive in essence rather than merely deficient in operation. In Erving Goffman's classic *Asylums* (1961), the incarceration of inmate populations could not possibly reflect humanitarian intent. The total transformation of the inmate's sense of self admits to no other purpose than coercion. Not coincidentally, although hardly noticed by his first reviewers, Goffman rejected any historical or developmental understanding of asylums, seeing them as beyond history, as unchanging essences.

During the 1960s, these laudatory and condemnatory images of the mental hospital were joined by more complex and necessarily more historical views. Gerald Grob (1966) contributed a detailed case study of the early nineteenth century's most influential institution, the Worcester State Hospital, and followed this with a comparative analysis (1973) of the many dozen institutions founded before 1875. He later produced a study (1983) of how American society faced the problem of mental illness in the period from 1875 to 1940. A more recent book (1991) brings the story forward to 1970, with the deinstitutionalization movement transferring care from asylum to community.

For Grob, humanitarian intentions were tempered by a changing social reality that gradually transformed the early nineteenth-century curative asylum into the late nineteenth-century custodial mental hospital. Grob (1979) viewed the American mental hospital as "not fundamentally dissimilar from most human institutions, the achievements of which usually fall far short of the hopes and aspirations of the individuals who founded and led them." The somewhat misleading label of "neo-Whig" has been offered as a summary of this position, though it clearly is a caricature of Grob's very complex stance.

A darker and more skeptical perspective challenged Grob's view. Beginning with Foucault's *Madness and Civilization* (1965), and culminating in the writing of David Rothman and Andrew Scull, an influential series of works presenting what has been termed the "social control" perspective were published during the 1970s. Though differing on many details, these writers saw the rise of asylums and mental hospitals as parts of the maturation of a society organized around the market place. Institutions were built as response to fears about disorder (Rothman 1971), or reflected the concern of an emerging bourgeoisie to protect its economic self interest (Scull 1977). To be sure, these exponents of the "social control" position were taking much more complex positions than the label affixed to their work implies.

As Dwyer (1988) has recently observed in her comprehensive account of recent work about the mental hospital's history, a new set of writers has tackled the historical problem of the asylum, generally setting a course somewhat between the revisionist or neo-Whig and the social control positions. These new voices tend to call attention to the complexity of the historical patterns they analyze, noting the degree to which neither of the earlier approaches captures all of the reality. Among the very best and complex accounts of the nineteenth-century asylum is her exploration of life in two New York asylums (Dwyer 1987).

Several important questions about American mental hospitals remain unanswered, and it is to these that the present study is directed. First, the earlier debate contrasted humanitarian intentions with institutional realities, suggesting (but not really proving) that the typical mental hospital *declined* in quality. But only one institution (the Worcester State Hospital) has been studied for a long enough period of time to assess change in institutional performance, and with ambiguous results. On the one hand, studies by Grob (1966) and Morrissey et al. (1980) suggest significant change in the hospital as an organization, not merely changes in the characteristics of patients admitted to the institution (although both changes are assumed to have occurred). On the other hand, Bockoven's (1956) assessment of the long-term trend in the recovery rates of the institution suggest an early decline, followed by many decades of stability. Did the hospital change in significant ways, or was there only a change in the type of patient admitted? Did the increasing admissions of the elderly, with poor prognosis of recovery, doom the state hospital to an almost purely custodial role? Was the early success of the mental hospital in the era of moral treatment followed by a real decline in the efficacy of care? These questions require a longer period of study than much of the recent research literature on mental hospitals employs. Moreover, the questions assume that adequate "outcome measures," or ways of assessing the effect of care upon patients, can be compared across a relatively long period of historical time. The present research will inquire into the adequacy of these measures, and discuss the degree to which these questions can be answered retrospectively.

A second broad question concerns the environment. Previous research on the American mental hospital frequently viewed it as a tightly bounded system, in one case even comparing it to a small society (Caudill 1958). Much of the evidence about the institutions successfully studied has been gathered from the internal documents and annual reports of each institution. But if we are to examine the external environment, we should look at the organization in its communal and societal environment—reflecting Rothman's suggestion that we need to link the mental hospital to the surrounding society. As will be argued later in more detail, this is all the more true if we accept the assumption of current organizational theory that change in organizations comes largely from without. So this book examines how influences far beyond the institution's walls combined to change its character. Policy, funding, the changing role of psychiatry, the increased involvement of families, and the patients' rights movement all affected the mental hospital's life.

A third broad question deals with the historical era of the study. Historical accounts of the mental hospital have generally been confined to the nineteenth century, while sociological discussions usually focus on contemporary events, rarely looking at more than the very recent past. The result of these practices is that we now know a lot about mental hospitals before the turn of the present century, and have some impressive portraits scattered through the period from the Second World War through the early

days of deinstitutionalization. With the beginnings of deinstitutionalization, contemporary researchers largely abandoned the study of the mental
hospital, no doubt believing that its imminent demise made it an unlikely
subject of study (Gallagher 1987). By contrast, an extensive literature grew
about new mental health care institutions, with separate journals publishing studies of community mental health care and partial hospitalization.
This book examines a mental hospital from its mid–nineteenth-century
origins to the present. The disadvantages (such as not enough time elapsing
to assess the recent history of the institution and lack of access to historical
documents beyond those in the public domain) are more than outweighed
by the advantages, for the most part because a long time span allows a more
adequate understanding of how an organization changes.

A fourth gap concerns the nature of the mental hospital. No study
explicitly examines the mental hospital in the light of current theory and
research about organizational dynamics. While much of the historical literature implies that the mental hospital proved an unwieldy, unresponsive,
and almost unchanging instrument in the hands of its founders and their
successors, no study has yet examined whether this might be as much the
product of its organizational features as of the characteristics of its patients
or staff and the absence of effective therapies. Several of the most promising
advances in organizational studies (such as neoinstitutional theory and
population ecology) have occurred quite recently and are not reflected in
even the most recent wave of scholarship about the history of social control
(Scull 1988) or the asylum (Dwyer 1988).

ORGANIZATIONAL PERSPECTIVES

What can we learn about mental health policy by focusing on the state
mental hospital as an organization, and how should we examine its history?
This book examines the organizational history of the American mental
hospital by providing a comparative case study of the Buffalo State Hospital. In addition to those aspects of the hospital's history that previous historical research suggests as important, I begin by reviewing the major perspectives on organizational foundings and development employed in recent
studies of organizations. While there are, of course, diverse perspectives on
organizations, several main approaches are of particular value to this study.

Focal-Organization Perspective

Much of the literature on organizations written before the 1970s adopted
this perspective, usually providing a single case study of a particular organization at a single point in time or over a very short period of time, and
assuming the organization to be a self-contained and independent entity. A
central theme of this approach is to view organizations as rational tools for

the attainment of goals, at least to some degree the reflection of the goals of their founders, managers, or directors. This leads toward a tendency to think "anthropomorphically" about organizations, as if they were themselves social actors trying to achieve goals.

In general, the focal-organizational perspective tends to assume that organizations are able to change easily. March (1981: 563) argues that, in the face of the appearance of their resistance to change, in fact they are "frequently transformed into forms remarkably different from the original." Though organizational change cannot be controlled arbitrarily, nonetheless organizations "are continually changing, routinely, easily, and responsively." In the words of its foremost critics, the focal-organization approach views organizations as "rational, flexible, and speedy adapters to changing environmental circumstances" (Hannan and Freeman 1989: xi).

Can state hospitals change? Sometimes the application of the focal-organization approach to the study of state mental hospitals has resulted in research that tends to confirm the ability of an organization to change in the face of new circumstances (for example, Shulman 1969; Levine 1980; Pinchoff and Mirza 1982). The more common view, however, is of the state mental hospital as an actor frustrated in its ability to achieve contradictory goals.

One of the classic studies of state mental health care might be grouped under this perspective. Ivan Belknap's *Human Problems of a State Mental Hospital* (1956) examined daily life at "Southern State Hospital," based on extensive field work over a three year period. Belknap (1956: xi) argued that "nearly all these hospitals have become organized in such a way during their historical growth that they are probably themselves obstacles in the development of an effective program for treatment of the mentally ill." After a detailed analysis of the organizational problems of this state hospital, Belknap concluded:

> one fact seems to stand out: from the time of its foundation the hospital has been defined as an institution which must carry out two contradictory and essentially unrelated functions. One of these functions was that of treating the mentally ill. The other was that of serving as a more efficient poor farm, with more centralized organization. The isolation of the hospital, its self-contained industrial and agricultural functions, its general low status, and its constitutional responsibility for the indigent insane are all facts which speak plainly. (Belknap 1956: 204)

Erving Goffman's *Asylums* (1961), among the most influential and important works of American social science, painted a vivid picture, in the most somber hues, of inmate life inside a state hospital. Goffman's participant observation inside St. Elizabeth's Hospital (a federal psychiatric facility which functioned very much like a large state mental hospital) was the most often used to assess models employ challenging, if not daunting, approaches, limiting discussion and debate to a select few (Young 1988). Finally, the seemingly endless debate among social scientists about the proper mixture of meaning and measurement usually is resolved in the direction of a highly positivistic emphasis on measurement, yet remarkably little discussion of even basic issues such as reliability and validity, let al.one questions of causal inference, are routinely presented (Lieberson 1985).

A central question awaiting further clarification concerns one of the key differences between the focal-organization and population ecology approaches: how much do or can organizations change? Singh (1988: 322) observes that "the relative role of adaption and selection processes in population change is still an open question." Singh notes that organizational ecologists have looked to founding and death processes to understand how populations change over time "with the assumption that organizational forms do not change significantly over time. Although this is a critical assumption, it has not been addressed empirically."

Marxist and Critical Theories of Organizations

A very different form of organizational perspective—Marxist and critical analyses of social control organizations—focuses less on the internal organization questions noted above, and more on the connection between social control organizations and societal elites.

Reviewing historical and sociological studies of social control, Scull (1988: 685) notes that it has "suddenly acquired a new cachet," in part showing the impact of the work of such scholars as Goffman and especially Foucault. The new work developed in contrast to an older tradition that viewed social control as the expression of "fundamental shared needs," in that it sees "the relationships between 'society' and 'social control' as problematic and contingent over space and time." This new work emphasizes historical study of the apparatus of social control "fashioned through the visible hand of definable organizations, groups, and classes, rather than being 'naturally' produced by the invisible hand of society" (Scull 1988: 686).

Scull's own work (1975, 1976, 1979, 1989) constitutes one of the most successful and thorough explorations of this terrain, in that it examines in detail the development of the psychiatric profession in the United States and Britain and the incarceration of the insane in asylums and mental hospitals, largely at state expense. Employing a sophisticated historical analysis of the interaction of class interest, professional knowledge, state development, and social control, Scull's work implies assessment of mental hospitals as anything but simple instruments wielded by a knowing elite, and moves the study of social control well beyond the confines of an "instru-

basis for a series of searing images of the degradation of inmate life inside a huge federal hospital, differing only in minor details from life in the larger state hospitals of the late 1950s. Goffman's argument implies as well that state hospitals further undercut the mental stability of those unfortunate enough to be admitted (see Gronfein 1992).

The balance of the research produced by focal-organizational studies of state mental hospitals shows little evidence that they function as adaptive organizations in the short run; nonetheless, the record is mixed. The strengths of the focal-organization perspective would seem obvious. Research guided by this perspective yields vivid, insightful, and detailed portraits of the daily life of an organization. The analysis usually makes use of "experience near" language and concepts (Geertz 1983: 57), which present a high degree of verisimilitude and seem to promise insight into the actual workings of the organization. But the weaknesses are also noteworthy. Are these typical organizations? How much change actually takes place over time, particularly over the long run? Even when change can be identified as occurring, how much change results from the conscious or intended efforts of participants (including managers and directors), and how much stems from unconscious or unintended adaptation to environmental forces? These are important questions that the focal-organization approach does not (and perhaps cannot) address.

Institutional Theories of Organization

During the 1970s, students of organization began to move away from models that stressed rationality as the key to understanding organizational change. In part, this shift was a reaction to the tendency to interpret organizational structure as the product of technical production processes operating at the core of a particular organization. In part, the change was due to a new appreciation of the important role the broader culture played in shaping organizational behavior. This led to an interest in the specific cultures of organizations (Ouchi and Wilkins 1985). Leadership in organizations could be understood by contrasting the frames within which leaders formulated behavior (Bowman and Deal 1984, 1991).

One major direction has emphasized the institutional environment (understood in broadly cultural terms) as a major force shaping organizational behavior. While significant differences exist among the adherents of this position, several key themes bring some unity to what we call here "institutional theories of organization." Thus, Meyer and Rowan argued in a widely cited paper that organizations come into being in contexts with strong normative expectations: "Professions, policies, and programs are created along with the products and services that they are understood to produce rationally . . . That is, organizations are driven to incorporate the practices and procedures . . . institutionalized in society" (Meyer and

Rowan 1977; in Meyer and Scott 1983: Ch. 1). Those organizations that do so have much higher chances of surviving than those that do not.

As the title of their paper, "Institutionalized Organizations: Formal Structure as Myth and Ceremony" implied, a highly institutionalized organization's formal structure could be examined as "myth and ceremony," not just as some rational means for attaining organizational goals. The subparts of organizations were often "loosely coupled," a phrase introduced into the literature in a study that probed the reasons why actual classroom behavior had become disconnected from formal and public educational goals (Weick 1976).

The institutional approach has generated some provocative and useful arguments about the direction of organizational development. A central theme of Weber's early work on bureaucratization was the seemingly inexorable "rationalization of the world" that proceeded with the development of capitalist economic growth, imprisoning more and more inside the "iron cage" of bureaucratic work organization. DiMaggio and Powell (1983: 147) note that the bureaucratization of the state and the corporation predicted by Weber has been largely achieved. Structural change that makes "organizations more similar without necessarily making them more efficient" is now driven by other forces. Three processes push organizations toward greater similarity, or what they term "institutional isomorphism":

1. *coercive isomorphism*, resulting from both informal and formal pressure exerted by other organizations;

2. *mimetic isomorphism*, in which organizations faced with uncertainty model themselves on others; and

3. *normative isomorphism*, largely the product of professionalization, through which professional cultures are diffused through a set of organizations.

Over time, these three sources of isomorphism should produce greater and greater similarity across different organizations in a particular sector of activity.

The institutionalist approach in organizational studies has already proved to be stimulating and provocative, moving the focus of analysis away from an overreliance on rational and anthropomorphic models. But it is not without its own set of limitations. Key concepts such as "loose coupling" are used without precise definition, and become almost ritual incantations that replace rather than refine analysis. It is often unclear what agent or agents produce the effects; instead, impersonal social forces (described in sentences featuring the passive voice; see Becker 1986: 7–8 and 79–80) arise out of modern society to bring about events. As DiMaggio

(1988: 3) notes, institutional theory often 'defocalizes' interest and agency, stressing instead "the identification of causal mechanisms leading to organizational change and stability on the basis of preconscious understandings that organizational actors share independent of their interests." Data are used to illustrate but not to test ideas, resulting in only modest progress and in theory that is not robust (Meyer and Scott 1983: 105).

Population Ecology of Organizations

The most dramatic shift in organizational studies in recent years has occurred as a result of the rise of the "population ecology of organizations." The shift began with its founders' discontent with existing focal-organization approaches. Thus, Hannan and Freeman (1989) were dissatisfied with the drawbacks of this approach, particularly with its assumptions that organizations adapted easily and quickly, that organizations could be understood anthropomorphically, and that diversity in organizational populations could be explained by individual adaptations. In several key papers (Hannan and Freeman 1974; 1977), they argued for models drawn from population ecology, emphasizing selection as the central process in explaining change in organizational populations.

The population ecology of organizations developed by Hannan and Freeman (1989) includes several unique features that separate it from competing approaches in organizational studies, most importantly its stance about how little individual organizational forms change. Unlike earlier approaches, the ecological approach assumes that powerful forces within and outside organizations press toward structural inertia. Change among organizations largely occurs at the population, rather than at the individual level, and is the product of differential founding and mortality, not of adaptation. Thus, the student of organizations should shift his or her focus away from short-term adaptations of the largest or longest-lived organizations, viewed cross-sectionally or over fairly short time periods. The focus of study should therefore be toward the dynamics of population change, necessarily over the full histories of populations. Finally, research on organizations should develop "tight links between theory, models, and empirical research," eschewing the tendency to develop each of these areas in relative isolation from the others.

To be sure, the population ecology approach has several key problems, some of which are shared with its competitors. Important concepts—such as "competition" and "legitimacy"—remain either undefined or unmeasured (Zucker 1989). Particularly troubling is the fact that, despite its commendable interest in assessing the long-term history of entire organizational populations, the conceptualization and measurement of historical context remains primitive and even antagonistic to genuine historical discourse (Isaac and Griffin 1989; Zucker 1989). The quantitative methods

mentalist" theory of the state or its constituent organizations (Harring 1983: Ch. 1).

A central issue posed by Marxist and critical theorists of social control "points to economic structures and to the activities of the state as crucial explanatory variables" (Scull 1988: 687). On the one hand, the founding and growth of state mental hospitals were part of the enormous expansion of the "institutional state" in nineteenth-century America (Katz 1978), and, along with schools, functioned as one of the central forces in the development of the "semiwelfare" state. On the other hand, mental hospitals were part of the immense reorganization of daily life carried on during the development of capitalism. Thus, Braverman presents a vision of the growth of both the mentally ill and the institutions created to house them. As capitalism develops,

> the care of humans for each other becomes increasingly institutionalized . . . the massive growth of institutions stretching all the way from schools and hospitals on the one side to prisons and madhouses on the other represents not just the progress of medicine, education, or crime prevention, but the clearing of the marketplace of all but the "economically active" and "functioning" members of society, generally at public expense and at a handsome profit to the manufacturing and service corporations who sometimes own and invariably supply these institutions. (Braverman 1974: 279–280)

Marxist and critical approaches to organizational study demand attention to the role that elites—professional, class, or political—play in founding and directing organizations, and push investigation into the interests, both material and ideological, that shape governance. While not without their own drawbacks, particularly a tendency to reduce ideas to mere ideologies and to credit elites with more foresight and coordination than perhaps deserved, Marxist and critical approaches do focus, more sharply than any other approaches, on the links between an organization and its surrounding environment.

LINKING ORGANIZATIONS AND HISTORY

Having reviewed several of the leading approaches in organizational studies, we can now return to the question of examining the history of American mental hospitals. If the goal (Rothman 1971) is to develop a history of the mental hospital that "carefully and imaginatively" relates its history to that of the surrounding society, then the previous section's discussion should suggest several bridges between organizational analysis and historical development. The preceding discussion is suggestive but not exhaustive, and is meant to present in a very schematic form the quite different concerns that each of the perspectives has about the development of an organizational form like the state mental hospital. When combined, the approaches help to illuminate different aspects of organizational change (DiMaggio and Powell 1983: 157).

The goal, then, is to build a model of the state mental hospital that is both truly historical and truly sociological (Skocpol (1984). Using such an approach means moving beyond the tendency, embedded deeply in some modes of organizational analysis, to ignore historical context in favor of an ahistorical preoccupation with structure. As Fombrun (in Carroll 1988: 236) has argued, "For organizational researchers, this means that quantitative data describing the historical record of organizational foundings and closings should increasingly be supplemented with 'thick description' (Geertz 1973), both of the data collection and the societal context in which the data were produced."

Aside from his own work, Andrew Scull's (1977: 11) call for "an historically informed macrosociological perspective on the interrelationships between deviance, control structures, and the nature of the wider social systems of which they are both a part and an essential support" has not generated much of a research literature about the asylum or mental hospital. While there are exceptions (Morrissey et al. 1980; Lerman 1982; Brown 1985), psychiatric sociology has remained largely ahistorical, atheoretical, and isolated from research developments in such fields as the sociology of work, social history, organizational sociology, political sociology, and social movements. This is true despite the fact that the first century of American mental health care was a period in which immense organizations, founded by social movements and funded by the states, came into being, forming the organizational basis of modern concepts of mental illness and psychiatric care, and also creating much of the American "institutional state" (Katz 1978).

A major resource for wedding historical and organizational analysis is Stinchcombe's widely cited essay on "Social Structure and Organizations," which has proved to be seminal in the rise of both neo-institutional and organizational ecology approaches. The heart of Stinchcombe's contributions to the new movement in organizational studies asserts that "organizational forms and types have a history, and . . . this history determines some aspects of the present structure of organizations of that type. The organizational inventions that can be made at a particular time in history depend on the social technology available at the time" (Stinchcombe 1965: 153). Stinchcombe argues that organizational foundings occur in spurts, and that the organizations established during these spurts share characteristics that endure well beyond their founding.

Both institutional and population ecology approaches have drawn heavily from Stinchcombe's arguments, in that they emphasize the normative environment shaping organizational foundings or those structural features at birth that influence later mortality. Either approach points to the importance of examining closely the conditions under which organizations are brought into being, as well as how the particular historical context of organizational founding shapes structure.

MAXIMALIST ORGANIZATIONS

My examination of sociological approaches to the study of organizations has up to this point been broad, in that I have presented ideas about the study of organizations in general. Mental hospitals, however, are better understood as a special kind of organization. Thus, in order to extend recent work in the sociological study of organizations to make it more applicable to state mental hospitals, I argue here that these institutions are best understood as "maximalist organizations." I use this term to highlight the special character of organizations such as state hospitals, in particular their high structural inertia and low mortality: once born, they change relatively little and have long lives. Here the term "maximalist" is used in direct contrast to the "minimalist organizations" examined by Halliday, Powell and Grandfors (1987), who discussed state bar associations for the period 1870–1930 as examples of minimalist organizations. I argue here that mental hospitals, particularly the larger ones founded at state expense in the latter part of the nineteenth century, are an extreme example of nonminimalist organizations.

Halliday, Powell, and Grandfors describe four core dimensions that differentiate minimalist and nonminimalist organizations:

Initial cost. Minimalist organizations can be founded with limited or very limited labor commitments or capital investments. Halliday et al. note that, in contrast to minimalist enterprises, organizations such as newspapers require substantial capital, while others such as restaurants have considerable labor commitments. As discussed below, maximalist organizations such as mental hospitals have both extensive capital and labor expenditures. In nineteenth-century America, mental hospitals were among the most expensive expenditures of state governments; only canals and prisons rivaled their cost to governments such as New York's. In the twentieth century, mental health systems grew to be one of the largest, and sometimes the largest, components of state government.

Maintenance costs. Organizations differ in the poverty or abundance of their resource environments. Minimalist organizations can subsist on almost no maintenance. By contrast, maximalist organizations such as mental hospitals require at least the committment of the costs of full daily maintenance on a 24 hour, seven-day-week basis for their residents, plus whatever treatment costs are incurred above those of custody. Costs of maintenance of their extensive physical plants tend to be a considerable part of their overall budget.

Reserve infrastructures. Minimalist organizations can supplement their own resources by calling on the reserves of others when necessary; for example, state bar associations use the resources of law firms when their own are insufficient, while small businesses use the resources of family members. Nonminimalist organizations have few such "shadow" organizational structures or reserves. Maximalist organizations like mental hospitals guarantee their own resources, duplicating even such generally available ones as electrical generating and heating plants, acute care facilities, surgical wards, kitchens, and workshops.

Adaptiveness. The low labor and capital commitments and expenditures of minimalist organizations leave them able to change in response to their environments, and what Halliday, Powell and Grandfors term "normative flexibility" permits them to alter their conception of organizational mission. By contrast, nonminimalists change less quickly and flexibly. Maximalist organizations change slowly if at all, given both extensive labor and capital commitments; their legal charters and administrative structures usually force a very stable mission that cannot easily be altered.

Two other dimensions define a subclass of minimalist organizations such as state bar associations, which in contrast to the previous four dimensions, are actually shared by maximalist organizations like state mental hospitals. These two dimensions include:

Niche definition. State bar associations and many other minimalist organizations have well-defined niches requiring little or no defense. Mental hospitals, which are shaped by professional domination and state-granted monopoly, also have easily defended and clear niches.

Norms of competition. Minimalist organizations such as bar associations have norms that discourage direct competition. Mental hospitals tend to segment markets on the basis of ability to pay, so that private hospitals compete only with each other and public hospitals deal with most long-term patients. Public hospitals usually have monopolies over all publicly supported patients in a geographical district. These last two dimensions—well-defined niche definition and norms against competition—act individually and jointly to virtually eliminate competition among these types of organizations.

TOWARD A NEW UNDERSTANDING OF STATE HOSPITALS

In tracing the development of the American state mental hospital as a special organizational form, I examine it as a special case of a "maximalist organization." At several points I use data on the entire population of mental hospitals in the United States, examining a survey of the whole set of organizations at a single point in time or exploring data on mental hospitals over their entire history. I also explore one hospital, the Buffalo State Hospital, in depth, in part by examing the circumstances under which it was founded. While this study does not neglect the internal events that make up part of the Buffalo State Hospital's history, it does place more emphasis on the external environment of the institution, looking first to the Buffalo medical and social environments during the hospital's early days, and then to the broader Buffalo community. I argue that the institutional environment that made up New York's mental health care population was the major environmental factor in its development, with national mental health issues of secondary but growing concern. I also examine the "shock" that came to this more or less stable system with the era of deinstitutionalization—a process that involved policy changes, funding changes, changing attitudes within psychiatry, and the rise of new organizational forms within the mental sector.

Thus, this book really has two subjects: a single organization over its life span, and a population of similar organizations for its history. Moreover, the book looks at this particular organizational form through the lens of institutional theory, concentrating in particular on those processes known to sociologists as institutional isomorphism, which pushed the population of mental hospitals toward greater similarity.

The centrality of the environment in contemporary organizational theory is not matched by any developed definition of what composes an environment. This study contributes to that need by providing an elaborate mapping of the environment of the institution, with particular attention to how it changed over time. Several changes are noteworthy, including the demography of the patient population, the changing ideas of effective treatment, and changes in the governance of the institution, which ranges from a small group drawn from Buffalo's emerging professional and business elites to a bureaucracy of rapidly growing complexity. But consistent with the organizational theory we have developed, this study pays closest attention to how the standards for what constitutes an adequate state mental hospital changed. These standards constitute a central part of the normative environment that shaped the organization. To be sure, there was often a considerable gap between standard and actuality, but it is the thesis of this book that even with the considerable gap, standards shaped organizational reality. Unlike organizations whose performance can be easily measured, state hospitals are organizations whose existence and funding depend on their presumed conformity to external standards.

Chapter 2

The Natural History of an Organizational Form: The State Mental Hospital

Providing a framework for understanding state hospitals as organizations involves sketching their natural history—their formation as a species and the foundings of individual hospitals, emulation across the states, expansion, and a recent period of closings and transformations. The goal of the following analysis is to specify those vital events for state mental hospitals. First, this analysis clarifies the reasons why state mental hospitals can best be understood as maximalist organizations. Second, study of these vital events constitutes a strong comparative approach that extends understanding of state hospitals as organizations. Third, such a comparison makes a clear case for why the Buffalo State Hospital is a representative example of the entire population, in that its vital events are typical of the entire form. This explicit and extended comparison of individual case with the entire population over its whole history presents a strong argument for the generalizability of this study's findings, and provides a solid basis for the analysis of public policy.

According to a central argument of population ecology (Hannan and Freeman 1989: 66–68), powerful inertial forces usually preclude organizations from achieving dramatic adaptational change. Diversity within organizational sectors tends to come instead from organizational births and deaths, both of the same species and competing species, and not from change of existing organizations. The American mental health care industry, particularly that part which deals with the seriously mentally ill, is an excellent example of this tendency. State hospitals were (and to a surprising extent, remain) the organizational form that deals with the seriously mentally ill. Since coming into widespread existence in the past century, their survival and very modest internal change gave the mental health sector a stable backbone, particulary during the period from the mid-nineteenth century to the 1960s. When change came, it took four forms: a dramatic decline in the number of residents in state mental hospitals, the closing of several dozen hospitals, additions of hundreds of community mental health centers and public outpatient facilities as well as several new state psychiatric hospitals, and modest but significant changes in state hospitals adapting to the changing institutional scene (Kramer 1977; see also Dorwart and Epstein 1993).

Population ecology suggests examination of the entire history of the population of state hospitals. As with the study of other organizational forms (Hannan and Freeman 1989; Carroll 1987), the data for such a task were not easily assembled (see Appendix A), but do allow an exploration of the entire population of institutions over a full historical period, one of the longest periods yet examined in the organizational studies literature.

THE RISE OF THE ASYLUM

The earliest institutional responses to the problems of the mentally ill were modest in scale and reached only a small portion of those known to be afflicted (Grob 1973). During the early eighteenth century, several eastern cities established almshouses in which some proportion of their inmates were mentally ill, while some colonies forced the construction of poor-houses, with some of their capacity given over to the insane. The incarceration of the insane within the walls of the almshouse or poorhouse was the most common, if increasingly disvalued, institutional reaction to the problem of mental illness until the early twentieth century. Conflict between advocates of local care of the insane in the county poorhouse and state care in the new asylums and hospitals would become a major factor in shaping the growth of state hospitals (Katz 1986: 99–103).

In 1752, a group of Philadelphians led by Benjamin Franklin brought into being the first hospital in America (Tomes 1984: 22–27). Two rooms in its basement were reserved for persons "deprived of their reason," and inmates were sporadically incarcerated there during its first decades. But this modest beginning led, over time, to the development of a separate institution that would play a leading role in the development of other mental asylums and the profession that evolved out of asylum-keeping.

The first separate public institution for the mentally ill opened in 1773 in Williamsburg. The Public Hospital for Persons of Insane and Disordered Minds had 24 cells, a keeper's apartment, and a meeting room for its Court of Directors (Zwelling 1985: 1). For several reasons, however, this institution failed as a model for public institutions in other colonies. Grob (1973: 28–29) has argued that the Public Hospital's very small size, its essentially local character, the disruption caused by the American revolution, and the very different social character of life in the new republic all militated against its reproduction in other states. In similar fashion, several public institutions of very modest size were opened in other colonies or states but did not serve as a pattern for other foundings.

Instead, several other potential models for the care of the insane were opened. In 1774, the governors of the new hospital being built in New York City instructed its supervisors to use part of its cellar "for the reception of Lunaticks" (Grob 1973: 30), and in 1808 a separate department for the insane was opened. Between 1811 and 1822, "a short lived spurt in the founding of private mental hospitals in the Northeast" (Grob 1973: 51) led to the opening of the McLean Asylum in Boston, the Friends' Asylum in Philadelphia, and the Hartford Retreat. Grob notes that these institutions hardly reflected planning and study, but were responses to local conditions in each community. In any case their financial support precluded admission to all but the affluent or a few cases supported by charity. Similarly, the few proprietary institutions created during the early decades of the nineteenth century necessarily were restricted to the most wealthy families.

In contrast to these local efforts (which failed to be imitated elsewhere), the founding of the Worcester (Massachusetts) asylum (Grob 1966; Morrissey et al. 1980) was the beginning of a significant period of institutional expansion in America. The Worcester asylum was a model for care that mixed both custody and therapy, implying the possibility of recovery from insanity and cessation of the burden of public support (Grob 1973: 111–112). Worcester was notable for fusing medical leadership with state funding. Under the stewardship of Samuel Woodward, Worcester presented an image of successful public care for the insane with prudent management of a large organization.

The boundaries between "public" and "private" were far less sharply drawn in this period. The first private (or, as they were often called, "corporate") institutions often received state funding for some of their patients, and private monies sustained many of the inmates in public asylums. But perhaps even more important were the forces that influenced the different types of asylums in the first half of the nineteenth century. A decisive development in the proliferation of new institutions was the formation of one of the nation's first national professional associations.

The creation of The Association of Medical Superintendents of American Institutions for the Insane (AMSAII) (McGovern 1985) in 1844 was a crucial step forward in the movement to build asylums. Grob (1973: 132–33) notes that AMSAII reflected both the mental hospital and the social needs and interests that had shaped its early growth, particularly the fusion of dependency and institutional treatment with psychiatric theory. AMSAII rapidly became the virtually unchallenged source of expertise available to guide each state's decision about when and how to open a state institution.

AMSAII's meeting each year brought together the leading figures in establishing and administering mental institutions. Common origins, management of similar institutional problems, membership in AMSAII, and visits to each other's institutions all combined to produce a more or less homogeneous view among the first generation of AMSAII members. Discussion and dissemination of their ideas was advanced in the pages of the *American Journal of Insanity* (AMSAII evolved into the American Psychiatric Association, and its journal into the *American Journal of Psychiatry*).

Finally, Dorothea Dix—an important nineteenth-century reformer—(Tiffany 1891) provided indispensable leadership. Her success was due in part to her mobilization of physicians as leading actors in her campaign, which built directly on their rising influence in the community. Dix traveled extensively throughout the United States during the critical period when many of the states were considering the development of their first public asylums, and served as the catalyst for successful appeals to their legislatures. Grob (1966: 107–108) notes that she was responsible for founding or enlarging over 30 institutions and for helping stimulate government to broaden its role in providing institutional care and treatment of the mentally ill.

The confluence of these many streams—small and successful private institutions such as Pennsylvania, the impressive model of the Worcester asylum, a national body like AMSAII developing a more or less cohesive ideology of care in the pages of the *AJI*, and Dorothy Dix's leadership of state drives for the opening of institutions—led to a wave of asylum-building. States did not innovate, since they did not open institutions independently invented within their borders. Rather, the states practiced the emulation of a model that fused the key features of early models such as Pennsylvania and Worcester, under the professional hegemony of AMSAII. Grob (1973: 112) points out that emulation was often the uncritical adoption of innovations from one area to another.

Later chapters will examine how emulation shaped the origins and development of the Buffalo State Hospital, one of the several hundred similar organizations eventually opened across the United States. We now turn to the creation of the social form that was emulated, and then to an examination of the process of emulation as it occurred throughout the states.

THE "PROPOSITIONS" AND THE CREATION OF AN ORGANIZATIONAL FORM

Michael Katz has observed that the asylum, like the school, brought an entire profession into existence. But the origins of the organizational form of the state mental hospital demonstrate the opposite argument as well, for the profession played a powerful role in shaping the details of the form. This can be seen most clearly in its success in propounding two sets of "Propositions," agreed-upon and taken-for-granted rules for founding and staffing asylums, in the formative years of the wave to establish state institutions

(Eisenhauer 1984). While AMSAII made other resolutions about the care of the insane, these two sets were particularly important in defining the state mental hospital as an organizational form.

At its annual meeting in Philadelphia on May 21, 1851, AMSAII voted to accept the "Report on the Construction of Hospitals for the Insane" offered by its standing committee. The committee crafted a report (see Appendix B) that contained "the well ascertained views of the body in reference to many points in regard to which there was no difference of opinion." The 26 propositions spelled out in considerable detail the size, location, grounds, design, ventilation, lighting and heating systems, and construction of the ideal hospital. Particularly crucial for establishing the organizational form was the fourth point: "No Hospital for the Insane should be built, without the plan having been first submitted to some physician or physicians, who have had charge of a similar establishment, or are practically acquainted with all the details of their arrangements, and received his or their full approbation."

The second set of AMSAII propositions, "On the Organization of Hospitals for the Insane," were developed by a standing committee and presented to the general meeting in 1853. These propositions (see Appendix B) defined the duties of the Board of Trustees, the Superintendent, Assistant Physician, Steward, Matron, Apothecary, Chaplain, and Supervisor. The fourth article gave virtually unlimited power to one man, the Superintendent. The eleventh proposition demanded a ratio of no lower than one attendant for every 10 patients, and noted that an even richer staffing level was desirable.

Embodied in these propositions are several of the most enduring characteristics of state mental hospitals as maximalist organizations: high initial and maintenance costs, organizational independence, well-defended niches and low competition, and high inertia and low adaptiveness. The details of construction, including the spacious grounds and fireproof buildings, guaranteed very high initial and later maintenance costs. The generation of all the necessities of life for a large resident population (with relatively long lengths of stay, even in the early days of asylum operation) implied organizational independence, enhanced by the distance each hospital would be from a large town or city. Creation of the state asylum involved the development of an organizational niche by passage of commitment law as well as by the granting of commitment authority to physicians and courts. State institutions had a legal monopoly on involuntary admission, and competition with other institutions was minimized. Later chapters in this book will examine the degree to which structural inertia and low adaptiveness describe much of the history of a state hospital beyond its founding years.

The establishment of the state hospital as an organizational form represents a particularly clear example of institutionalization of an organization (Hannan and Freeman 1989: 56–57). State governments reproduced the state asylum across the country during the nineteenth century, granting it the dominant role in the structuring of public mental health services. The state asylum became the natural, or taken-for-granted, institutional response to mental illness, with all but a small proportion of patients sent to it for care.

The importance of the AMSAII Propositions is not that they were followed literally in every instance. In fact, even their author, Thomas Kirkbride, was unable to conform fully to the rules in his own institution (Hurd 1914 I: 221). Yet they show how successful professional practice could shape institutional development through the cultural hegemony of AMSAII. As Tomes (1984: 265) notes, "The particular era of asylum medicine in which Kirkbride came to maturity gave his success in hospital practice a significance beyond the walls of his own institution . . . his approach to hospital management profoundly influenced a whole generation of American asylum doctors." And they, in turn, as one of the first sets of experts to guide the development of the 'institutional state' (Katz 1978: 354–69), shaped the growth of an organizational form defined by the AMSAII Propositions.

To be sure, later standards would modify some of the details of the propositions, most notably the 1866 decision by AMSAII to increase the maximum number of patients to 600 (Hurd 1914 I: 220). But continuities in the norms and even the language would remain striking. Indeed, even after the considerable changes brought by deinstitutionalization and the creation of national accreditation and certification, standards for mental hospitals remain recognizable descendants of the AMSAII Propositions, in that they still address issues of medical control, physical environments, and staffing ratios (see Appendix B).

DiMaggio and Powell (1983) have sought to explain the tendency toward similar structure, or "isomorphism," in modern organizations. The major force promoting similarity in structure is competition among firms within a market. But public mental hospitals do not compete in this way, for the most part because they have a monopoly on the dispensing of inpatient mental health services in a given area. A second major force promoting similarity is bureaucratic coordination by some centralized agency. But for much of their history, public mental institutions in this country were free of control from centralized authority, with at most a state-level agency attempting governance and direction. Only during the past several decades have national forces (accreditation by a national organization, oversight by federal certification) begun to act in this fashion, and even these are hardly uniform in their impact.

In the absence of market or bureaucratic pressures toward isomorphism, what accounts for the similarity among public mental hospitals? Later chapters will assess whether these institutions have become more similar over time; our concern here is with the establishment across the states of very similar institutions during the nineteenth century. To answer this question, then, DiMaggio and Powell (1983) point to three mechanisms of institutional isomorphic changes—coercive (formal and informal pressures exerted by other organizations and cultural expectations for organizations); mimetic (imitation fostered by uncertainty); and normative (largely promoted by professionalization).

Historical scholarship on the state mental hospital (Dwyer 1988) reveals an unusually clear example of institutional isomorphism, showing how it developed into a cohesive organizational form primarily through the shared culture of AMSAII, which anticipated the impact of professional cultures on many other areas of life in twentieth-century America. The coercive pressure of the AMSAII Propositions, the powerful mimetic effect of the Worcester asylum, and the increasingly cohesive professional doctrine developed among the superintendents led to the reproduction of this organizational form. The orthodoxy of AMSAII's original members would later be challenged (Grob 1973), but not before it had affected the establishment of the state hospital in most states. Later chapters will provide a set of concrete examples by exploring how a single mental hospital was influenced by these forms of isomorphism.

By the early 1850s, the spread of the state mental hospital through emulation was well launched. The AMSAII Propositions, the influence of AMSAII and Dorothea Dix on the appointment of a superintendent, and the inheritance of a common set of problems and constraints all acted to reproduce the features of the state mental asylum across the states. Organizational rivals such as the poorhouse continued to lose ground in competition with the new asylums. The state hospital proved to be the organizational form most readily duplicated across the states, with little competition from other possible alternatives such as private asylums or general hospitals until the mid-twentieth century. In the absence of efficacious new therapies, the increasing size of the state hospital, expanding to meet a rising overall population as well as the burgeoning population of cities, was a decisive factor in pushing the institutions toward custodial care.

The maximalist organization of the nineteenth-century state asylum contained within it the possibility of the largely custodial state hospital of this century. No necessity forced this transformation, but several events made it likely. As resident populations and state costs grew, per capita appropriations for state care fell (Bockoven 1956), and the inherent tendency of the organizational form toward custodial care became the dominant force directing daily life in the state hospital (Belknap 1956). Another major force pushing toward the custodial state hospital was the incarceration of increasing numbers of elderly, many of whom had a very poor likelihood of recovery; throughout the twentieth century, the proportion of elderly would climb

(Malzberg 1964). An institution that began its life as the pride of state reformers eventually became "the shame of the states" (Deutsch 1948).

Figure 2.1 presents a broad picture of the number of state mental hospitals from before the American Revolution to the present. The overall trends are clear: state mental hospitals grew in number until well into the twentieth century, and then leveled off and fell slightly in number during the past few decades. Perhaps surprising in this figure is how small the actual decline in the number of mental hospitals has been, despite the dramatic declines in the inpatient census produced by the initial wave of deinstitutionalization.

Figure 2.2 charts the number of openings of state hospitals. While hardly random, the pattern certainly does not show "spurts" of foundings, as suggested by Stinchcombe (1965) and discovered for other organizational forms such as newspapers (Carroll 1987), state bar associations (Halliday et al. 1987), and labor unions (Hannan and Freeman 1989). These data suggest that an initial waving of foundings results in this organizational form becoming the "taken-for-granted" response to the problem of mental illness. Once the first wave of foundings has taken place, states open mental hospitals (now fully legitimized organizational responses to mental illness) to cope with increases in potential admissions. These second wave and later foundings are driven by bureaucratic and political decisions about the expansion of state facilities for the mentally ill.

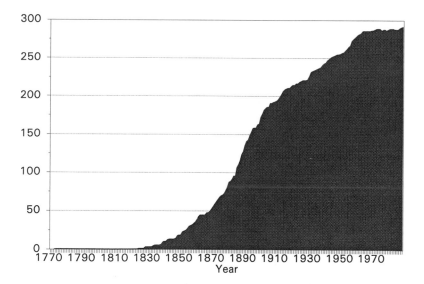

Figure 2.1
Number of State Hospitals, 1773–1988

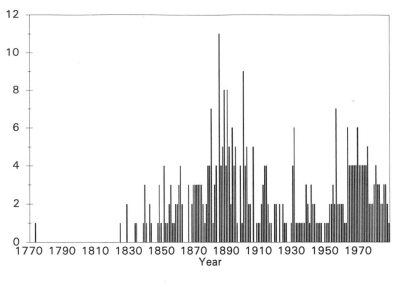

Figure 2.2
Openings of State Hospitals, 1773–1988

EMULATION ACROSS THE STATES

If theory suggests examining the environment to understand the spread of organizational form (as in Delacroix and Carroll 1983), what environment should be studied to understand the rise of public mental hospitals? The difficulty of defining organizational environments is clearly exemplified in the case of mental hospitals. The first wave of foundings—such as those of Worcester (Massachusetts) and Utica (New York)—shows states establishing one institution near the center of the state to serve its entire population. But, as the early and pioneering research of Edward Jarvis (Grob 1978) demonstrated for Massachusetts, use of the hospital varied inversely with distance from it. A second wave of foundings sought to build more hospitals to serve areas and districts distant from the central institutions. Local or regional environments within a state combined with statewide environments became important for these foundings. Finally, as the larger states developed central bureaucracies to manage their emerging mental health care systems, mixtures of local, regional and statewide environments (with primary emphasis on the statewide level) returned to importance.

The state mental hospital differs in its bounding from other organizations previously studied by population ecologists. The bounding of its environment is not limited to the local service area from which it draws clients and other resources. Each hospital is created and funded by the individual state, and draws its clients almost exclusively from state, or sub-state, service or catchment areas. In a real sense, there is no national system of public mental hospitals, but rather, 50 state systems. As discussed below, the federal government played almost no role in the provision of mental health care to the civilian population until after World War II, with the exception of several federal institutions such as St. Elizabeths Hospital. Its advent was among the most dramatic changes of the many that transformed mental health care during the last few decades.

UNDERSTANDING FOUNDINGS AND THE SPREAD OF REFORM

Delacroix and Carroll (1983; see also Halliday et al. 1987: 459) note that two research traditions deal with organizational births. The first tradition studies entrepreneurs, and emphasizes the psychological, social, or economic characteristics of founders. The second tradition, influenced by Stinchcombe (1965), looks at organizational and environmental issues conducive to foundings and at the imprinting of new organizations with cultural characteristics at the time of founding.

The first tradition is well represented in the historical literature on the asylum (for a recent comprehensive review, see Dwyer 1988; for specific discussions see Grob 1966 and 1973; Dain 1971; Tomes 1984; Dwyer 1987; McGovern 1985; Hurd 1914). By contrast, Grob (1983: 343) notes the paucity of attempts to use social science methods to study the spread of reform across the states. An ecological approach puts emphasis on those social and economic factors that make environments more or less fruitful for the founding of institutions. Ecological studies of the foundings of particular organizations have tried to examine those factors that play a major role in explaining the founding rate (Halliday et al. 1987; Knoke 1982; Sutton 1988; Hannan and Freeman 1989). This approach considers the temporal, spatial, and social dynamics of reform (Knoke 1982).

To help us understand when, where, and why the state mental hospital first appeared in each of the states, I will use a statistical approach called "event history analysis" (A more elaborate explanation of this is found in Appendix A). In event history analysis, the central issue to be explained, the dependent variable, is the underlying transition rate that indicates when a state moves from having no mental hospital to first opening. Event history analysis assesses how a predictor or set of predictor variables accounts for changes in this rate. To study influences on the founding of state mental hospitals, the date of founding must first be established. For the purposes of this study, I used the date when a state began to admit patients into its first institution. Other events in the process of founding a state hospital might well have been the focus of study, but I wanted to look at the event that culminates all of the work of founding a maximalist organization (Hannan and Freeman 1989: 147–49 discuss the founding process in general terms; Grob 1973: 112 discusses nineteenth-century mental institution founding processes). The date that each state opened its first institution is used to construct the underlying rate.

Following is a brief discussion of each of the predictor variables used in this study of foundings:

Temporal Patterns

Though all the states eventually opened mental hospitals, the timing of opening represents an important datum. Unlike other innovations recently studied by social scientists, such as reforms in the control of delinquency (Sutton 1988), the passage of compulsory school attendance laws (Robertson 1980), or workmen's compensation (Pavalko 1989), the timing of the appearance of the state mental hospital unfolds across the country over an extremely long historical period. The first public institution was opened in Williamsburg in 1773, when Virginia was still a colony; while Montana in 1912 was the last to open an institution. I created variables that measure the number of years since the founding of the first public institution at Williamsburg. I also created variables that indicate three different periods which historical research (Grob 1973) on the founding of American hospitals has documented as important. The first, from 1773 to 1829, bounds the earliest years of state development, and is the reference category used in the following analysis. A second period, from 1830 to 1869 (beginning with the organization of the Worcester State Hospital and ending with the aftermath of the Civil War), and a third from 1870 onward (defining a postbellum period of state expansion) allow comparison.

Spatial Patterns

Like other innovations (Knoke 1982; Smith and Hanham 1981; Sutton 1988), the founding of mental hospitals is expected to follow a definite spatial pattern. Particularly in the era before the rise of rapid transportation and ready communication, "contagious-expansion diffusion" was expected to produce a pattern of diffusion where the founding of a hospital in one state led to the founding of hospitals in immediately contiguous states. To model this process, a variable measuring the distance between the capital of the leading innovative state and each of the other state capitals was created. Several other variables indicate the location of a state within one of the U.S. Census regions (Northeast, North Central, West, with South as the reference category in the following analysis).

Social Forces

In addition to temporal and spatial factors, several social factors seem particularly important to include in models of the founding of mental hospitals. Like many other innovations, we expect the diffusion of the mental hospital to follow population growth (Knoke 1982; Smith 1984). The largest states should be early adopters, followed in general by smaller states, exhibiting a pattern of "hierarchical diffusion." Thus, a model of the spread of reform should include a variable of state population size at each decennial census.

Like many other social innovations, mental hospitals probably reflected the growth of cities. As the country urbanized, social disorder (and the fear of social disorder) grew apace. Cities were not merely the most visible arena for disorder, they were also crucial centers for the response to disorder and the creation of new forms of social control (Starr 1982: 72–73). Thus a measure of the percent urban of the population was also included.

One of the most dramatic social changes of nineteenth-century America was the arrival of ever-increasing numbers of immigrants. With different national cultures and religious backgrounds, the newcomers posed a formidable challenge to American institutions and arrangements, and provoked increasing anxiety about rising disorder. Grob (1966: 203–208) has discussed the degree to which the cultural gulf between the asylum superintendent and his increasingly foreign born patients was a factor in reshaping the nineteenth-century mental institution. But did the increasing social heterogeneity of their populations actually lead states to open mental institutions? To tap this dimension of change, I included the variable of the percent of the population foreign-born.

Population growth, urbanization, and diversity were not the only dramatic social changes that probably played a part in the creation of asylums. The transformation of the economy by industrialization reshaped social relations across the country, provoking the development of new social institutions. Katz (1978: 7) notes the close temporal connection between the increasing social and economic complexity associated with industrialization and the creation of public educational systems, with public mental hospitals a part of the growth of the "institutional state." Industrialization is tied to the formation and development of new social classes: the concentration of wealth and civic influence in the hands of the commercial and manufacturing leadership, and the unprecedented growth of a working class. Thus, the percentage of the population in manufacturing enters the models as another variable (Scull 1989: 214–21).

As mentioned earlier, physicians played a leading role in the founding of mental hospitals, particularly state hospitals. For this reason it is assumed that the degree of organization of physicians plays an important role in foundings. As a measure of the professionalization of medicine, the number of physicians and surgeons was also included in the analysis. (The number of surgeons is a very small fraction of the number of physicians, and is included to keep the definition of the data the same from one census to another. For a discussion of the social composition of American physicians in the nineteenth century, see Rothstein 1972: Appendix IV.)

DYNAMIC MODELS OF THE SPREAD OF REFORM

Data were gathered on the contiguous states and territories from each decennial census; to simplify the presentation that follows, I will refer to all of them as states. West Virginia, whose boundaries included a mental institution opened by its parent state, is deleted from the following analyses, as are Alaska and Hawaii (due to the recency of their statehoods). Yearly estimates of the values of each variable were generated using linear interpolation (Allison 1984: 38). (Definitions and sources are given in Appendix A.)

Having described the predictor variables used here to study the rise and spread of state mental hospitals, I will briefly explain how event history analysis (Allison 1984) is used to test the hypothesized relationships. Since measurement is possible only for yearly units of time, a "discrete-time method" (Allison 1982; 1984: 14–22) is used to examine the timing of the opening of each state's first public mental institution. Each state is represented by a data record for each year, beginning with its organization as a territory or admission to the union as a state and for each ensuing year until the opening of the state's first public mental institution. Thus the number of records define the "risk set"—those states still "at risk" at the beginning of each year of founding their first institution. Once a state has founded its first institution, it is no longer at risk and is deleted from the next year's list of states at risk. Each record contains information about whether the founding of the state's first public mental institution happens in that year (a censor variable coded "1"), or doesn't happen (the same variable coded "0"); all of the independent variables take on the values of that year. In this way, a state that persists in not founding its first institution until late in the process is found in the "risk set" until quite late, and contributes all the information about the changing values of its independent variables until then. By contrast, a state which founds early (such as Maine in 1840) contributes only the information of its first year in the risk set. As Allison (1984: 19) notes, this approach deals directly and effectively with both the problems of censoring and time-varying explanatory variables.

In a more technical sense, the focus of the discrete-time model is the risk of a state opening a mental hospital for the first time. The observational data about hospital openings are used to estimate a hazard rate, the unobserved rate of those states at risk of opening a hospital in the next year that actually do so. This rate is dependent upon the values of the explanatory (or independent) variables.

The measures of temporal and spatial diffusion were available for the full set of states beginning with their organization as territories or admission to the union. For the other social factors, however, data could not be collected earlier than the 1840 Census. Thus, the results are presented in two sets. The first examines the opening of hospitals from 1773 to 1912 for all states (excluding Virginia and West Virginia), with predictor variables (covariates) for the time and space variables. The second covers the period from 1840 to 1912, with full data for all five other covariates or predictor variables. The values for each decennial census were interpolated to yield measures for each year (Allison 1984: 38).

Following Allison's (1984) approach to discrete event-history analysis, I used logistic regression to generate the estimates of the effects presented in Table 2.1 (for a similar approach, see Pavalko 1989). The findings reported for the first model confirm the historical judgment that the founding rate increased significantly after the advent of the Worcester State Asy-

Table 2.1   Estimates of Temporal, Spatial, and Social Effects on the Rate of Opening First State Hospital, 1773–1912

Variable Name	Estimate	Standard Error	Coefficient/SE
I. Time and Space Model (1773–1912)			
Constant	-2.92273	.31877	6.51658
Middle period (1830–1869)	2.27194	.62104	3.65831
Late period (1870–1912)	3.52454	.68852	5.11896
Northeast	.42888	.45952	.93331
North Central	.32892	.40754	.80708
West	-.55694	.44660	-1.24706
Number of state-years: 1864			
II. Social Variables Model (1840–1912)			
Constant	-1.73589	.14965	21.81101
% Urban	.03556	.01868	1.90352
Physicians	.00058	.00014	4.19188
% Foreign Born	.00368	.01652	-.22241
% Manufacturing	.06812	.04056	-1.67953
Number of state-years: 825			

lum, and accelerated even more after the Civil War. The rate of asylum-building reflects a "bandwagon" effect in which the founding rate sharply rises after a period of early innovation. The Worcester Asylum was the model that most of the states followed in developing their own institutions (Grob 1966). However, regional location alone was not a significant predictor of change in the founding rate, once time period is taken into account. Unlike other innovations which diffused from one state to geographically neighboring states, the opening of state hospitals shows no regional effect. Perhaps the national character of AMSAII was of more importance in shaping adoption.

The results from the second model are more surprising. The number of physicians in a state proves to be the only significant predictor of an increase in the founding rate. (But bear in mind that, as was noted earlier, the number of physicians is so highly correlated with population size that the effects cannot be separated statistically.) The founding of asylums turns out to be strongly correlated with the number of physicians in a state.

The only other predictor that approaches significance is urbanization. Cities provided the organizational base for physicians and their allies to launch efforts to open mental hospitals. By contrast, and despite the persuasive hypotheses that link them to the opening of mental hospitals, the presence of a foreign-born population and the industrialization of a state prove of negligible importance in explaining the opening of state hospitals.

It is important to point out that these results are suggestive, rather than conclusive, given the paucity of other explanations that can be included in the model. However, they do point in the same direction: toward an understanding of the spread of the mental hospital across the American states largely as the product of the professionalization of medicine and the urbanization of the population. To be sure, these two variables are not unrelated, yet they are not so highly correlated as to be indistinguishable. Cities proved to be the basis of many other organizational efforts (Stinchcombe 1965: 151–52), including those such as general hospitals, universities, and medical schools. As my case study of the Buffalo Asylum makes clear, the decision to found a mental hospital drew on the organizational resources increasingly found in cities, involving doctors in collaboration with civic and class leaders coming into power in the growing cities of the country.

States, then, opened their first mental institutions largely as the result of the number of physicians and level of urbanization, not as the result of immigration or industrialization. Sponsored by local physicians who were influenced by a national movement launched by Dorothea Dix, mental institutions were seen as an indispensable part of state government, not as a reform mandated by industrialization or immigration. By the end of the nineteenth century, almost all of the states had opened at least one mental institution. Until the 1950s, this expansion matched or outpaced population growth.

EXPANSION OF THE STATE MENTAL HOSPITAL

The expansion of the state hospital has several dimensions. After founding their first hospitals, many states opened a few, and in some cases, many other hospitals. Institutions founded to care for a few hundred patients were often expanded to several times their original size. The result was an enormous increase in resident population in public mental hospitals throughout the past two centuries, with a very sharp decline after 1955. Other public facilities that cared for the insane—most notably, the poorhouse, usually funded by local aid—lost ground in the competition with the state hospital, and by the early twentieth century closed their doors or gradually were transformed into other types of institutions, such as the public old-age home (Katz 1984). As the state hospitals expanded, the character of state control changed, moving toward the large public bureaucracy model. In the larger states, centralized bureaus that provided not only oversight but direct governance were founded to supervise the rapidly growing hospitals.

While the population ecology perspective on organizations has tended to emphasize the sheer existence of different organizations, their differential growth is of course also significant (Carroll 1987). A close look at the data (not presented here) on foundings shows how rapidly the public institutions overtook private ones. Whether one examines the relative numbers of each type of institution or, even more dramatically, looks at the number of admissions or patients under care, it is clear that public care for the insane had become the modal and then dominant form of care in the United States soon after the Civil War. (As we shall discuss below, much of the twentieth century shows essentially the same pattern, changing only with the coming of deinstitutionalization starting in the mid–1950s.) Put another way, most patients in American mental hospitals were confined inside the walls of public institutions for most of the previous and this century.

Although public institutions predominated over private ones, neither category was completely homogeneous; different forms of public and private asylums came into being (Hurd 1914; Grimes 1934). While the public hospital dominated care for over a century, the persistence of the private hospital (augmented by spurts of new foundings) is worthy of study in its own right. Accessible only to the rich and affluent until the rise of private insurance (Starr 1982), the private hospital played only a small role in care of the mentally ill before the end of World War II. However, it served as an important comparison for each new generation of critics of public care, serving as a model (if an imperfect one) of what care for the insane could and should be. Its dramatically smaller size, better physical conditions, and almost luxurious staff-patient ratios made it seem superior to state care (Grimes 1934; for discussions of different organizational subtypes, see Dywer 1987; Hurd 1914 I: Ch. 11; Spaulding 1986).

Fragmented and decentralized decision making about the mentally ill has characterized much of the national experience. Though the superintendents of institutions remained members of a national organization, the individual states chose their own paths toward the asylum. No national policy existed, nor would one come into being even in a primitive form until well after World War II. The nineteenth- and early to mid-twentieth-century United States is accurately described as a "weak state" (Hamilton and Sutton 1989) that had no national policy about the care of the mentally ill. Even before the Civil War, considerable differences emerged among the states in the intensity with which they devoted resources to the mentally ill. What is striking about the American experience is how unequal the states were, and are (and, after the collapse once again of an effort toward national health reform, apparently will be for the foreseeable future) in their provisions for the mentally ill. Current critics of state policy (for example, Torrey, Wolfe, and Flynn 1988) claim that the quality of care a chronically mentally ill American receives today is as much a product of the state he or she lives in as any other factor. An examination of nineteenth-century data would support a similar generalization for the middle of the last century.

Why did state hospitals grow so considerably between the Civil War and World War II? Some of the early growth came from the successful effort of reformers to shift the public institutional care of the insane from poorhouses and county facilities to state hospitals. Sutton (1991) presents a tightly argued empirical demonstration of a "demand-side" explanation. Rather than examine putative changes in the numbers of the so-called "insane," Sutton examines characteristics of the American states that might be associated with the expansion of asylum populations from 1880 to 1920. The decline in the use of almshouses, along with growth in state fiscal capacity, the amount of time since statehood, and competition for votes all were tied to larger asylum populations. Sutton's quantitative models tend to support quite firmly Grob's historical narratives, with both approaches seeing the expansion of the asylum as an alternative to the development of comprehensive national policies to deal with dependency. But Sutton's "state centered approach" ignores the actual identity and behavior of state officials or of asylums. Staples (1991) employs a more qualitative and narrative style to argue a similar point: he sees the growth of state mental hospitals in large part as the reflection of the increasing ability and need of the developing state apparatus to control deviant and dependent populations.

What did the officials who ran state hospitals or the agencies that operated them think were the causes of their growth in the early twentieth century? The authors of an important attempt to study state hospitals after World War II (Council of State Governments 1950: 33–34) listed seven factors as influential in the growth of hospital populations. First, general population growth implied that "there are simply more people who could have a mental disease." Second, the aging of the general population put more people into the older age brackets "where the highest incidence of mental disease has always fallen." More older people thus implies more people in mental hospitals. Third, providing more hospital beds meant an increased hospital population, given the constant pressures of overcrowding and need exceeding capacity. Fourth, "both the medical profession and the general public know more about mental disease, and have been increasingly willing to utilize mental hospitals. Confidence in the hospitals has grown." Fifth, "the concept of mental disturbance has broadened. Formerly, only the severest types of mental illness were considered for hospitalization, but patients are now drawn from a wider and wider range of disturbed conditions." Sixth, increased life expectancy implied longer duration of hospital life. Over time, mental hospitals extended lengths of patient's stay, because of "higher standards of psychiatric care, because of the inability or unwillingness of the community to find places for them, or because of the shortage of social workers for aftercare." Finally, increased urbanization meant decreased tolerance for deviant behavior and perhaps higher rates of mental illness: "the rushing tempo of urban life today . . . *may* act to produce more disturbed people; it *does* act to make it more difficult for the disturbed person to get along in the world outside the hospital." Much more historical research must be done to assess how well these factors explain how state hospitals grew to house more than a half-million Americans by the 1950s.

DEINSTITUTIONALIZATION AND BEYOND:
CLOSING STATE HOSPITALS

To conclude the analysis of state mental hospitals as maximalist organizations, we turn to a brief discussion of the patterns of closings. Later chapters will return to the historical sequence begun in this chapter with the discussion of foundings.

Figure 2.3 presents a picture of the number of closings of state mental hospitals. The pattern is strikingly different from other patterns of organizational closings (Singh and Lumsden 1993: 164–76) such as labor unions and newspapers, which usually show either a liability of smallness (with smaller units closing earlier than larger) or a liability of newness (with newer units having higher mortality than older and more established units). American mental hospitals, by contrast, show a remarkable pattern of mortality. Most of the several hundred created since 1773 are still in

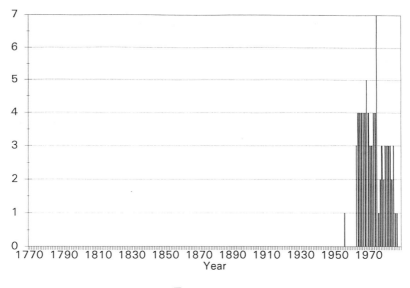

Figure 2.3
Closings of State Hospitals, 1773–1988

existence. Of those that closed, neither smallness or newness is linked to mortality. Rather, these closings reflect a period of unique organizational turbulence that began shortly after World War II, and whose main events are usually summarized as "deinstitutionalization" (Bachrach 1978; Brown 1985; Lerman 1982; Talbott 1979). Closings occurred in a sharp wave, almost a spike, that began in the 1960s and continues to the present. This underscores how strikingly different a maximalist organizational form is from other types, a finding with important policy implications.

While the initial phase of deinstitutionalization was viewed at the time as a simple reflection of the use of powerful new drugs in psychiatric hospitals (Scull 1977: Ch. 5), research has broadened the number of factors that must be taken into account to shed light on what happened. The other important factors hypothesized to explain the closings of state hospitals include growing and cumulative professional and public hostility toward the state hospital; new models of care such as psychiatric rehabilitation; the growth of state government costs; a fiscal crisis initiated by the explosion of welfare spending in the 1960s; the rise of Medicare and Medicaid; the advent of a for-profit nursing home industry; expansion of other mental health organizations; federal funding for the development of community mental health organizations (CMHCs); policy changes at the state level; and a series of Supreme Court and other legal decisions that mandated treatment of patients in state hospitals while restricting admissions.

To explore these issues, I developed and tested models for the closing of state hospitals. The unit of analysis is the state, and the dependent variable is whether or not a state government closed any of its hospitals. (Each of the fifty states is coded a 0 if no hospital was closed, and 1 if it closed one or more of its hospitals.) As Appendix A explains, I used a variety of data sources to establish whether each of the many hundred state hospitals remained open, or closed. Appendix A also gives the source of data for the explanatory variables.

Table 2.2 presents the results of the analysis. Since the dependent variable is a dichotomy (that is, it only can take on two possible values, zero or one), logistic regression was used to explore whether the independent variables can account for closing. This analysis studies state policy: do the variables that describe each of the states help explain why a state closed at least one hospital?

The explanatory variables include some of the most important reasons advanced for the state decision to keep open or to close hospitals. One variable evaluates the state's history of deinstitutionalization—the overall percentage decline in the resident population in state hospitals from 1955 to 1984. Another set measures the appearance of organizations within a state

Table 2.2   Logistic Regression Estimates of the Effects on State Closing of Mental Hospitals

Regression Variable	Coefficient	SE	Coefficient/SE
% Deinst. (1955–1984)	.08222	.03676	2.23631
CMHC's (1977)	.06578	.03808	1.72746
Unionization	1.60944	.68920	2.33522
% Nursing Homes*	-.00476	.00258	-1.83820
% State Expenditures*	.00168	.00158	1.05615
% Federal Revenue*	.01494	.01228	1.21776
Industrialism (1970)	.72318	.32738	2.20902
Affluence (1970)	.52000	.31408	1.65565
Northeast Region	.56798	.74196	.76553
North Central Region	.76392	.67306	1.13500
South Region	-.39304	.62026	-.63367

*Percentage change, 1980 versus 1960 or 1961.

that offer alternative institutional care for the same population once housed in state hospitals—the number of community mental health centers (CMHCs) in 1977 (a year for which data were available, and also well situated within this historical period), and the percentage increase in nursing home beds. Another set of variables assesses state financial pressure (percentage growth in state expenditures) and federal support (percentage growth in federal revenue). To assess the role public employee unions play in slowing or arresting states from closing hospitals, a dummy variable (a dichotomous variable that indicates the presence or absence of some condition) indicating those states with powerful state hospital workers' unions is incorporated (Torrey, Wolfe, and Flynn 1988: 11–12). Two overall measures of the socioeconomic level of the states were also included: industrialism and affluence (Morgan and Hirlinger 1989). Finally, to explore the impact of location, dummy variables about the state's location in the Northeast, North Central, or South entered the equation (with states in the West serving as the referent group).

Table 2.2 shows that only a few of these plausible variables actually helps explain the variation from state to state in the policy to close a state hospital. The percentage measure of deinstitionalization, overall industrialism, and unionization proved to be statistically significant predictors of closing, while the other variables did not. So, other things being equal, states that carried out inpatient reductions most fully also chose to close at least one of their hospitals. Those states highest in industrialism also elected to shut down one or more of their state hospitals. Finally, and counterintuitively, states with powerful public employee unions were likely to close a state hospital. This may indicate that public employee unions are most successful in attracting members in those states that most threaten their source of livelihood, and that unionism is the result of the threat of closing more than it is the cause of staying open. (This analysis is only suggestive, and a more definitive answer must await studies that disentangle the timing of union growth and state policy.)

To turn to those variables that did not prove significant, the most surprising findings concern the seeming lack of impact of the growth of alternative institutions for the care of the seriously mentally ill. Neither CMHCs nor nursing homes appear to directly affect state policy decisions about the closing of state hospitals. It is entirely possible that their effects are more on the daily operation of the state hospitals. Critics such as Torrey (1988) have suggested that, despite the anticipated role CMHCs were designed to play in the care of the seriously mentally ill, they have in fact largely cared for other populations, including what he terms derisively the "worried well." CMHCs probably compete (and successfully so) with state hospitals for skilled personnel, including clinicians such as psychiatrists, psychologists, and social workers. Similarly, nursing homes probably provide care to patients who once might have been housed in state hospitals, and accounts have been published that depict nursing homes as serving as community-based "back wards." But a more precise delimitation of their roles vis-à-vis the state hospitals must still be drawn.

Two very different public policy variables, which were included to explain the closing of state hospitals as a function of the changing financial role of the federal government, or of the growing fiscal crisis of state government, failed to attain statistical significance. In this respect the present analysis has produced findings similar to those on changing state policy about the control of juvenile delinquents. Sutton (1988: 222–31) found little support for these broad theories about the changing character of social control in advanced capitalism proposed by Scull (1977).

Further work about the closing of state hospitals, and about the broader process of deinstitutionalization, will probably have to move in the direction of "bringing the states back in," to modify a phrase first used in the singular to discuss the need to understand the impact of the modern state on social policy (Evans et al. 1985). Current research about American social policy notes its exceptionalist character, particularly the fragmentation across the states and other subnational units of policy decisions (Hamilton and Sutton 1989). The analysis presented here suggests that efforts to improve our understanding of the history of mental health policy must take into account decision making in state capitals as well as in Washington. Other chapters in this book make clear that much of state policy about mental illness also reflects the behavior of the maximalist organizations that have for so long made up much of the public mental health care sector.

Among the most important questions to clarify is that of the mania for closing institutions that swept across public mental health care in this period. State hospitals, once created to lessen the stigma facing the mentally ill in poorhouses, became stigmatized themselves. Some of the shift in perspective can be observed by comparing the view of the state hospital in Ward's (1946) *The Snake Pit* with Goffman's (1962) *Asylums*. In the former, the hospital is shabby, but in the latter it is sinister. We see poor care in the former, but reprehensible treatment in the latter. The patients of the *Snake Pit* are simply not helped very much by their stay at the institution; the inmates of *Asylums* are actually harmed by their incarceration. A major factor in this shift was the rise of a vigorous patients' rights movement as well as a dramatic change in professional values about community care.

This analysis has clarified the fact that most state hospitals remain open, though with considerably smaller inpatient populations. But the public image of the state hospital has become less clear. Several reasons can be suggested now, with further exploration of this question provided in the chapters that follow. Social problems rise and fall in public arenas (Hilgartner and Bosk 1988); serious mental illness has declined in salience, overshadowed by mental health (that is, psychiatric and psychological care for a larger but less impaired population than those with serious mental illness), crime, drugs, homelessness, and other issues. Psychiatry has continued to withdraw from its former base in the state hospitals and has shifted some of its attention away from the problems of the seriously mentally ill (Abbott 1988; Torrey 1988). Federal health care policy issues have overshadowed those issues defined as state questions, making state mental health care (and its pivotal institution, the state hospital) a much less visible public issue.

Finally, the great decline in inpatient population makes state hospitals seem less important, while other mental health organizations have increased in number and visibility. Reflecting both reaction to stigma as well as the addition of new functions, many state hospitals changed their names. Thus one NIMH listing (in 1990) of "state and county mental hospitals" enumerated 286 institutions. Only 79 bore the name "state hospital," with 66 different phrases used to identify these organizations. The organizations themselves have become more complex, performing, in addition to their traditional role of long-term inpatient care of the seriously mentally ill, a multiple set of functions. These include short- and intermediate-term inpatient care and outpatient care, and operation of community residences, combined with such nonpsychiatric functions as serving as "a modern day almshouse," an asylum of last resort, and a large public employer (Goldman et al. 1983).

STATE MENTAL HOSPITALS AS MAXIMALIST ORGANIZATIONS

This chapter has argued that state mental hospitals are best understood as maximalist organizations with unique vital events. State mental hospitals were not founded in spurts, like so many other organizations, but were opened over a very long historical period. State mental hospitals, unlike other organizations, are not subject to either the liability of newness or smallness. Nor, however, are they "immortal," as government bureaus have been characterized (Kauffman 1976). Rather, we have seen that state hospitals have their own distinctive pattern of mortality, closing in a wave that followed a sharp decline in patient population and preceded an anticipated but largely unactualized increase in competing organizations of supposedly better quality. As a leading critic (Talbott 1979, cited in Torrey 1988: 376) noted, "The chronically mentally ill patient has had his locus of living and care transferred from a single lousy institution to multiple wretched ones."

By the late nineteenth century, public asylums had become ubiquitous; a century later, despite sharp criticism, virtually universal condemnation, public commitment to close them, and wholesale population decline, they remain ubiquitous, a tribute to their endurance (Morrissey et al. 1980;

Rothman 1971: Ch. 11). No state to this point abandoned the state hospital completely, for all 50 states still have at least one currently open (for a discussion of alternatives, see Goldman et al. 1983; Carling et al. 1987; Dorwart and Epstein 1993).

Emulation accounts for the appearance of the state hospital in each of the American states. Mental hospitals became part of the expected set of services provided by a state rather than an innovation triggered by certain population or other levels. Industrialization and immigration failed to account for its diffusion. By contrast, the number of physicians in a state was tied to the opening of its first state hospital, a fact that underscored its medical origins.

The impact of deinstitutionalization, aside from profound decline in the number of inpatients and a few closings, included the transformation of many state hospitals by adding new functions to the old base of inpatient care. Stigmatization provoked name-changing, with organizational survival masked by a new image compatible with the orthodoxy of community care and the decline of medical dominance.

Mental hospitals are among the most substantial of organizations, their social structures fused to imposing physical structures. But as political and cultural organizations, their operation, indeed, their very survival depend upon how they are interpreted by their publics, and how their managers and staff interpret them to their publics. Organizations acclaimed as innovations worthy of emulation in the past century were defamed as anachronisms worthy of abandonment a century later, with equal paucity of evaluation of the actual outcomes of care (see Grob 1991). A permanently successful organization had become a permanently failing one (Meyer and Zucker 1989). Much of their recent history—including both a mania for closing them and considerable pressure to "reform" them through accreditation—can be understood by their shifting public policy image.

Whatever else they are, state hospitals are survivors. To assess how little or how much they have changed over time, the following chapters examine in detail how one representative state hospital adapted over more than a century since its founding. While it is a unique organization, its vital events fit that of the form quite well. It opened as the Buffalo State Asylum for the Insane in 1880, during the period which saw most other foundings throughout the United States. Renamed a hospital in 1890, it grew to many times the size intended by its founders. During deinstitutionalization, its inpatient population declined sharply and it added hundreds of outpatients, and it now operates community residences as well. It continues to exist, though under yet another name—Buffalo Psychiatric Center rather than Buffalo State Hospital—which reflects its changing role.

Chapter 3

"A Most Noble Charity":
The Birth of a State Asylum

The previous chapter discussed the basic vital events of foundings (or births) and closings (or deaths) that shaped the growth and development of the state mental hospital as an organizational form. To help understand how individual hospitals actually evolved, we need to examine the founding or birth of one representative state hospital, the Buffalo State Asylum for the Insane, later known as the Buffalo State Hospital and now the Buffalo Psychiatric Center. The founding process for a maximalist organization like a mental hospital often involves the commitment of massive resources even before the organization begins to function. In the case of a state mental hospital, the state government has to pass legislation, raise funds, call into being planning bodies, and finally erect a building of great size and cost. This chapter describes in detail how such an undertaking was launched more than a decade before the first patient was admitted.

While the primary method of analysis I use in this chapter and the next is historical, I also use two organizational approaches to explain how broader cultural standards leave their imprint on an organization even before birth. The population ecology perspective places central emphasis on organizational births. Births create a species; given organizational inertia, few organizations will evolve so much in their later lives that they become members of different forms. The neo-institutionalist perspective, on the other hand, has largely ignored organizational births, tending instead to look at much later stages of organizational development, as mature organizations adapt to changes in their institutional environments. In the case of the state mental hospital, standards were not only invoked by the founders but were followed closely in planning and developing both the physical and social structure of the new asylum. While this chapter tends to emphasize physical form, and the next one concentrates on organizational issues, we should understand that in the maximalist organization the two are fully interdependent.

In his classic *The Mentally Ill in America*, Albert Deutsch treats the opening of the Buffalo Asylum in just one sentence: "In the decade 1871–1881, four additional state institutions for the mentally ill were opened"; a note specifies," The Buffalo State Asylum was opened in 1880."[1] Deutsch's words assume that the expansion of state mental health care beyond the founding of the first wave of asylums was merely a quantitative increase in state expenditures. A closer look at the history of the Buffalo Asylum shows a more complex process at work, in which in addition to statewide pressure for reform, the class, civic, and professional interests of the leading figures in the Buffalo medical community shaped state expansion to their own ends.

The Buffalo Asylum was a product of the rise of medicine as a profession in Western New York. With the opening of the Erie Canal in 1825, Buffalo entered a period of rapid economic and population growth virtually unrivalled by other American communities.[2] As the community grew, so did the number of medical practitioners. By 1845, Buffalo had a total population of nearly 30,000 persons, and the census showed 78 physicians and surgeons. Buffalo's medical men (no women were physicians) faced many of the same problems typical of American practitioners before the Civil War. Patients skeptical of the doctor's abilities often chose lay practitioners or members of one of the many healing sects which flourished at the time. Many doctors learned by apprenticeship, and formal education was primitive in both form and content, with students exposed only to one or two years of didactic lectures. What knowledge physicians accumulated could not easily be shared, for formal means of transmitting knowledge were scarce. Finally, many physicians had to supplement their low income by farming or other occupations. Far from being prestigious, medical practice was often a marginal undertaking.[3]

Beginning in 1845 with Austin Flint's founding of the *Buffalo Medical Journal*, a generation of Buffalo physicians began the long struggle for professional recognition.[4] The *Journal* improved the communication of medical knowledge and facilitated the organization of the regular physicians into medical societies. By providing them a forum for their political and social views as well as medical discoveries, the *Journal* allowed physicians to publicize their deliberations. The *Journal's* most active writers formed an elite coterie of professional activists who shaped local reform in medical education and institutional development.

Aside from Flint, the most important figure in Buffalo's medical community was James Platt White. His lifelong commitment to raising the standards of medical education reflected his own experience as a member of a medical generation educated in the early nineteenth century. He was born in eastern New York in 1811 and moved with his family to Western New York in 1816, a time when such a move was "an emigration to the West."[5] After acquiring a classical education, White studied law, but quickly abandoned it to enter medicine. He attended a course of medical lectures at Fairfield, New York, "then the seat of a flourishing medical school," and returned to Western New York in 1832. His preceptors, two leading doctors of Buffalo, asked him to aid the nearby village of Black Rock, which had been struck by a cholera epidemic. White's heroic efforts were well remembered later, and were the basis of his rapid rise in the Buffalo community. He returned to his medical studies, receiving a degree from Jefferson Medical College in Philadelphia in 1834. In the next year, White began his practice in Buffalo, and in 1836 married Mary Elizabeth Penfield. It was an auspicious match, since her wealthy background tied him to the fortunes of Buffalo. With the income generated by his medical skills and his flourishing practice in obstetrics, White was able to avoid the penury typical of many doctors of the time.

Toward the end of his lengthy career, White would address a medical audience about clinical instruction, "a topic with which I am never wearied. It has been uppermost in my mind during the last thirty years."[6] Recalling for his audience the early 1840s, he noted:

> For a long time the defects in the system of medical instruction in the neighboring colleges at Fairfield, Geneva, and Willoughby had been the subject of remark upon my medical associates and myself. It was on all hands agreed that the great *desideratum*, clinical instruction, could not be supplied in these rural schools. Without an opportunity to apply at the bedside the precepts inculcated in the lecture-room, the system of teaching by lectures can never be successful in making good practitioners.
>
> Moved by these considerations, and influenced partly, no doubt, by the hope of personal professional advancement, if they could show they merited it, two or three young men, after careful deliberation, set about procuring a charter for a medical college.

White recalled that other Buffalo practitioners not only refused to participate but even tried to "discourage" the undertaking. But the medical college, called the University of Buffalo, was a success, and the college's young leaders, White and Flint, found their rise in medicine assured. Flint later characterized White's professional advancement in obstetrics as "quick and rapid . . . In a very few years he had in this respect outstripped not only his competitors of equal age, but his seniors [and] . . . secured and maintained a degree of success to which but few attain."[7]

James Platt White was the University's first Professor of Obstetrics and Gynecology. For the first three years of its existence, the University held its lectures in a small building, formerly a Baptist church. The first course of lectures began on February 24, 1847, with 66 students registered. Millard Fillmore, then president of the United States, was appointed its first chancellor, a position he held until his death in 1874.[8]

Flint and White also hoped to establish a general hospital, an enterprise which had to be postponed because of volatile political developments stemming in part from ethnic and religious conflict. Following the completion of the Erie Canal, large numbers of immigrants, particularly Irish and German Catholics, began to settle in Buffalo. John Timon, appointed the first bishop of the Diocese of Buffalo, began a remarkably successful program of founding Catholic institutions, at least in part because of the increasingly hostile reaction of Buffalo's Protestant elite to the immigrant influx. In 1847, Timon invited the Sisters of Charity to come to Buffalo. In 1848, they opened the city's first hospital, the Buffalo Hospital of the Sisters of Charity.[9]

The hospital had accommodations for 100 patients, and received some public funds. In return, no inquiries were made about the religious background of prospective patients. Flint served as attending physician, and White as consulting surgeon. Soon after the hospital opened, another cholera epidemic struck Buffalo. The hospital admitted 136 patients with the disease, 52 of whom died. The Protestant physicians of the city, including leading figures such as Flint and White, praised the courage of the Sisters of Charity, an unusual act during a time of increasing religious tensions. Notably, it was about this time that Bishop Timon chose James Platt White as his personal physician.[10]

The University constructed its permanent building on the corner of Main and Virginia Streets. The new building was immediately adjacent to the Buffalo Hospital of the Sisters of Charity. Bishop Timon permitted, for a small fee, the use of the hospital for clinical instruction. Medical students received bedside training under the supervision of an attending physician or surgeon.

Flint later characterized White's teaching as "direct, forcible, and practical." During the first three years of instruction, White followed the customary pedagogy of the day, lecturing to students about childbirth and showing them illustrations from medical texts.[11] Unless they served an apprenticeship, medical students would not observe an actual delivery until they were in practice.

In January 1850, White learned that Mary Watson, a young unmarried Irish woman, was expected to deliver within a few days. She was persuaded to leave the Erie County Alms House and live with the University's janitor and wife in the basement of the Medical College. Each member of the medical class was allowed to listen to the fetal heart by means of a stethoscope, with White continuously in attendance. After labor began, each student was permitted to make vaginal examination, though only by touch, since direct observation would have violated the obstetrical etiquette of the day. All of the students were gathered around White while he attended the delivery, the first time in the United States that medical students saw a live birth.[12]

As word of this first American example of "demonstrative midwifery" became public, Buffalo physicians and the press debated the issue. A newspaper published an article by a writer identified only as "L" attacking White for exposing his patient to the "meretricious curiosity" and "salacious stare" of his students and thereby committing a "gross outrage upon public decency for the purpose of furthering his own professional reputation."[13] A sensational trial followed, with White suing Dr. Horatio N. Loomis for libel. White was unable to prove Loomis was the author, but the case attracted national attention to the issue and "demonstrative midwifery" became a standard part of the medical school curriculum.

White's medical and social interests were broad, and during the 1860s he joined other Buffalo physicians in lunacy reform. Like other physicians of the day, he had no formal training in the care of the insane, but viewed with considerable professional pride the movement to establish insane asylums whose superintendents were medical men.[14]

For the insane in Western New York, however, institutional care was given primarily by the Erie County Alms House, or, for a few, at New York's only state asylum at Utica. Buffalo's medical elite praised the doctors of Utica, but had nothing but contempt for the keepers of the Erie County poorhouse. The Buffalo medical community shared the concern of Dorothea Dix over the operation of the poorhouse, focusing not on its facilities per se but on the lack of medical treatment.[15] With its extremely high mortality rate, the poorhouse was without doubt the least healthy environment in the county. The editor of the *Buffalo Medical Journal* complained, "The whole policy of the Poorhouse is niggardly and mean. Cheap provisions, cheap doctors, cheap nurses, cheap medicines, cheapness ever is the rule, forgetting that higher policy which find true economy in a humane policy."[16] Of particular concern was the "diet of the house—a diet which exceeds, in its accurate estimate of the starvation point, anything which Dickens ever described."

The physicians' campaign was successful, and Erie County opened a new poorhouse six miles north of the center of Buffalo. A separate building was provided for the insane, and the diets of all the inmates improved somewhat. At the suggestion of Bishop Timon, Sister Rosaline Brown visited the new poorhouse. She found the general quarters to be clean, but was shocked by the condition of the insane. Like Dorothy Dix before her, she was horrified to see inmates shackled to the walls and tied to furniture. Determined to create a more humane institution for their treatment, she succeeded in opening in 1860 the Providence Lunatic Asylum, located on a property sold to her by Austin Flint and adjoining White's farm.[17]

White's ties to Bishop Timon probably account for his brief direct involvement with the Providence Asylum. In 1862, White began service as its physician, caring for the physical needs of its few patients, while the nuns tended to their "moral treatment." White was succeeded in this role in 1863 by Julius F. Miner, the editor of the *Buffalo Medical Journal*, who informed his colleagues of the success of the Asylum:

> It is incredible what effects are often produced upon diseased minds by what may be termed moral treatment, and though it may be confessed that medicine, as such, has only an indirect application to the disease of the mind, still we are not without means of cure. Employment, diversion, amusement, social opportunity, change of scene, &c., is our moral materia medica, more powerful for good, in diseases of the mind than the actual materia medica in diseases of the body.[18]

The Buffalo medical elite was optimistic about moral treatment as a conscious effort by medical men to treat rather than merely confine the mentally ill. In stark contrast to the Providence Asylum, a statewide investigation in 1865 by lunacy reformers produced a chilling portrait of the incarceration of the insane at the Erie County poorhouse.[19]

Of the 500 hundred inmates of the poorhouse, 121 were labelled lunatics. Almost half of that number were of the mild type, yet only two had been treated in an asylum. The very mild type lived with the general pauper population. Not all the insane had beds, with 20 sleeping on straw that was changed every week or two. During the winter, roughly the same number had no shoes or stockings. After noting that there were no accommodations for the various grades of the insane, that other paupers cared for the insane, and that a physician visited them only twice a week, the inspecting physician concluded that the poorhouse was "not suited to the favorable care and treatment of the insane." "In fact," he argued, "the State of New York should maintain, at this place, a charity like the Utica Asylum, as it would confer a great benefit upon society. I assume the responsibility of urging some action in behalf of the insane of Western New York commensurate with the importance of the subject, the interests of humanity, and the dignity of the state."[20]

That the Erie County Poorhouse insane were given relatively good treatment compared to that provided in other parts of the state may explain the Legislature's passage of a bill creating the second state asylum, to which county almshouses were to send the pauper insane. The new asylum, named the Willard Asylum after the report's author, was only a partial victory for the state's lunacy reformers such as John P. Gray, superintendent of the Utica asylum. With his own institution badly overcrowded, (Utica AR 1864: 12; Utica AR 1864: 18), Gray had been imploring the state for new institutions.[21] The Willard Asylum, however, was to be an institution for the incurably insane. Gray had won only part of the argument: the county poorhouses were to be emptied, but the incurable insane were simply to be moved from a local "receptacle" to a state-operated one.

The decision to build the Buffalo State Asylum for the Insane can be viewed as the result of the conjunction of professional, political, and class interests. Led by John Gray, the medical profession was the most active agent in pressing statewide for more asylums. Allies in Albany such as Senator Tweed and his Tammany colleague Governor Hoffman had ample political motivation to oblige them, in part by increasing state expenditures on public works to strengthen their political grip on the state's electorate.[22] On the local level, James Platt White played the central role in the creation of an asylum for Western New York. His experience with the patients of the Providence Asylum must have provided a vivid contrast to the incarceration of the insane in the Erie County poorhouse. In February, 1869, White and several other "thoughtful citizens of the city of Buffalo, aided by Dr. Gray of Utica," began the first steps to found an asylum. White wrote to the leading physicians of Western New York, asking them to obtain signatures of "influential citizens" on a petition to the Legislature "praying that body to establish an asylum for the insane to accommodate this part of the State."[23]

The New York State Legislature's bill creating the Asylum called for the Governor to appoint commissioners to choose a site in the eighth judicial district in the western part of the state. The commissioners consisted of John Gray, James Platt White, and three other physicians from Western New York. With Gray in the chair, the commission met in Buffalo in July of 1869. The state gave White and his fellow commissioners a free hand in the setting, design and execution of the building.[24] Gray's eminence as superintendent of the state's most important institution and the other commissioners' lack of experience in asylum management led to the decision to adopt the propositions of the Association of Medical Superintendents of American Institutions for the Insane (AMSAII) as "the proper basis upon which the different sites should be considered and the final determination made."[25]

By the late 1860s, these propositions and the codification of asylum practice by Thomas Story Kirkbride of the Pennsylvania Hospital for the Insane represented the orthodoxy of those men who ran most of the public and private asylums in the country.[26] However, both professional and lay critics were attacking the orthodoxy, questioning the claims of high cure rates and charging abuse and mismanagement. While Gray's professional ties to Kirkbride made his insistence on them unexceptional,[27] what was surprising was the commissioners' decision about a site for the asylum.

The Asylum's By-Laws faithfully quoted the superintendents' first proposition calling for every hospital for the insane to be "in the country, not within less than two miles of a large town, and easily accessible at all seasons."[28] After visiting Lockport, Warsaw, Westfield, Batavia, Attica, and Buffalo in October, 1869, the commissioners voted the next month to locate the asylum on a 200-acre lot to be donated by the City of Buffalo.[28] In every respect the design of the hospital was carried out in perfect conformity with the AMSAII propositions, with one major exception: the site selected was well within the municipal boundaries of a very large and rapidly growing city. The lots adjoining the site were parcelled out and in several instances were already in residential and industrial use.[29]

Why did the commissioners violate the first and simplest of the AMSAII propositions? Their decision was not a simple miscalculation of the direction that Buffalo's growth would take, but quite the opposite. The asylum commissioners were meeting in the offices of the Buffalo Park Commission, just then embarking on a dramatic intervention in shaping Buffalo's growth. Beginning in 1868, the city had employed the firm of Frederick Law Olmsted and Calvert Vaux to plan its park and parkway system.[30]

The answer can be found by examining Olmsted's plan for Buffalo. Figure 3.1 presents the plan (in a version published in 1881), with downtown Buffalo appearing in the lower left, the Niagara River and the Erie Canal on the left, and the dark areas and lines representing the immense set of parks and parkways which Olmsted designed for the city. The plan's title refers to both a "Park System" and a "General Plan of the City." The "State Insane Asylum" (in the upper left corner) was intended to be part of both. The Asylum is on the north end of Richmond Avenue, a dark line running vertically toward the left of the map, which links several of Olmsted's major circles. Its grounds are the west border of Buffalo's largest park, identified in the drawing simply as "The Park."

Olmsted's plan for the Buffalo Asylum grounds (Figure 3.2) faithfully followed the second of the superintendents' propositions of 1851, requiring each hospital for the insane to have no "less than two hundred acres of land devoted to gardens and pleasure grounds for its patients." Olmsted suggested to the architect that the hospital buildings be placed as indicated in the plan, maximizing the amount of light on its wards.[31]

The influence of Buffalo's business class in the creation of civic institutions was central in the city's donation of the land and perpetual free water in exchange for the Asylum's location. As an observer noted at the ceremony laying its cornerstone, the Asylum was viewed as an important part of the social development of the city of Buffalo:

> The decade of years from 1870 to 1880 will stand in the future annals of the city as an epoch in which a spirit of enterprise—long slumbering under a mist of doubt and apprehension—sprang into full life and vigor, and by the inception of grand schemes of public improvement, convinced the public mind that the growth and prosperity of the city depended upon the successful forwarding of works designed to benefit, instruct, and amuse all classes of citizens.[32]

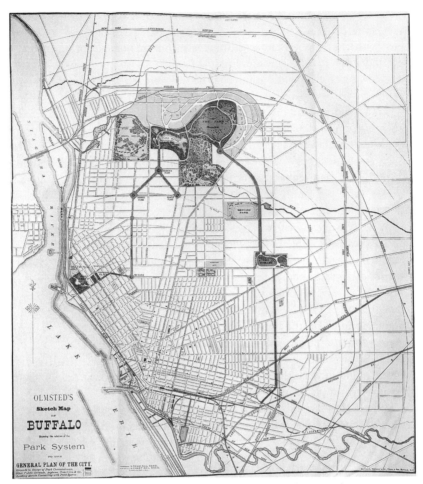

Courtesy National Park Service, Frederick Law Olmsted National Historic Site.

Figure 3.1
Map of Buffalo

The Asylum was listed along with several other civic ventures of major proportions, such as the new city park, a normal school, and the new city and county hall. All of these efforts involved the city's business class in a new level of coordination.

Unlike most nineteenth-century physicians, James Platt White was a secure member of this class. After Austin Flint moved to New York City in 1859, White assumed the mantle of Buffalo's leading physician. Flint would later note that "Dr. White furnished an instance, certainly rare in this

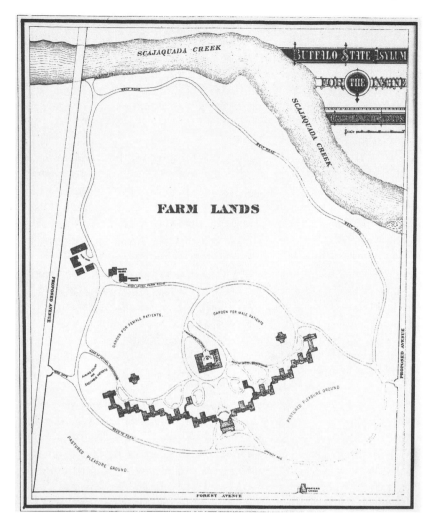

Figure 3.2
General Plan of Grounds for the Buffalo State Asylum

country, of wealth acquired by the practice of medicine."[33] During the last decade of his life he launched a successful project as an entrepreneur. At the time of his death in 1881 he had built the "White Fireproof Building," which at the time was considered the "finest business edifice" in the city.[34] The minutes of the Asylum's Board show him to be a vigorous and experienced business manager. White ran the asylum's affairs as its president until his death in 1882. During this period the state government provided only funding and sporadic oversight, with daily management resting in White's hands. He was part of several post-Civil War ventures launched by the city's Protestant elite that marked their formation into a self-conscious and increasingly confident coterie. White played a role in the founding of the Buffalo Historical Society, the Young Men's Association of Buffalo, and the Buffalo Fine Arts Academy. At the time of his death he was president of not only the Insane Asylum, but also the Church Home and, most significantly, the Buffalo Club, then, as now, a central institution for bringing together Buffalo's elite.[35]

The location of the Asylum in Buffalo was also the culmination of White's commitment to the professionalization of medicine. As a founder of the University of Buffalo and the first practitioner of "demonstrative midwifery," White had long insisted on the importance of clinical training. While he confessed little knowledge of asylum practice, he had, as president of the New York State Medical Society in 1870, taken up the cause of reform in the teaching of "psychological medicine" in the medical curriculum.[36] White and Gray had become allies in convincing the state's medical colleges to offer this subject, and Gray had published an editorial about it in the American Journal of Insanity.[37] Gray argued that the separation of the asylums from the medical colleges was a major obstacle to progress in psychological medicine. The Buffalo Asylum was clearly intended to be a major advance in the teaching of psychological medicine, an important enough desideratum to override the superintendents' propositions. The Asylum's location near the University and the offices and residence of Buffalo's medical elite would allow clinical instruction in psychological medicine to be practiced in the most advanced asylum for the insane in the United States.

The choice of an architect was also in the hands of the commissioners, who issued informal invitations to several architects to submit preliminary drawings. Two sets were received, one from a Rochester architect, A. J. Warner, and the other from a young architect then living in New York City, Henry Hobson Richardson.[38] Richardson had also been invited to compete for the building of Buffalo's Christ Episcopal Church in 1869, but had received support from only one member of the building committee, and so the contract was given to a Boston architect. Richardson's one supporter on the committee was White.[39] Richardson was given the Asylum commission, and Warner was named supervising architect.

John P. Gray designed the plan for the building's interior, which was incorporated into the architect's final drawings with only one minor change.[40] Once again, Gray took for his model the orthodoxy of the 1850s and 1860s. His plan was an elaboration of the famous "Kirkbride" or linear plan, the model for asylum construction during these decades (see Figure 3.3).

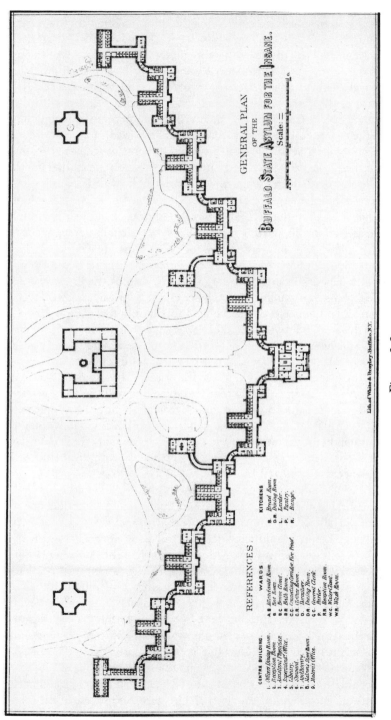

GENERAL PLAN
OF THE
BUFFALO STATE ASYLUM FOR THE INSANE.

Scale: ═══

REFERENCES.

CENTRE BUILDING.

1. Officers Dining Room.
2. Reception Room.
3. Assistant Physician.
4. Superintendent Office.
5. Library.
6. Steward.
7. Apothecary.
8. Matrons Store Room.
9. Matrons Office.

WARDS

A.B. Attendants Room.
B. Bed Room.
B.C. Broom Closet.
B.R. Bath Room.
C. Connecting Corridor, Fire Proof.
C.R. Clothes Room.
D. Dormitory.
D.R. Dining Room.
G.C. General Clerk.
P. Parlor.
R.R. Reception Room.
W.C. Water Closet.
W.R. Wash Room.

KITCHENS

B. Bread Room.
D.R. Dining Room.
L. Larder.
P. Pantry.
R. Range.

Lith. of White & Brapley, Buffalo. N.Y.

Figure 3.3

General Plan of the Buffalo State Asylum

The linear plan embodied several of the most important of the superintendents' propositions, making it possible to classify patients into different wards on the basis of their behavior and treatment needs.[41] As elaborated in the writings of Thomas Story Kirkbride, the linear plan allowed for the most efficient management of a hospital for the insane. It permitted the separation of the sexes into individual wings of the institution, with the superintendent's offices and living quarters, reception rooms, and apothecary in the center building. Each wing had separate wards for eight classes of patients of each sex. The most disturbed patients were placed in the wards furthest from the center, with the infirm placed on the ground floors. The influence of the Kirkbride plan was considerable, with Kirkbride consulted directly in the building of at least 35 hospitals.[42]

While faithful to the general ideas of the linear plan, Gray's plan for the Buffalo Asylum differed in some important ways. In addition to its location, the Buffalo Asylum was designed for 500 patients, twice the number Kirkbride thought of as a maximum, but consistent with the current standards of the superintendents' association. Gray also took the linear plan to its logical limits by expanding the number of wards for each sex to eleven, and increasing the length of the building to almost a half mile.[43] He followed in this respect Proposition 25 of AMSAII, which called for the rooms of the most excited class (those likely to be unruly or violent) to be placed only on one side of the hall of each ward. in sum, as Gray noted, "this institution is the first and only one in which the principle has been fully carried out . . . as the building . . . has a southern exposure, and the windows are large and numerous, the wards are most favorably arranged for light and thorough ventilation."[44] To put the matter simply but accurately, one of the most important exponents of the prevailing orthodoxy designed what he considered the perfect asylum, blending orthodoxy with his many years of experience at Utica.

White had determined the site of the Asylum, and Gray its floor plan. The exterior design was left to Richardson. According to Kirkbride, one of the main advantages of the original AMSAII principles was that they allowed large hospital buildings to be constructed at very low cost. Kirkbride chose to illustrate his views with a lithograph of the Alabama Hospital for the Insane, the first built according to the principles "in all its details."[45] White apparently intended something quite different than a plain, unadorned, and cheap structure like the Alabama Hospital, however. Again, White's membership in Buffalo's business elite is significant, because this elite had embarked on a program of civic improvement and embellishment involving considerable public and private expenditures.[46] The Asylum was to be Buffalo's largest and finest public building.

Richardson's final elevation of the Asylum (Figure 3.4) represents a major new development in American architecture, his first use of the "per-

Figure 3.4

Richardson's Elevation of the Buffalo Asylum

sonal interpretation of medieval forms" that brought him eminence and that now is labelled the Richardsonian style.[47] As Gray noted in 1872, "The buildings are to be substantial and durable, without ornamentation or attempt at exterior effect, beyond what their extent and massiveness will produce."[48] Its effect must have met White's expectations perfectly, given how Flint described White's own style of living: "without ostentation, his family lived in a manner befitting his wealth and social position." Considered on its architectural merits alone, the building probably deserves Ochsner's judgment that it "is an outstanding example of nineteenth-century institutional architecture."[49]

Richardson chose locally quarried material for the building, employing a reddish-brown sandstone with a rugged face; he later approved the use of red brick to save costs in the construction of the outer wards. In June, 1871, ground was broken on the project, but the first of a long series of interruptions in the work delayed the laying of the cornerstone until September 18, 1872.[50] The economic troubles of the 1870s and a series of political conflicts over the asylum's governance caused further delays.[51] The central building and two eastern wings were finished by 1880.

White had constructed an asylum that was a monument to the orthodoxy of superintendents such as Gray, who selected his protege, Judson Boardman Andrews, as its first superintendent.[52] Andrews accepted his mentor's insistence on the physical causes of insanity, and the care of the insane primarily with medical, not moral, treatment. The University of Buffalo appointed Andrews its first Professor in Insanity, and announced that students would be trained at the splendid new hospital.[53]

White, now 70 years old, proudly watched Andrews assume his superintendency over the Asylum's first patients on November 15, 1880. The first acts of patient abuse at the new asylum allegedly happened only 15 days later.[54] After suspending the two attendants charged with "bringing the patients to time," White once again chose a public hearing to defend his innovation, but with more mixed results than in the Loomis case. White hired the prominent Buffalo attorney Grover Cleveland to represent the Asylum. The Commissioner in Lunacy, John Ordronaux, found two attendants innocent of the charges of abuse, but later suggested to the Board of Managers that they be discharged because they brought discredit to the institution. White soon retired from the Board's presidency because of failing health, and died several months later. Flint noted in his eulogy for his old friend and colleague that he "died with his armor on," while travelling to perform an operation in a village near Buffalo.[55]

The enduring achievements in architecture and urban planning that were part of the birth of the Buffalo State Asylum were, of course, only a part of the institution's complex history. Like many other public asylums founded during a time of optimism about the curability of insanity, that later history saw a steady increase in the number of patients at the expense of quality of care. Richardson's asylum buildings were intended to house 500 patients, many of them in private rooms and all in spacious wards, as early photographs of the Asylum show.[56] The hospital eventually contained over four times that number, with beds jammed by the dozens into these corridors. Increasing numbers of committments were not accompanied by corresponding increases in space or staff, producing, by the early twentieth century, many of the problems faced by the typical American state hospital.[57] Despite these later problems, the plans for the Buffalo Asylum described in this chapter are precise images of the care for the insane that reformers such as James Platt White sought. Missing from them, however, and from much of the asylum's later history, are the innovative professors of psychological medicine whom White intended would walk these halls, in the words of S. Weir Mitchell, "preceded and followed . . . by clever rivals, or watched by able residents fresh with the learning of the schools."[58]

The next chapter turns to the question of the organizational structure of the Asylum. Before turning to that issue, it is important to note how, at its birth, the Asylum fit several of the most important organizational issues discussed earlier. At its birth, the Asylum's physical structure showed the effects of a powerful imprinting of cultural expectations about what a proper asylum should be. The existing professional and popular standards for the care of the insane were met almost perfectly. Given the Asylum's conformity with the traditional norms about state asylums, it is paradoxical that it was designed with the most innovative ideas about architecture and urban planning. At its birth, the Asylum fit perfectly the definition of a maximalist organization and, as we have seen, was the visible center of efforts to reform care of the seriously mentally ill.

NOTES

1. (Deutsch 1949: 256). Other histories of the expansion of state care for the insane provide similar comments on the opening of the Buffalo asylum (as in Hurd 1914 v. II: 178–86). During the past twenty years, much has been written about the rise and development of the mental hospital. The most important student of this issue is Gerald N. Grob (see Grob 1966, 1973, 1983). The last contains a very useful review of primary and secondary sources for the study of the care of the mentally ill in North America, including a list of the often polemical literature that has been written to some degree in response to Grob's work. (For a recent discussion of the debate, see Brown 1985).

2. Discussions of Buffalo's economic growth during the nineteenth century include Goldman (1983); Harring (1983); Hill (1923); Katz, Doucet and Stern (1982); and Stern (1979).

3. On the status of nineteenth-century physicians, see Starr (1982: esp. Ch. 3).

4. *Buffalo Medical Journal* 1 (1845: 162–63). My generalizations about Buffalo's physicians are based on my reading of the *Buffalo Medical Journal* and its successor, the *Buffalo Medical and Surgical Journal* (referred to in these notes as BMJ and BMSJ) from its founding in 1845 to the early 1870s. On the historical importance of the *Journal*, see Lily Sentz, "The *Buffalo Medical Journal, 1845–1919.*" *Bulletin of the Medical Library Association* (July 1985): 278–82. A useful brief history of the *Journal*, the Buffalo medical community, and Buffalo's hospitals can be found in Potter (1895). An informative recollection of early Buffalo medicine was given by the *Journal's* first editor shortly after he left Buffalo to move to New York City: Austin Flint, "Address Before the Erie County Medical Society." BMSJ 1 (1861) 1–12. For a detailed portrait of a similar group of physicians in nearby Rochester, see Edward C. Atwater, "The Medical Profession in a New Society, Rochester, New York (1811–1860)." *Bulletin of the History of Medicine* (1973): 221–35 and (1977): 93–106.

5. Biographical information about White is taken from *Memorial: James Platt White, 1811–1881,* a 65–page pamphlet probably printed in 1882 by the faculty of the University of Buffalo; an original copy is in the Medical Archives of the State University of New York at Buffalo. This *Memorial* contains a lengthy memoir by Austin Flint, along with speeches, editorials, and formal motions in honor of White given by the many organizations and societies which he led or served. It is invaluable in assessing his role in mid-century Buffalo. Other typescript biographies of White, his wife, and his adopted son by an anonymous twentieth-century author are in the collections of the Buffalo and Erie County Historical Society. For useful assessments of White's career, see Oliver Jones, "A Bench Mark for Obstetric History in the United States." *Obstetrics and Gynecology* (1974): 784–91; and "Our First Professor of Obstetrics, James Platt White (1811–1881)." *The Buffalo Physician* (1974): 42–47.

White's membership in Buffalo's upper class was in part due to his marriage. An anonymous biographer of the Whites wrote, "Dr. White had to struggle for his education; she had every advantage given her. He came from a farm, she from a "big house," in the English sense, where she had been surrounded with every refinement and every luxury. She had the penetration to perceive the underdeveloped, even crude youth going heroically about Black Rock on his cholera calls the man whom her husband was to become. Her breeding tempered his rugged strength without weakening it . . . she largely inspired and molded her husband's public career." Unsigned and undated typescript biography of Mrs. James Platt White, manuscript collections of the Buffalo and Erie County Historical Society.

6. *Transactions of the Association of the Alumni and Officers of the Medical Department of the University of Buffalo, for the Years 1875–1876–1877.* (Buffalo: Hansman and Burow, Printers, 1877): 29. The University's success might be judged by the size of the group listening to White's after-dinner speech to its alumni; 150 guests attended the banquet at the Tifft House, with White responding to a toast to "Our Alma Mater."

7. Austin Flint, "A Memoir of Professor James Platt White, M.D.," *Memorial: James Platt White* (Buffalo, 1882): 4.

8. Potter (1895).

9. On Buffalo's volatile ethnic and religious history, see Goldman (1983: Chs. 4 and 5); for a more complex view, see David Gerber, "Ambivalent Anti-Catholicism: Buffalo's American Protestant Elite Faces the Challenge of the Catholic Church, 1850–1860." *Civil War History* 30 (1984): 120–43. A detailed description of Buffalo's population before the Civil War time is provided by Laurence A. Glasco, *Ethnicity and Social Structures: Irish, Germans, and Native Born of Buffalo, New York, 1850–1860.* (New York: Arno Press, 1980). On the career of Bishop Timon, see Timon (1862) and Deuther (1870).

10. Deuther (1870: 298).

11. "his object was sound teaching, the value of which was to be verified at the bedside." Flint, *op. cit.:* 4.

12. On the importance of White's innovation for American medicine, see Virginia Drachman, "The Loomis Trial: Social Mores and Obstetrics in the Mid-Nineteenth Century," in *Health Care in America: Essays in Social History,* ed. Susan Reverby and David Rosner (Philadelphia: Temple University Press, 1979): 67–83.

13. A full account of the trial and the reactions of the popular and medical press are provided in Frederick T. Parsons, *Report of the Trial, The People versus Dr. Horatio N. Loomis, for Libel* (Buffalo: Jewett, Thomas and Co., 1850).

14. The *Buffalo Medical Journal* provided frequent reports about asylums such as Genoa (BMJ 1 (1846): 202), Utica (BMJ 1 (1846): 271–75), the Salpetriere (BMJ 2 (1846): 397), Worcester (BMJ 2 (1847): 689–90), Eastern Lunatic Asylum of Virginia (BMJ 9 (1853: 254), and presented

reviews of books about asylum-keeping (as in *BMJ* 10 (1854): 249–250". Austin Flint's attitude toward the care of the insane under medical management was probably typical of Buffalo's leading physicians. Commenting on the annual reports of asylums in several states, he wrote: "We have reason to feel proud of the scientific attention now being given in this country to that department of medicine which concerns mental disorders." (*BMJ* 2 (1847): 689–90). He had earlier indicated his own evaluation of the relative standing of asylum-keeping in a comment about the "mammoth Asylum" at Utica, a "charity-palace" whose superintendent, Dr. Amariah Brigham, published the *American Journal of Insanity*. Flint praised Brigham for being "actively and efficiently engaged in promoting and diffusing knowledge in this not least, if not the highest brand of medical science." (*BMJ* 1 (1846): 271–75)

15. Dix visited the poorhouse in 1844, just after Erie County voted to change its name to the "County Hospital for the Insane." After describing its inadequacies, she commented, "It will require a great many votes to convert that little building, with its few cell-rooms, into a hospital, or even an asylum." See Dorothea L. Dix, *Memorial To the Honorable the Legislature of the State of New York*, reprinted in Dix (1971: 23–24).

16. *BMJ* 12 (1856): 184–86. The Erie County Poorhouse is one of the very few to be studied systematically by an historian (see Katz 1983: 57–89). Two helpful papers on the development of Erie County welfare institutions have been written by Charles L. Bland (1975 and 1976).

17. Deuther (1870: 278–80). On the founding of the Providence Retreat, see *Providence Retreat. Seventy-Fifth Anniversary Souvenir History: 1860–1935* (Buffalo: Sisters of Charity, Providence Retreat, 1935): 9–10. See also Paul (1984).

18. "Providence Insane Asylum." *BMJ* 3 (1863): 66–69.

19. Willard (1865).

20. Willard (1865): 33–35.

21. See especially *Twenty Second Annual Report of the Superintendent of the New York State Lunatic Asylum, for the Year Ending November 30, 1864* (Utica: New York State Lunatic Asylum, 1864), 12–13, and *Twenty Fifth Annual Report . . .* (Utica: 1867): 16–19. See also the unsigned article, almost certainly by Gray, attacking special facilities for incurables: "The Willard Asylum, and Provision for the Insane." *American Journal of Insanity* 22 (1865): 192–212. For the opposing medical viewpoint, favoring development of asylums for incurables, see Cook (1866).

22. The links between nineteenth-century lunacy reform and the

need to spend state money for purely political reasons have not yet been adequately examined. Governor Hoffman played a central role in the great expansion in state care for the insane in New York, beginning to assume national leadership among the states in mental health care during this period.

23. *Proceedings in Connection with the Ceremony of Laying the Corner Stone of the Buffalo State Asylum for the Insane in the City of Buffalo. September 18, 1872* (Buffalo: White & Brayley, Printers, 1872): 28–29. An original copy of this document is in the Director's Office of the Buffalo Psychiatric Center (BPC), the current name for the institution.

24. The act of the Legislature and interim report on its implementation are found in "Report of the Commissioners to Locate an Insane Asylum in the Eight Judicial District, New York." *New York State Senate Documents, 93rd Session* 1 (1870).

25. *The Buffalo State Asylum for the Insane. By-Laws and Acts Authorizing Location, Appointment of Commissioners, Organization, etc.* (Buffalo: Warren, Johnson, & Co., Printers, 1871): 5–6. This document, an original copy of which is in the Director's Office of BPC, presents the AMSAII Propositions adopted at its annual meeting in 1851. White's relative lack of interest and, presumably, lack of knowledge about the treatment of insanity can be judged by the very few titles about it in his extensive personal library. It contained seven issues of the *American Journal of Insanity*, a single annual report from the Asylum at Utica, and a copy of Bucknill's *On Insanity*. The extensive writings of such American experts as Kirkbride, Brigham, and other superintendents are noteworthy by their absence. See *Catalogue of the Medical Library Donated to the University of Buffalo by James P. White, M.D.*, leatherbound manuscript, Medical Archives of the State University of New York at Buffalo.

26. Thomas Story Kirkbride, *On the Construction, Organization, and General Arrangements of Hospitals for the Insane* (Philadelphia: Lindsay and Blakiston, 1854). The orthodoxy is analyzed in depth by Gerald Grob in the works cited earlier. An invaluable assessment of Kirkbride's career is presented by Tomes (1981 and 1984). For an examination of Kirkbride's theories in the context of the professionalization of medicine, see Eisenhauer (1984).

27. Gray's prominence in the leadership of his profession is described by his protege in Judson B. Andrews, "Memoir of John Perdue Gray, M.D., LL.D." *American Journal of Insanity* 44 (1887): 21–32. For a portrait of Gray at the height of his national eminence, see Rosenberg (1968).

28. *Report of the Commissioners, op. cit.* 2–9.

29. *Atlas of the City of Buffalo, Erie Co., New York. From Actual Surveys and Official Records* (Philadelphia: G.M. Hopkins & Co., 1872): 100–101.

30. As the architectural historian Charles Beveridge has noted, this plan holds "a special place in the history of American city planning," since it was the first of many such plans designed by Olmsted and "the first demonstration of the form he hoped the expanding American city would take." (Beveridge in Banham 1981: 15).

31. "State Provision for the Insane. Buffalo State Asylum—Its History and Description," *American Journal of Insanity* 29 (1872): facing page 4. This unsigned article, almost certainly written by John P. Gray, is accompanied by several fine engravings, including a detailed plan of the grounds by "Mr. Fred. Law Olmsted, the celebrated landscape architect."

32. *Proceedings in . . . Laying the Corner Stone, op. cit.* 3.

33. The class structure of nineteenth-century Buffalo has been studied with great precision; see Katz, Doucet, and Stern (1982).

34. The "White Fireproof Building" was located on a triangular block of land across Erie Street from St. Paul's Episcopal Church; it was bounded by Main and West Swan Streets. see *Insurance Map of Buffalo, New York, Vol. 1* (New York: Sanborn Map & Publishing Co., 1881): Plate 13.

35. My conclusion about White's direct control over the Asylum's affairs is based on my reading the minutes of its managers: *Board of Managers. Record. Buffalo State Asylum for the Insane.* bound manuscript, Director' Office storeroom, Richardson Building basement, BPC. White's institutional memberships and accomplishments are described in detail in his *Memorial.*

36. James P. White, "Address before the Medical Society of the State of New York," *BMSJ* 9 (1870): 295.

37. "Clinical Teaching and Pathological Investigations in Insanity." *American Journal of Insanity* 26 (1870): 408–426. This unsigned article is almost certainly by Gray. It quotes extensively from White's address to the Medical Society. Noting that it is "greatly to be regretted that so large a majority of institutions for the treatment of the insane are remote from established medical schools," the article states that the commissioners of the Buffalo Asylum, "having this view, and being all medical men, gave unanimous preference to Buffalo." With the Asylum near the medical college, "the advantages of clinical instruction can now be realized." For a key statement of how the Asylum served Buffalo civic interests along with supporting the teaching of "psychological medicine" at the University of Buf-

falo, see "Editorial Department. Buffalo State Asylum and Clinical and Didactic Teaching in Medical Colleges upon the Subject of Insanity." *BMSJ* (1870): 421–23. This celebrates the location of the asylum in Buffalo, and quotes liberally from the *AJI* editorial and White's presidential speech.

38. For a biography of Richardson, see Hitchcock (1966).

39. Ochsner (1982: 65).

40. "State Provision for the Insane": facing page 6.

41. *Ibid.*: 7–9.

42. "The Kirkbride Plan: Architecture for a Treatment System that Changed." *Hospital and Community Psychiatry* 27 (1976): 473–77.

43. Several of the original plans, dated December 1869 and drawn by a J. A. Fleming, are at BPC's Work Control Center. The only major difference between them and the 1872 illustration cited above is the reversal of the angle of the last ward building. Richardson met with Gray in Buffalo in mid-December, 1869. Richardson's initial impulse reflected his experience as a student, and his unfamiliarity with American mental hospital design. His sketchbook, now in the Houghton Library at Harvard University, contains a set of "plans, elevation, and a thumbnail sketch for a hospital with pavilions connected around a courtyard." This design is close to the pattern of a French general hospital which he had worked on as a student. But his pencilled notes below the sketch reject his own sketch, noting "I much prefer Dr. Grays [sic] system" (O'Gorman 1974: 212–13).

44. "State Provision for the Insane" *loc. cit.*

45. Kirkbride *op. cit.*

46. David Gerber argues that the Protestant elite of antebellum Buffalo had been badly shaken by the challenge of Bishop Timon's success in institutional development. With the completion of St. Joseph's Cathedral in 1855, Buffalo Catholics had built the city's most impressive cultural institution. The Protestant reaction was ambivalent, leading to a new interest in civic embellishment. The new Asylum was part of the movement to improve Buffalo's cultural resources. See David Gerber, "Ambivalent Anti-Catholicism," *op. cit.*

47. Kowski (1980b; see also 1980a).

48. "State Provision for the Insane," *op. cit.* 10.

49. Ochsner (1982: 79).

50. "Proceedings in . . . Laying the Corner Stone," *op. cit.*

51. These conflicts are described in some detail in the first ten *Annual Reports* of the Board of Managers of the Asylum.

52. A brief biography of Andrews is presented in Hurd (1914 IV: 340–42). Andrews shared Gray's belief that insanity was due to lesions in the brain, and stressed a healthy diet as a response to the physical disease that was insanity.

53. Andrews resigned a year before his death in 1894.

54. *Stenographer's Minutes of the Inquiry of Commissioners of Lunacy Respecting Charges Against the Buffalo State Asylum for he Insane.* (1881) Bound typescript, Medical Archives of the State University of New York at Buffalo.

55. Flint, "Memoir," *op. cit.*

56. "Thirty-First Annual Report of the Buffalo State Hospital to the State Commission in Lunacy for the Year Ending September 30, 1901." *Thirteenth Annual Report of the State Commission in Lunacy* (Albany: the Commission, 1902): between 736–37.

57. See Grimes (1934). The last patients housed in Richardson's buildings moved to other buildings in the early 1970s. Except for three outer buildings on the east wing demolished to make room for a rehabilitation building, the original buildings still stand, though with considerable deterioration on many of the wards. The central building housed the Director's Office until 1993 and other administrative functions until 1994. The buildings have increasingly become the focus of preservation activity in Buffalo, but their size and construction make them difficult targets for restoration.

58. Mitchell (1894).

Chapter 4

Organizational Development: How the State Asylum Became the State Hospital

To create an asylum was not only to erect a set of buildings, no matter how centrally important that task was to nineteenth-century reformers. The creation of an asylum also required the formation of a new organization built around a staff capable of running the institution. The issue of staffing is examined here first in terms of the Buffalo State Asylum's founding, with particular emphasis on the implications for its organization and staffing. The Asylum's efforts to solve its most important staffing question—the role of the attendant in daily life at the hospital—are also considered.

The Asylum's physical plant both reflected earlier models of care for the insane yet also modified them for post-Civil War Buffalo. The Asylum's management, labor force, and patient population both resembled earlier examples yet differed in certain crucial respects. Like the other asylums then in operation in New York, the Buffalo Asylum was managed on a day-to-day basis by a local Board of Managers selected by the governor from Buffalo's business and medical elites. In the late 1870s, the Board turned to the task of creating the social structure of the hospital. The presence of Dr. Gray, medical superintendent of the New York State Asylum for the Insane (at Utica), was again critical, for the Board of Managers chose as the Buffalo Asylum's first superintendent Gray's protege, Dr. Judson B. Andrews, who had served for the past 13 years at Utica, nine of them as Gray's first assistant. Care for the insane at the Buffalo Asylum would be shaped by Andrews' experience at Utica and the new problems he would find at Buffalo.

THE SUPERINTENDENT

Andrews, in Gray's opinion, was "thoroughly qualified" for his new position in Buffalo (Utica AR 1880: 61; "AR" is used to abbreviate "Annual Report"). His biography (Hurd 1916 IV: 340–42) shows certain elements common to other successful asylum superintendents of the late nineteenth century, though his attainments were well above average. Born in Connecticut in 1834, he graduated from Yale in 1855, and taught school for several years before beginning his studies at Jefferson Medical College in Philadelphia in 1857. After Andrews returned to teaching in Saratoga County, New York, the Civil War broke out. The death of a local military leader "aroused his patriotic ardor," and he joined the 77th Regiment, New York Volunteers. With Andrews its elected captain, the regiment took part in the Richmond campaign. Andrews' failing health, however, forced him to resign, and he returned to Yale to complete his medical studies, graduating in 1863.

Andrews received a commission as assistant surgeon and returned to the Union army later in the year. His new regiment took extremely heavy casualties in the battle of Cold Harbor, with the largest number of members killed (129) in any single engagement during the war. Andrews participated in several other major battles, and was present at the Confederacy's surrender at Appomattox.

After the war, Andrews began his career at Utica under Gray. While the Asylum at Utica was opened during the era of "moral treatment," Andrews' service there exposed him to a new phase in the state treatment of the insane. In this new phase, asylum superintendents presided over far larger patient populations, usually crowded into buildings planned for fewer patients. Unlike the earlier era, insanity was presumed to be curable if treated during the earlier phase of the disease. Dr. Gray was the leading figure in the assumption that insanity was a disease of the brain, always attributable to some lesion that would eventually be treatable through medical intervention. Gray led the way in requiring autopsies of asylum patients, and his annual reports during the years Andrews served as his assistant often included lengthy and detailed reports of the pathologist's search for these lesions. Gray's ideas played a role, though perhaps a more modest one than he might have relished, in the demise of the moral treatment of insanity, and its replacement by a fully medical model for the treatment of the insane (Bockoven 1956). While moral treatment may have never fully disappeared from the American mental institution, the arrival of larger and larger patient populations, many of them elderly and with poor likelihood of recovery, made moral treatment increasingly impractical.

With a background that mixed military command with the practice of asylum medicine, Andrews assumed his superintendency on October 1, 1880; the first patients, transferred from the Asylum at Utica, were admitted six weeks later. By the end of the year, 50 patients were being treated: "The Buffalo State Asylum for the Insane is now launched on its career as an institution devoted to the care and treatment of the insane." (AR 1880: 2) By the end of the decade, almost ten times that number were under care.

ATTENDANTS

The optimism that attended the opening of the asylum was rapidly called into question, as the Board of Managers reported in their report of the first full year of patient care: "The asylum is a hospital in which the judicious and proper care of patients is the first and highest duty of *all* connected with its management. It was erected, organized, and is conducted as such. It had scarcely been opened for the reception of patients, before it was violently and maliciously assailed. It was alleged that patients were abused and violently treated in the asylum" (AR 1881: 6; emphasis in original).

The Buffalo newspapers published lengthy stories about the allegations of an attendant, Frank P. Churchill, who charged that two other attendants, Robert H. Jones and J. F. McMichael, "had, to his personal knowledge, habitually maltreated patients confided to their care." After an investigation by the State Commissioner in Lunacy revealed the charges to be questionable, the Board of Managers took no further action in the matter.

Starr (1982: 345) has noted that the newspaper scandal is a periodic feature of the history of mental institutions, and that it takes two forms, the scandal of repression and the scandal of neglect. In the first, people who are not mentally ill are railroaded into institutions against their will. While the Buffalo Asylum was not spared this type of scandal during its first decade (see AR 1883: 6; AR 1885: 11), our focus here will be on the second, in which patients are alleged to receive little or no treatment, or are claimed to be the victims of abuse, violence, or even murder. The professional staff are rarely the targets of this second type of scandal. Most of the blame is placed on the attendants who have the most direct contact with the patients.

The location of the Buffalo Asylum no doubt exacerbated the serious problems of securing a stable workforce of reliable attendants. Unlike an established institution like Utica, the Buffalo Asylum had to recruit an entirely new staff in a very competitive labor market. Except for a small Catholic institution, there were no other asylums nearby from which experienced attendants could be drawn. The proximity of the settled part of Buffalo was so close that the Asylum would be under the very close scrutiny of the many newspapers, whose circulation wars could only be helped by lurid asylum scandals. Finally, wages at the Asylum were kept very low, with the typical attendant during the 1880s making less than half that earned by workers in manufacturing or railroads.

In 1884, the Buffalo Asylum paid its 17 male attendants salaries that ranged from $20 to $28 per month, room and full board included (State Board of Charities 1884: 131–33). By 1890, these rates had been raised by roughly two dollars a month, so that males were being paid wages of from $264 to $336 a year, room and board included (Commission in Lunacy,

1890: 71). By contrast, the average annual earnings in 1890 were $475 for nonfarm employees, $439 for manufacturing, and $560 for railroad employees. Women received considerably less for the same work, usually only about two-thirds that of men. While this inequality was criticized by the State Commission in Lunacy, which noted that women "usually give more hours to the service, and are more industrious, faithful and painstaking, as a class, than an equal number of men" (Commission in Lunacy, 1890: 221), nonetheless, the prevailing inequalities in the labor market permitted the State to keep the wages unequal.

The value of room and board is difficult to estimate. The attendants were given the same food as that given to the patients. Dr. Andrews' Annual Report (AR 1883: 30) presents a "Table of Diet" that promised meat or fish at least one meal a day and often twice a day: "This diet was changed from time to time, and enlarged by varieties in vegetables in season." In fact, the Asylum's farm was something of a failure during its first decade of operation. The soil was regularly blamed for the poor production of vegetables. The value of room is even more difficult to estimate. On the one hand, the Asylum building was very well-designed. During the very coldest days of the Buffalo winter in February 1886, for example, the outside temperature averaged only three degrees; the Asylum's wards were kept at 70 degrees (AR 1886: 8). On the other hand, most of the attendants lived immediately adjacent to their patients. The following Commission in Lunacy (1890: 223) observation almost certainly fits life at the Buffalo Asylum:

> When it is remembered that the duties of this class of employees require them to remain in immediate contact with the insane for many consecutive hours daily, and necessitate a submission on their part to rigid rules of discipline and constant control of demeanor, it will be seen that while on duty they must of necessity be under constant and severe strain . . . these employees should be provided with comfortable quarters quite apart from the wards, thus insuring to them when off duty that undisturbed rest and quiet which is so essential to their mental and physical well-being.

Asylum life for the average attendant was a combination of a long and demanding day, followed by something other than "undisturbed rest and quiet."

Not surprisingly, then, Andrews' annual reports during the 1880s often note with gratitude almost no turnover in his medical and supervisory personnel, but comment frequently on the difficulty in keeping attendants. Until the 1880s, learning the job of "attending upon the insane" was an informal matter. What skill or success in treatment attendants developed was either intuitive or the result of years of experience. The need to recruit a large staff immediately upon the opening of the Buffalo Asylum, combined with its urban location (and accompanying competition from other employers) and a difficult patient mix, made the development of more formal training techniques more likely.

The patients admitted to the asylum presented formidable nursing and management problems. In today's language, virtually all were admitted involuntarily. From the very first admissions, the Asylum received a large number of chronic insane whose prognosis for recovery was presumed low. In the first year of operation the Asylum admitted 219 patients (AR 1881). Almost 40 percent of the admissions were cases of insanity of more than two years' duration, making them unlikely prospects for cure. Over a third of the patients were judged to be either homicidal or suicidal; 18 were brought to the Asylum in some form of restraint. Almost a quarter of the admissions had substantial physical injuries, including 32 who were "broken down by intemperance and vicious habits and indulgences." Figures for the rest of the decade are similar, with some years presenting even more physical impairment.

DAILY WORK LIFE AT THE ASYLUM

The Asylum's daily work life in the early 1880s can be reconstructed at least partially from a detailed portrait of its daily life on November 28, 1883 (AR 1883: 35–44) and an account of a visit by members of the State Board of Charities (1884: 131–35; 150–56) on October 2, 1884. The former document gives a picture of how Andrews tried to organize the Asylum's staff; the latter, a glimpse at what informed visitors, usually somewhat sympathetic to the goals of the asylum, though a bit critical of actual conditions, saw.

The Asylum had a small staff to care for its patients. In 1883, for example, the Asylum had a daily average of 301 patients under care (AR 1883: 33–44). To assist Dr. Andrews, there were two other physicians, one for males and one for females. The other resident officers were the steward, who was in charge of purchasing, male personnel, and the farm; and the matron, responsible for female attendants, care of the sick, clothing and bedding, and "oversight of the domestic affairs of the household." The treasurer, a non-resident officer, controlled finances and receiving and spending money. A medical student with experience in a drug store was employed as an apothecary.

The rest of the direct patient care was in the hands of attendants during the day, and two "night-watchers," one for each sex, during the night. A ward had between 25 and 38 patients, with an average of 27.8 on the six female units and 33 on the five male ones. During the day, each ward had three attendants assigned to it. The "attendant in charge" received orders either directly from a physician or through the steward or matron. The attendant in charge was responsible both for the care of the patients and the conduct of the other attendants. On most wards, two other attendants were assigned, one to assist in patient care, the other to operate the dining-room. On wards housing the most disturbed patients, a fourth attendant was assigned.

Dr. Andrews' own words present a very detailed job description for the nonmedical direct care staff of the early 1880s:

> There is one supervisor in charge of the women's, and one of the men's department. Their duties are, as the name implies, supervisory. They communicate with the medical office, receive and introduce new patients to the wards, instruct attendants in their duties, distribute medicines, accompany the physician in his daily rounds, see that his directions are carried out in making all changes from ward to ward, and all details of patients for outside labor. They make a list of the clothing of patients when admitted, and collect it when discharged, and arrange for visits between patients and their friends as directed by the medical officers. In the performance of their duties they are constantly on the wards of their respective divisions and have the fullest opportunity to oversee the conduct of the attendants in their intercourse with and treatment of patients. They are promoted from the most experienced attendants. The wards on which they reside are in telephonic communication with the medical office, and they can at all times receive immediate direction in every case of necessity, or summon a physician at once. Their position is one of great responsibility, and requires persons of judgment and intelligence. (AR 1883: 33–34)

Below these two supervisors were the several grades of attendants. Again Dr. Andrews provides a description of their duties:

> The attendant in charge is responsible for the conduct of the other attendants, and for the care of the patients on the ward. He receives instructions and orders directly from the physicians or through the supervisor. He looks after the sick, attends to the bathing, the changes of clothing, and has the care of the same, and is required to know intimately all the patients under his charge, and report to the physician of their health, their appetite, habits, and peculiarities; whether they manifest suicidal or violent tendencies, the delusions expressed, and changes in their mental or physical condition. The second attendant assists in the domestic duties of the wards, in getting patients up, making their toilet, afterward in their occupation, exercise and amusements. The dining-room attendant has charge of the dining-room, sets the table, distributes the food to those at the general table and the extra diet to the sick, and is responsible for the good order and cleanliness of his department. He also, with the second attendant, takes charge of the patients in their walking and occupations. In the various duties of the wards the attendants are assisted by such of the patients as are willing to render aid, though they are not *compelled* to labor . . . The attendants are the constant companions of the patients,

they live with them, eat with them, sleep on the wards with them, and exercise over them such moral influence as they are capable of. (AR 1883: 34; emphasis in original)

An important role in the Asylum's workforce was that of night-watcher. From roughly 9 P.M. to 6 A.M., the direct care of patients was the responsibility of the man and woman assigned this position. While the other residential staff could be summoned in emergencies, the night-watchers were completely in charge of the Asylum during these hours, as Dr. Andrews informed his readers:

The night-watchers make the rounds of the wards early in the evening to inform themselves of any new patients who may have been received during the day, and of the arrangement for sleeping, of any changes from ward to ward, or in the condition of the sick. At nine o'clock they report at the medical office to receive instructions. They are given the names of any patients who may need their services, the sick and helpless, the suicidal and violent, and those who are indifferent in their habits. They visit every ward every hour, and seriously ill, or strongly suicidal or disturbed, every half hour. They give such food and medicine as the physician may direct, and if his services are required call him at once by telephone from his room. In case of need they call up an attendant from the ward. Special watches are detailed from among the attendants in any case where constant care is deemed necessary. The night-watchers remain on duty till the ringing of the rising bell, after which they make a detailed report for the information of the physician . . . A full report is made of any incidents worthy of note, as finding doors unlocked, lights burning, or any infringement of rules; the condition of the sick, the administration of medicines ordered, the occurrence of a fit; attempts to break out, violent conduct or disturbance of any character. These are written on separate sheets of paper and accompany the regular report. The carrying out of this system proves highly satisfactory in furnishing a complete record of the wards during the hours of the night. (AR 1883: 34–35)

Dr. Andrews presented the "Night-Watchers Report" for November 28, 1883. It showed the ward, name (only indicated by initial in this version), and condition at each hourly visit by the male and female watcher. Of the 165 male patients, 16 were at some point during the night either "awake," "noisy," "out of bed," "filthy," "wet," or "taken up," the last a term indicating that the watcher had helped a patient to the toilet. Of the 167 women, 24 were so described. Andrews concluded that the table "shows the thoroughness of the supervision of patients, which is maintained during the night" (AR 1883: 35–36).

Much of the attendant's work with patients involved the nursing of physical illnesses. In the early 1880s, nursing had not yet become a distinct occupation apart from the other work of the attendant. Andrews' essay implies that nursing duties were the common concern of attendants and even supervisors.

A major part of the role of attendant was to help patients engage in various occupations. Using a system similar to the one that Gray developed at Utica more than 20 years earlier (described in Utica AR 1876: 54–63), daily records were kept by the supervisors on the type of work, if any, each patient performed. A table presented in Andrews' report shows patient labor statistics for November 23, 1883, "a fair exhibit of the occupation of the day." These statistics are intriguing, since they were published in considerable detail in the early reports of the Asylum and the several agencies that inspected the institution. Yet Andrews made clear in several of his reports that patient work was to be viewed entirely as therapeutic: "Employment in an asylum is strictly a medical question and should be directed by the physician and prescribed as medicine and diet are" (AR 1882: 24). He even questioned whether too much emphasis had been placed on patient labor in other asylums, agreeing with Gray of Utica that many patients had been overworked before their admission and required rest, not work (Utica AR 1876: 54). Gray observed that the great majority of his patients were "overworked, and undernourished people of both sexes. Many of them are old, and others are feeble, and suffer under chronic diseases and infirmities. They indeed need rest far more than work; rest of body and rest of mind" (Utica AR 1876: 54). Nonetheless, for those who could work and were willing to work, Andrews, like many other superintendents, viewed labor as a helpful therapy. He did not deny that it was equally beneficial to the institution, and each Annual Report contained fairly detailed estimates of work at the Asylum. In the early 1880s roughly three quarters of the patients performed some type of work on a regular basis. The published reports do not permit more than the crudest estimate of the value of this labor to the institution. The statistical tables report as employed "those who occupy themselves in any useful work for any length of time" (AR 1883: 41), and Andrews denied it was possible to calculate its value because it varied from "short periods" to "several hours."

The Annual Reports for this decade present an apparent paradox. Patient work is reported in considerable detail, yet its value is routinely minimized. The farm produced products valued at about 5 percent of the institution's annual budget, almost all of mending of clothing and bedding was done by patients, and much of the routine maintenance of the buildings and grounds was accomplished by patients supervised by attendants. The available evidence is consistent with several explanations. First, it is possible that Andrews' own explanation is correct—that the work patients did had therapeutic value. It is equally possible that, as later critics of the twentieth-century mental hospital often maintained, the Asylum was already exploiting patient labor to maintain itself, and had become something of an urban plantation (Grimes 1934; Deutsch 1948). Another likely explanation accepts parts of both of these views. Involvement of the insane in some type of labor was a central part of the "moral treatment" in an earlier phase of the nineteenth-century asylum (Bockoven 1956). Its inclusion in treatment was virtually inevitable in a new asylum, whether or not it produced much of value. It performed the useful function of allowing the nonclinical staff who operated the farm and maintained the buildings and grounds to perform limited tasks in patient care, almost a necessity given the small number of attendants employed by the hospital. The paradoxical character of labor's image in the annual reports probably can be explained by the effort that Andrews and other superintendents had to make to legitimate the relatively expensive care they provided to the insane. Asylums such as Buffalo were treating populations who in earlier decades were often incarcerated in county poorhouses. Nineteenth-century reformers from Dix onward argued passionately for the segregation of the insane from other types of paupers. This the Asylum certainly accomplished, but only partially and at considerable expense. County officials were required to send the insane to the Asylum, but they had economic motivation to err in the direction of keeping marginal types in their own poorhouses, since the cost of Asylum care was charged to county of residence. This may shed light on one of the major themes of Andrews' reports, which rarely failed to note how important prompt commitment to an asylum was if cure was to be effected:

> The natural tendency of such ideas of economy is to retain in county custody all of the insane that can be kept at home and to withdraw from the State asylums every case, at the earliest possible moment, and the question may fairly be raised whether all of the acute insane, and such as present a reasonable prospect of improvement, are sent to State hospitals as contemplated and required by law. Whether they are sent or not depends upon a belief in the curability of the case; and the important question of whether a patient is likely to be benefitted by medical care and treatment, avowedly a difficult one for an expert, is left to a county official to decide off-hand. It is not strange, then, that the county asylums should receive the benefit of any doubt that may arise, and that they contain patients who have never had the advantage of treatment in any State institution. (AR 1887: 41)

ORGANIZATIONAL INNOVATION: THE TRAINING SCHOOL

As noted earlier, the Asylum faced a serious problem in recruiting and retaining attendants, largely because the state was unwilling to provide wages competitive with Buffalo's new industries and old commercial enterprises. A long work day followed by an evening in close proximity to thirty or more insane posed serious problems. The sheer size of the building made supervision of staff even more problematic. The patients often had serious physical ailments in addition to their behavioral troubles, at least in part because of the Asylum's location in a big city.

Andrews was well aware of the importance of attracting and holding good attendants, and devoted a quarter of his report for 1884 to the problem. He began with a premise: "It is a self-evident fact that much of the success which attends the conduct of an asylum depends upon the character of the attendants, who are necessarily intrusted (sic) with the immediate care of the patients" (AR 1884: 26). The selection and training of attendants was a difficult task for the physician, requiring

> not only time and patience, but the exercise of wise discrimination in judging of character and of adaptability to the work to be performed. To make a good attendant requires a combination of original qualities which are to be further developed by constant supervision and instruction. The requirements are good health, patience, kindness of disposition, intelligence, a fair degree of education, and that coolness and self-control which enables one to meet successfully the varying states of patients and retain their respect. Added to this, there must be a fidelity to the trust reposed, a willingness to receive direction and reproof and a love for the work. To obtain such as approximate to the requirements is at times, and in some locations, a matter of serious difficulty. (AR 1884: 26)

The problem was not a lack of applications, for Andrews implied that many obviously unfit candidates had appeared at the Asylum. Some misperceived what the work required. With an obvious reference to the county poor houses, the frequent target of hostile comments from the asylum superintendent, Andrews commented that many applicants "were imbued with the idea—a heritage of the past—that as attendants upon the insane, they are simply keepers or wardens, who are to receive large pay for very little work." Others wanted the job as a sinecure, complete with good medical care for their approaching old age. Still others saw it as a temporary job until a better one came along in a different line of work. Some were too young, had "questionable habits," or lacked education or intelligence. Finally, some of the applicants admitted they had been fired by other asylums for cause.

At least some of those unfit for work as attendants were screened out by the new state civil-service requirements of literacy and references of good character. Andrews noted that this reform had little effect at his institution, which had made similar requirements before and did not award jobs through patronage. Awareness that the examination was required and that the attendant was part of the public service of the state would "tend to elevate the character of the applicants." Applicants were also required to sign an agreement that they would work obediently for a year. The first month's wages were held until the end of the year. If the attendant performed adequately, the wages were finally paid.

Until October 1883, the introduction of the attendant to his or her duties was informal, consisting of whatever comments were made during the course of a work day by one's supervisor. At that point a more formal approach was taken to training, which developed into the first training school for attendants of both sexes in an American asylum, and the first in a public mental hospital. It is not clear whether the Buffalo experiment is a case of the diffusion of an innovation or an independent invention. A year earlier the training of female nurses of the insane was begun in the McLean Hospital (near Boston), reflecting similar developments in the Boston City Hospital (Cowles 1916). Almost certainly, a physician of Andrews' stature would have been aware of the Boston experiment. The movement to train nurses set in motion by Florence Nightingale in England had reached the United States through Elizabeth Blackwell, the first American woman physician (Bullough and Bullough 1978: 106ff). The feminist movement and The Civil War had both accelerated interest in training nurses, and during the 1870s training schools were created in several hospitals, though on a limited scale.

Insane asylums such as McLean and the Buffalo Asylum had one characteristic that made them more fertile ground for innovation in this area than hospitals were. Asylums had medical superintendents, while hospitals were virtually all run by lay trustees (Cowles 1916; Rosenberg 1981). The Buffalo Asylum's need to create a new work force and the transiency of its attendants, combined with patients requiring considerable nursing, all played a role in making the institution of the training school more likely. Andrews' own background, including his extensive Civil War experience and his tenure at Utica, made him more than likely to view improvements in the training of attendants as an important step.

The first year of the school consisted of a series of lectures given during the winter months by the assistant physicians. When summer came, the attendants were judged to be too busy outside to participate in formal training. The content of the training was first described by Andrews in the Asylum's Annual Report for 1884:

> The rules are fully explained, and the reason for them, and their importance stated. After this, lectures are given in physiology, hygiene, and the art of nursing; they are taught what to do in case of accident, of injury, how to control hemorrhage, to perform artificial respiration, to count the pulse, to take temperatures and to observe symptoms. In short, the instruction, so far as practicable among the insane, is made to conform to that given in a regular training school. (AR 1884: 28–29)

One of the assistant physicians, William D. Granger, later published a slim book that allows an examination of the content of the instruction. He notes in his preface: "The lectures were given to the class almost as they appear in these pages" (Granger, 1886: iii). The first three chapters presented some ideas on "The Nervous System and Some of Its More Important Functions," "The Mind and Some of Its Faculties," and "Insanity; Or, Disease of the Mind." The anonymous review that appeared in the *American Journal of Insanity* (Anon. 1886a) comments that in these three chapters, "The author has done wisely in not attempting . . . more than the merest outline of anatomy and physiology, and that in the simplest language." These three lectures probably had the consequence of establishing both the medical authority of the lecturer and the fact that insanity was a disease to be diagnosed and treated only by a physician. They have no real relationship to the remaining seven chapters in the book, which are more practical in character.

The lectures are important primarily because of what they say about the role the attendant must play in the Asylum's work day. They do not attempt to "professionalize" the role of the attendant. There is no attempt to pass on a theoretical body of knowledge or a special ethical responsibility; certainly no independent or collegial form of organization is advocated. Almost the opposite: the role of the attendant is to be obedient to the orders of the physician or other officer of the asylum. What skill the attendant eventually learns in the care of the insane will come primarily through learning the everyday routines of the ward while occupying the lowest position in the asylum's hierarchy. In beginning his chapter on "The Duties of an Attendant," Granger provides an answer to the question of what an attendant should first learn:

> These many duties are not quickly nor easily learned, and the new attendant must be willing to fill, at first, a minor position, to begin at the beginning and learn gradually all the details of ward work; he must acquire habits of caution and watchfulness, and learn in a general way the care of the insane, before he can assume a position of authority over other attendants, the control of a ward, and the responsibility of the direct care of patients.

Granger admitted that the position of attendant was "often a trying one," but alluded to several sources of motivation. Attendants and patients developed "many delightful friendships." Attendants should practice the Golden Rule, "Thou shalt love thy neighbor as thy self." They should care for their patients as they would want someone to care for their mother, sister, or brother. Finally, Granger reminded them that their contract with the Asylum created "mutual legal responsibilities." They should try to conduct themselves so that when they leave their position at the Asylum, it is with "universal respect."

Another important theme in Granger's lectures concerned observation of patient behavior. The Asylum building was so large, and the patient population so numerous, that the superintendent and his assistant physicians had to depend largely on the observations of their subordinates to manage both the asylum as an institution as well as the care of individual patients. Granger advised the attendants to rely on written notes. "In practice, written notes taken at the time, are extremely valuable in teaching close and accurate observation, and cultivating an ability to clearly express to others the result." He presented a "system of observation" that suggested the attendant observe 21 different aspects of the patient's health and behavior, ranging from the "effect of medicine," the condition of various organs, appetite and sleep patterns, to the mental condition, habits and general conduct of the individual.

For three attendants (and frequently fewer) on a ward with 30 patients, making observations on only a portion of these items would be a formidable task, much less writing up detailed written notes. But Granger argued that the attendants had to be aware of individuals, not just the ward as a whole, and to be alert to what he called "silent symptoms," the withdrawal of the patient from life on the ward.

Consistent with Andrews' philosophy of asylum life, Granger placed great emphasis on involving the patient in some type of work. "Of all things, idleness and loafing are the worst . . . asylum life should be made as home-like, pleasant, and natural as possible." Patients should work as much as possible, though "overwork is as bad as idleness." Granger told the attendants that they should not sit idle themselves, but presumably should engage in whatever occupation their charges were pursuing. Patients were to be encouraged to care as much as possible for themselves, and in general to live as they might outside the asylum. Efforts to break the tedium of ward life should include daily walks on the grounds, if possible. Patients should have their own clothing, "in all well-regulated asylums," and bathe weekly or even more often if necessary.

Granger's lecture on the care of the violent insane suggested that the attendant study closely the pattern of behavior that provoked the violence. Usually it was possible to discover the cause of the problem, and then the attendant would be able to remove the cause in the future. If the patient had to be restrained, other attendants could be summoned. Three attendants were necessary to hold a violent patient, and from four to six to carry the patient. Restraint could only be employed at the order of a physician, and a restrained patient could never be left alone. Similarly, seclusion of the patient had to be immediately reported.

Other chapters in Granger's book discussed the use of the most common medicines and therapies, such as opium, chloral, dry and moist heat, and the use of hot baths and wet packing. Brief sections described a series of clinical procedures that must have been the subject of classroom demonstrations, since the book contained no illustrations. The attendants were taught how to give hypodermic injections, forcible feeding with the stomach tube, and the use of "nutritive enemata." Granger also explained how to deal with emergencies such as suicide attempts and how to accomplish artificial respiration.

The initial set of lectures were a success. All but two of the attendants employed at the Asylum attended them and displayed a "gratifying interest." To be sure, they also were reported to "find it a recreation and relief from the monotony of their daily work" (AR 1885: 26). Though more women than men participated, the men demonstrated "equal if not a greater" interest. A special report to the Board of Trustees was followed by the unanimous resolution that a training school be established. A committee developed a plan for the school and wrote a circular that announced its formation. Students admitted to the school were hired as attendants at the lowest pay grade. Each of the two years of the course ended in an examination that, if passed, brought an increase in compensation. After passing the first year's exam, attendants received a raise of $3 per month and two weeks' paid vacation. Successfully passing the second exam brought an added $3 per month as well as a "certificate of qualification as trained nurses and attendants." Graduates of the school who were placed in charge of wards were to receive an additional $2 per month. Acceptance of the pay created the obligation of remaining on the staff of the Asylum for at least one more year.

The creation of the training school was "approved and commended" by the State Board of Charities (AR 1885: 26), which viewed its establishment as "the beginning of a new era in the selection and proper qualification of attendants for the insane." The initial evaluation by the asylum's medical superintendent was equally positive:

> The advantages so far derived have more than repaid the labor expended. There have (sic) been an improvement in the order and discipline of the asylum, and the *morale* of the service has been elevated. The patients are treated with a more intelligent consideration, and as a consequence there are fewer complaints. The sick are better cared for, self-reliance cultivated, and emergencies are most successfully met. The power of observation is quickened, and changes in both the mental and physical conditions are more readily appreciated and more generally reported. We feel assured that a higher and better standard of care has been attained, and that thus the desire of the board, as expressed in the circular, will be more fully reached by the continued instruction. Whether the special training and the improved pay to those who succeed in completing the course of instruction will accomplish the second object— permanency in the occupation of attendants—cannot now be determined. We must leave the decision of this question to abide the results. (AR 1885: 26–27)

By the next year, Andrews had more evidence, all of it positive, about the impact of the training school (AR 1886: 31). The quality of service had been "improved and elevated" generally. Two patients were saved from suffocation by the use of artificial respiration learned at the school. "Without this prompt action death would have occurred before the physician, who was summoned at once, could have reached the ward." The training school apparently also had an impact on the retention of staff, since all of the graduates of the school still remained in the service of the asylum and had been given positions of "greatest responsibility" on the wards.

The first graduating ceremony was conducted on April 20, 1886. In attendance were the Board of Managers, the president of the State Board of Charities, and the State Commissioner in Lunacy, who also gave the main address. The Commissioner gave a brief history of treatment of the insane, telling the graduates: "from the preceding review it is apparent that your occupation has gradually developed from humble beginnings to the rank of honourable and useful profession." He predicted that within a decade no attendant would be employed in New York asylums who was not a graduate of a training school. Calling the school a "far-reaching reform," the Commissioner claimed that many asylums were preparing to follow Buffalo's example.

The professional reaction was also positive. Just a month after the graduation ceremony, Granger read a paper about the school to the fortieth annual meeting of the superintendents' association. The July issue of the *American Journal of Insanity* carried an account of the graduation ceremony by a "prominent physician" who was present (Anon. 1886b). The account included examples of the questions asked at the final examination of candidates. The 38 questions asked about insanity and the 15 about epilepsy clearly parallel Granger's text. By contrast, examples drawn from the 41 "miscellaneous questions" go considerably beyond the text into areas of practical nursing such as the "varieties of hemorrhage and the methods of arresting each" and "how should a room be disinfested after a case of contagious disease." The relatively greater attention to practical nursing is reflected in the 55 questions directed at midwifery and "monthly nursing," as compared with 14 about the nervous system and 18 about the mind.

The account also contains brief excerpts from three essays by the students read to the commencement audience. Judging from the excerpts, the anonymous correspondent is correct in concluding that the essays showed "the intelligence of the attendants and their thoroughness of operation." Mrs. Hobson's essay on "The Relations of Attendants to Patients" discussed the mission of her work:

> Attendants for the insane are more than nurses for the sick. They are ever on the watch, are the instruments of order and discipline, and to a great extent the active agents of moral treatment. To be with these poor sufferers and not take an interest in them is impossible. Sometimes humanity warms the interest and it is exalted into a principle, but if we go still far-

ther and religion animates it, happy indeed is the woman whose mind and moral nature are harmoniously engaged in the dispensation of mercy to her fellow creatures. (Anon., 1886b: 124)

Although both men and women attended the initial lectures of the training school, the first seven graduates of the school were women, as were a considerable majority of the graduates during the rest of the century. The development of mental hospital nursing as a largely female occupation was well under way in the mid–1880s in Buffalo.

The Buffalo training school for attendants evolved quite rapidly into a school of nursing during the early 1890s. The fact that, as early as 1897, the school was using a nursing textbook by P. M. Wise (1896) demonstrates how advanced that transformation had become. Wise's two-volume text, filled with dozens of illustrations and sophisticated scientific terminology, differs greatly from the relatively simple text by Granger, though it does cite the latter as a reference for the nursing of the insane.

The national impact of the training school movement launched by the Buffalo Asylum and McLean was substantial though incomplete. Granger (1916: 307) claimed it began at the 1886 superintendents' meetings, and within a few years several dozen schools were in operation. By 1906, 62 training schools in hospitals for the insane were in operation in the United States (Cowles 1916: 297).

More difficult to assess was the training school movement's impact on the general development of hospital nursing. The anonymous physician who wrote the very favorable account of the first graduating ceremony for *The American Journal of Insanity* was almost certainly Henry M. Hurd. Hurd, superintendent of the Eastern Michigan Asylum, was listed as present at the ceremony (AR 1886: 26), and was present at the superintendents' association discussion the next month, credited by Granger (1916) as the "birthplace" of training schools. As the first superintendent of the Johns Hopkins Hospital, Hurd played a leading role in the development of professional nursing in the 1890s. Isabel Hampton, whom he appointed superintendent of the new training school, often quoted Hurd's description of "the hands of the nurse" as "a physician's hands *lengthened out* to minister to the sick." Hurd (1914) later organized what stands as the most complete description of American mental hospitals. He gave a prominent place to histories of the training school movement at the McLean (Cowles 1916) and Buffalo (Granger 1916) Asylums.

FROM STATE ASYLUM TO STATE HOSPITAL

In examining the initial staffing of the Buffalo State Asylum, we have seen that the scale and physical location of the asylum, the urban population mix, and the military and professional experience of the institution's first medical superintendent can partly account for its development of the first public training school for attendants. An important question to address in the context of these observations is: What were the implications for the nearly 100,000 people who would be admitted to the asylum during its first century?

A provisional answer must begin by noting the significant contribution the professionalization of nursing made to the care of those asylum patients with physical illnesses, and to the growing number of elderly who would spend the last years of their lives on the Asylum's wards (Grob 1979). To simply dismiss this care as custodial, as if it were in some sense unimportant to the lives of thousands of people, would be as much in error as to praise it uncritically. By raising the quality of care, including purely palliative care, the training school improved asylum life for many of its patients. By protecting the Asylum's patients from the spread of infectious and nosocomial disease, lives were prolonged; this was particularly critical in an urban area like Buffalo, since the asylum grounds adjoined neighborhoods periodically swept by smallpox (AR 1890: 35) and diphtheria (AR 1888: 20).

Like many other health care and social reforms, there is another side to the story of the mental asylum training school. Like many other Progressive era reforms, the concept of the training school was initiated from above, by the medical superintendent and managers of the Asylum. It was intended to improve care and retain staff, on the terms defined by those who ran the institution. While clearly consistent with the efforts of Nightingale to professionalize nursing, the creation of the training school and its subsequent direction was always controlled by physicians and managers, at first locally and later in Albany. As in the American hospital schools of nursing, Nightingale's insistence on independent funding was ignored. Nursing for the insane would develop under the subordination of the physician in the hospital hierarchy of authority (Friedson 1970: 57ff).

The reform played an important role in the battle against the county poorhouse as a "receptacle" for the insane. Hospital superintendents like Andrews (AR 1888: 32) and lunacy reformers such as the State Commissioner in Lunacy (AR 1887: 40) could contrast the highly trained asylum attendant with the staff of the county house, who were distinguished by their low pay and absence of any training whatsoever. Image and reality, however, did not entirely match. The average attendant at the Buffalo Asylum during its first two decades did not graduate from the school. Rather than transforming the entire direct care staff, the training school in its early years functioned to produce a layer of supervisory personnel above the average attendant. Since the overall staffing of the asylum did not increase to keep pace with the growth in admissions, the training school's effect was even more modest.

Notably, the training school also played a significant role in the demise of what elements of moral treatment still existed at the Asylum in the 1880s (Bockoven 1956). The role of the trained attendant and, later, nurse, became increasingly technical in character, as comparisons of the training texts in use have made clear (Granger 1886; Wise 1896). By 1890, the image of the institution began to change quickly, as Andrews noted:

> Another act of the last Legislature is of such importance that reference to it should not be overlooked. We refer to the change in the nomenclature of all the institutions for the care and treatment of the insane in the State. The change of name from asylum to hospital is a step in advance which characterizes the progress of the age. Some may consider it merely a matter of sentiment, but it is of greater import than this . . . Who would not prefer to be sent to a State hospital rather than to a State lunatic asylum. The word hospital carries with it and enforces the idea of the treatment of the sick rather than that of a place of refuge and simple care. This is an index of progress. (AR 1890: 39)

Despite such proclamations, research under way even at that time at the Worcester State Hospital actually demonstrated that the moral treatment of the asylums of the early days of the nineteenth century had higher rates of recovery (not merely discharge) than the state hospitals of the end of the century (Morrissey 1980: 62; Bockoven 1956). Following a medical model that at the time had little to offer in treating insanity, the graduates of the training school were taught to view moral treatment as pre-scientific. Combined with other reforms of the 1890s, such as the opening of a pavilion for the medical treatment of acute cases and a pathology laboratory, the training school led to an increasingly greater emphasis on medical treatment that was necessarily custodial in character.

Finally, the training school, like its counterpart in the hospitals, functioned to guarantee a stable supply of men and women at low wages. During its first years of operation, attending the school resulted in increased pay, though still below that earned in other working-class occupations. In later years, nurses in training would receive even less pay than male attendants in training would. The practice of paying women a fraction of the wages of men would continue, and nursing's domination by the professional paternalism of medicine would deepen (Ashley 1976).

The training school, then, clearly failed to "solve" the manpower problem for the state hospital. What it did instead was to permit the hospital to function as an ever-growing custodial operation, with custody firmly under the control of a medical superintendent and with the upper layers of a supervisory hierarchy made up of physicians and nurses. While changes did take place, the everyday life of the state asylum of 1890 was remarkably the same as it would be more than a half-century later. For the most part the changes did not fundamentally alter the character of the institution. To take one crucial example, various therapies were tried, usually on a small portion of the population and usually with minimal if any effects on the outcome of their hospital stay. Some therapies, such as the various forms of hydrotherapy, provided some small measure of change. Others were terribly dramatic, such as the surgical practice of lobotomy, but were performed on a very small number of patients.

Earlier, we argued that state mental hospitals are best understood as maximalist organizations. Such organizations display an unusual degree of structural inertia, combined with very low mortality. Once founded and put into operation, maximalist organizations tend to survive with little or no change. At its founding, the Buffalo State Asylum fit closely the characteristics of a maximalist organization. Its early organizational development also fits the pattern of a maximalist organization. Change did take place, but organizational continuities were far more evident than disruption of what had become a very slowly-changing organization. The next chapter examines what daily life was like at the large state asylum of the late nineteenth century and at the huge state hospital of the first half of the twentieth century.

Chapter 5

The State Hospital:
Reform as Inertia

The transformation of the state asylum of the nineteenth century into the state hospital of the twentieth century involved several changes, including expansion in size, a shift in emphasis from individual treatment toward caring for masses of patients, and a medicalization of the culture of treatment. For the most part, that transformation has been documented by the published reports and unpublished writings of the physicians who ran the institutions. This chapter uses unpublished records as a source for understanding the transformation from asylum to state hospital, taking up a challenge in interpretation raised more than a century ago.

In 1847, Austin Flint, Buffalo's leading physician and editor of the *Buffalo Medical Journal*, told his readers of the pride he felt in the scientific attention and state funds being directed toward institutions for those "who suffer from the terrible calamity of insanity." Reviewing several reports, Flint concluded: "We trust that annual reports from the various lunatic institutions of our country, will be continued. They should be extensively circulated in order to sustain and promote public interest in the subject, and, after a series of years, the amount of statistical facts which will in this way accumulate, will furnish the data for important analytical results" (Flint 1847: 689–90).

Almost a half century later, the Philadelphia neurologist S. Weir Mitchell (1894) presented a very different view to the American Medico-Psychological Association, celebrating its fifty years of existence as the professional organization of lunatic asylum superintendents.

> Where, we ask, are your annual reports of scientific study, of the psychology and pathology of your patients? They should be published apart. We commonly get as your contributions to science, odd little statements, reports of a case or two, a few useless pages of isolated post-mortem records, and they are sandwiched among incomprehensible statistics and farm balance-sheets; and this too often is your sole answer. Where, indeed, are your replies to the questions as to heredity, marriage, the mental disorders of races, the influence of malarial locations, of seasons, of great elevations, all the psy-

chological riddles of a new land, a forming breed, never weary of quickening the pace, of inventing means of hurry—restless workers?

This chapter takes up the challenge of using statistics reported in the annual reports of the Buffalo State Asylum for the Insane and accumulated in the admissions books by its superintendent to address several crucial issues. First, what kinds of patients were admitted to the asylum? How were they diagnosed and treated, and with what outcomes? Second, did the waves of unemployment that washed over Buffalo contribute to the admissions, as one of the leading theories in psychiatric epidemiology has argued? Third, why did an institution such as the Buffalo Asylum rapidly move away from innovation toward stagnation?

Use of unpublished statistics as a primary data source also allows a very different view of the state hospital than given by official public statements such as governmental annual reports, which usually are crafted to present the institution's record in the most favorable light. Public utterances tell a story of an institution adapting to new developments in the care and treatment of the insane. As we shall see, careful analysis of unpublished data shows a quite different record, with remarkably little change over a long period of time (See Appendix A for a fuller discussion).

ADMISSIONS TO THE BUFFALO STATE ASYLUM

Comparing the admissions books for the decade of the 1880s of the three institutions that housed the insane in Western New York provides a convenient way to sketch their very different histories. Table 5.1 presents the type of information found in each institution's admissions book, along with the percentage of admissions for which entries were made. The table contains information on the Erie County Almshouse, the Providence Retreat, and the Buffalo State Asylum.

Data for the Erie County Almshouse, the target of Dorothea Dix's wrath when she visited it in 1844 and thereafter a major target for Buffalo's leading physicians, are shown in the first column. Dr. James Platt White of Buffalo, who in the years after the Civil War was the leading figure in the crusade to build a state asylum for the medical treatment of the insane in Western New York, contrasted the promise of such an institution with the hideous reality of incarceration in the almshouse (Anon. 1882). But as the first column of Table 5.1 shows, the poorhouse continued to record the admission of the insane through the 1880s.

The second column of the table presents data for the Providence Lunatic Asylum, which was discussed briefly earlier. A small institution founded in 1860 for the care of the insane in Buffalo, the Providence Retreat—as it came to be known—was founded by the Sisters of Charity, the same order

Table 5.1 Valid Cases for Admissions Register Data, Three Buffalo
Institutions Housing the Insane, 1880–1891

	Erie County Almshouse (N=333)	Providence Retreat (N=231)	Buffalo State Asylum (N=3,355)
Date of Admission	91.6	100.0	98.9
How Sent?	90.1	—	97.4
Sex	96.4	100.0	98.9
Age	99.9	99.6	98.9
Civil Condition	—	98.8	98.5
Number of Children	—	—	48.4
Occupation	13.5	98.3	95.5
Education	—	—	97.6
Religion	—	—	95.2
Habits	—	—	94.0
Country/State of Birth	—	97.4	97.0
County of Residence	—	95.7	96.6
Insanity in Family	—	—	24.4
Exciting Cause	—	—	77.0
Forms of Mental Disease	100.0	8.9	98.6
Bodily Disorder	—	—	33.5
Date of Attack	—	—	70.7
Number of Attacks	—	—	91.4
Number of Admissions	—	—	97.3
Age at First Attack	—	—	21.9
Date of Discharge/Death	—	36.8	72.8
Result	—	—	72.2
Observations	—	—	40.8
Number of Days	16.0	—	71.0

that had founded the city's first hospital in 1848 (Paul 1984). The Retreat was built on land owned by Austin Flint and sold to the Sisters when Flint moved his practice to New York City. By the 1880s, the Retreat admitted both the insane and inebriates.

The third column of the table summarizes the data coded from the first admissions book of the Buffalo State Asylum, which contains information on the 3,355 admissions from 1880 to 1891. Bound in leather and with its title stamped in gold, the book contains double-paged printed forms that allowed the entry of information about an individual on a single line. In addition to the person's name, the form asks for two dozen different pieces of information.

The three admissions books summarized in Table 5.1 are curious texts, whose composition and completion reflect the very different intentions and actualities in these three institutional responses to insanity. The paucity of data for the almshouse shows its character as a receptacle for the housing of the insane, and little more. By contrast, the Retreat's admission book testifies to the importance of communal identity in the care of the insane, and the mixture of medical and moral treatment provided to the small number of patients afforded its care. The last column shows the much more advanced form of medical model that Andrews intended to apply to his new patients. Andrews intended to use the resulting data to compile the information that appeared in the 21 regular tables he published in his annual reports to the Commission on Lunacy and, given his empirical bent and personal commitment to scientific research on insanity (see Andrews 1869, 1870, 1871, 1883, 1886, 1888, 1880, 1891), he almost certainly intended to achieve the "important analytical results" hoped for by Austin Flint.

Having made note of these useful observations, it should also be noted that the data in Table 5.1 support several conclusions about the methodological problems in using admissions registers as a source for the social history of the asylum. The paucity of information about the Almshouse inmates, for instance, has to be balanced against the even greater lack of other information about that curious nineteenth-century institution. As Michael B. Katz (1983) has demonstrated with these same data, almshouse registers are, in fact, invaluable sources for studying a crucial social institution. The column of data about the Almshouse was constructed from Katz's microfilms of the admissions register; only those cases in which insanity was clearly indicated were used in building the table. Similarly, the information about the Providence Retreat, though spare, is virtually the only information available about the institution's operation prior to the publication of its two reports in 1895 and 1900 and a prospectus in 1921.

In contrast, the State Asylum's admissions register is remarkably detailed and complete, lending some credibility to the idea that Andrews intended to use it for research. His bound case notes on each patient have survived as well, as has an index card system still in use more than a century later to keep track of new admissions. The administrative records of his administration have apparently not survived.

The coding of the data in the admissions registers presented the usual obstacles. Virtually all of the codes were constructed to allow capturing the greatest amount of detail. Every legible word was used in constructing the codes, and the handwritten entries were generally fairly easy to decipher. I used the occupational codes developed by the Philadelphia Social History Project (Hershberg and Dockhorn 1976), rather than contemporary sociological approaches (Hauser 1982; Treiman 1976a and b) because, while the latter claim to be universal in application, trial coding sessions showed the former much easier to apply to these nineteenth-century job titles. The only other problem, inevitable with coding primary sources such as these, concerns those entries that are blank. Do the 51.6 percent of the asylum's admissions that have no entry in the register's column for number of children indicate admissions without children, people who were beyond responding to this question, or simply cases whom Andrews never interviewed? Unfortunately, there is no satisfactory resolution to this problem.

The first methodological purpose to which these data can be put contributes to understanding the demography of the delinquent and dependent populations that made up the inmates and patients of these institutions. These data help describe the very different populations housed by each institution. This is particularly true for the poorhouse and the Providence Retreat, institutions about which we know little without these records. Even for the State Asylum, which published detailed tabular reports about its patients, the admissions register yields very rich evidence about issues not found in its annual reports and of significant interest to understanding its social history. Religion, fertility experience, whether the person was brought in chains (listed under "observations"), and how the person was sent to the asylum are variables that were not tabulated for readers of the annual reports. In part this reflects the role of the annual report, in which Andrews tried to present his asylum in the best possible light. The use of data in the reports is selective, presenting those tabulations required by the state along with those that demonstrated what a difficult but valuable task the asylum performed.

THE MEDICAL MODEL OF INSANITY

One of the most important factors in the transformation of the asylum into the state mental hospital was the replacement of the psychological view of lunacy known as moral therapy into a fully medical model of mental illness. The admissions register of the Buffalo Asylum presents detailed information on the alleged exciting cause of insanity, the form that mental disease took, and the outcome of care—all variables that can be analyzed quantitatively. These records, however, are also symbols of the attempt to use the medical model of caring for and curing the insane, and must be interpreted in the context of Judson Andrews' view of the nature of madness.

Just before he moved to Buffalo to take charge of the new asylum in 1880, Andrews (1880) presented his views on the nature and forms of insanity. A disciple of John P. Gray of the Utica Asylum, Andrews fully shared his mentor's physicalist views. Both believed that insanity was a disease of the brain alone, assuming a soul independent of bodily conditions. "The brain is viewed as the organ or instrument of the mind. Insanity is a complex affair, consisting of disturbed mental manifestations caused by disease of the brain." For Andrews, two powerful bodies of evidence supported these ideas.

The first was the results of scientific research. "In every case of insanity in which a thorough microscopic examination of the brain is made, evidences of diseased conditions are found. The belief . . . that insanity exists only with disease of the brain, have been confirmed." A second source of support was clinical. "The success of the modern treatment, which is founded upon this theory of the nature of insanity, attests its correctness." The campaign to build new asylums rested on high rates of cure, which cut the costs of state support via quick restoration of the individual to a productive role in the community.

Armed with both scientific and clinical evidence of the correctness of his approach, Andrews and his assistants applied his ideas in diagnosing madness in 3,355 admissions and readmissions between 1880 and 1891. He distinguished among several major forms of insanity for his readers, illustrating his 1880 text with a series of vivid sketches of mania, melancholia, and dementia. A brief summary of his ideas about mania will suggest the problems psychiatric nosology, or the classification or categorization of disease, faced in the 1880s.

Mania, "a state of mental exaltation," was diagnosed in all its forms in a total of 36.5 percent of the new admissions, and was by far the largest category of disease. Acute mania, found in 23.2 percent of all cases, was the "raving madness of popular belief" and was easily recognized. "Most cases present disturbances of health as precursors of the attack. There is sleeplessness, variability of the appetite, disturbance of the stomach or bowels, or the secretions of skin, kidneys, or other parts of the physical organism" (Andrews 1880: 620). The disease unfolded in a series of episodes of depression, elation, delusion, and suspicion, often ending in restless agitation, accompanied by threatening speech and even open violence. A wide variety of symptoms, ranging from "boisterous conduct" to violence, was present. The greatest liability to death was from sudden exhaustion, but "the tendency in simple acute mania is towards recovery,"

Table 5.2 "Forms of Mental Disease" for Admissions to the Buffalo State Asylum, 1880–1891

Disease	Number	Percent
Mania		
Acute mania	768	23.2
Chronic mania	277	8.4
Mania	1	.0
Paroxysmal mania	27	.8
Periodic mania	10	.3
Recurrent mania	15	.5
Subacute mania	108	3.3
Melancholia		
Acute melancholia	182	5.5
Chronic melancholia	37	1.1
Melancholia	706	21.3
Subacute melancholia	12	.4
Dementia		
Dementia	693	20.9
Dementia with epilepsy	32	1.0
Senile dementia	1	.0
Epilepsy		
Epilepsy	14	.4
Epilepsy with dementia	93	2.8
Epilepsy with mania	46	1.4
Epilepsy with melancholia	4	.1
Paresis		
Paresis	153	4.6
Not Insane		
Idiocy	8	.2

Disease	Number	Percent
Inebriety	70	2.1
Not insane	36	1.1
Opium habit	4	.1
Other, N.E.C.	12	.4
Total	3,309	99.9
(Missing data = 46)		

generally produced by rest, improved physical health, and diet, factors that the new asylum provided to its patients.

Mania of long duration led to a long series of delusions. Chronic mania, diagnosed in 8.4 percent of the admissions, was "rarely recovered from, and the tendency is toward a gradual decline of mental power." If the disease lasted for more than two years, recovery was virtually impossible.

Andrews presented detailed tables using these and several other noso-logical categories in his annual reports, including several rudimentary attempts at associating these disease categories with outcomes such as recovery or death. The image the reports present is of an asylum that applies complex scientific ideas to admit, treat, and cure mental disease. As Gerald Grob has pointed out, these categories were "functional and descriptive; they permitted psychiatrists to organize material and communicate with each other. But this nosology did not in any sense go beyond description to deal with etiology" (Grob 1985: 231).

RECOVERY AT THE ASYLUM

The problems of interpreting diagnosis apply with equal force to the judg-ment that a person had recovered. Table 5.3 presents the data about recov-ery coded from the admissions register; note that many cases have missing data because the admissions register was no longer used before an outcome had taken place. By the time the Buffalo Asylum opened, the profession of psychiatry had growing doubts about the meaning of recovery. Pliny Earle, a leading figure in the profession, published a series of studies that cast doubt on the accuracy of high recovery rates, which had served as the jus-tification for building institutions such as the Buffalo asylum. While Andrews remained convinced of the possibility of curing most cases of insanity, his own institution ended up only in the middle ranks of Ameri-can institutions in terms of the proportion of recoveries when Earle studied their rates in 1884 (Earle 1887: 213–14). Even Andrews admitted that "recovery" was a slippery concept:

> The question of recoveries in asylums depends so much upon the personal equation of the officers who make up the statistics, and upon the different methods employed and views entertained in regard to the subject, that a comparison between them is not only impracticable but useless. In this institution if cases of inebriety were discharged as cases of insanity recovered, it would increase the general average from thirty-one to thirty-five percent. If the asylum also took credit as cases of recovery for the large number of cases discharged as much improved, and most of which go on to final recovery, the percentage would immediately rise to more than forty-four percent. (AR 1888: 19)

A century later, measurement problems in psychiatric diagnosis and mental health services research remain serious (Lipton and Simon 1985; Taube, Mechanic and Hohmann 1989). Of what value are the data from the 1880s for quantitative research on the asylum's patients? Multiple regression analysis was used to explore whether the various demographic items (age, sex, and so forth) and diagnostic judgments (alleged exciting cause, form of mental disease) would prove helpful in explaining variation in length of stay among those who were discharged as recovered. Overall, a very small proportion of the variation (less than 4 percent) in length of stay could be explained statistically by the 19 independent variables. Only two variables—habits, an indicator of alcohol and drug use, and county of residence, an indicator of rural versus urban residence and all that implied in nineteenth-century New York—enter the equation with statistical significance.

Table 5.3 Results of Treatment at the Buffalo State Asylum, 1880-1891

Result	Number	Percent
Recovered	840	34.7
Improved	365	15.1
Unimproved	657	27.1
Inebriate	44	1.8
Morphine Habit	139	5.7
Suicide	1	.0
Transferred	1	.0
Died	376	15.5
Total	2,423	99.9
(Missing data = 932)		

Negative findings are often disappointing, but in this case they are illuminating. Given the state of psychiatric knowledge at that time, it is not surprising that Andrews' nosological categories cannot explain much about length of stay. However, I did expect to find some effects of sex, ethnicity (but not race, since almost no racial minorities were counted among the inmates), and class in predicting length of stay and reflecting differential treatment inside the asylum, but the analyses show no such differences. This is an important finding in its own right, since it challenges the notion that nineteenth-century psychiatry was largely or totally a form of social control directed at women, immigrants, or the lower classes. Whatever else it was, psychiatry as practiced in the Buffalo Asylum seems largely free of gender, ethnic, or class biases, at least as detectable through these methods.

But these findings are illuminating in another and far more important sense. From its earliest days, the Buffalo State Asylum under Andrews' leadership already exhibited the essence of the state mental hospital as an organizational form, since it was a maximalist organization that fused long-term custody for the seriously mentally ill with medical supervision. From its opening in 1880, the Buffalo Asylum used the conceptual apparatus of psychiatry—including standards for diagnosis, treatment, and discharge—to manage the care of the mentally ill. The care became more bureaucratized as the twentieth century saw increases in both inpatient numbers and in staff. Patient populations shifted somewhat, treatment modalities came into fashion and fell out of favor, and some aspects of daily life changed, but the essential features of state hospital life present at its opening persisted with remarkable stability over the better part of the next seven decades.

The management and culture of the state hospital were medical from the very beginning. But as the data for the 1880s show clearly, this meant relatively little for the outcome of care, either then or more than seven decades later. Andrews' own words summarize how difficult the task of measuring the effects of the asylum was:

> To give any idea of what has been accomplished in the work for which it was established is clearly impossible and has not been attempted. Statistics will give the number of those admitted to its benefits, and of those who have gone out from its walls. The words "recovered," "improved" and "unimproved" give the results of human judgment as to the mental conditions and probabilities for the future. The mere figures, however, tell us nothing of the suffering and sorrows of the sick or the sadness and heart-woes of the friends who have confided their loved ones to the care of the institution. They express nothing of the joy and happiness of those who have gone out "clothed and in their right mind," or of the hopelessness of those who have been returned to their homes or transferred to other institutions, unrecovered or unimproved. Human joys and sorrows are not to be weighed, counted or detailed in history: they are forever buried in the

breasts of those who experience them. It is only left for us to note the means provided to relieve the sufferings of our human kind, and the story shows how generously the State has dealt with this, one of its noblest charities. (AR 1890: 37)

AN UNCHANGING ASYLUM IN A CHANGING SOCIETY

Once founded, maximalist organizations change very little: was this true of state mental hospitals in the twentieth century? Judging by the annual reports issued to the public (see Appendix A), one could make a strong case to the contrary. Each succeeding year sees new innovations in medicine, psychiatry, or nursing; buildings opened or closed; staff changes ranging from new directors to deep cuts or generous additions to the hundreds of employees; scandalous reports in the press followed by praise for its human-itarian commitment; reorganizations or redeployments; and finally, admin-istrative reactions (ranging from bland bureaucratic musings about doing a good job with less than adequate resources to occasionally impassioned dia-tribes about how poor a job the state is doing in supporting the institution).

Annual reports of an institution use what might be termed a "discourse of institutional legitimacy": corporations report to their shareholders on how well managed a year has been; universities claim advances in teaching, research, and service; governments show their responsiveness to public need. State mental hospital annual reports are couched in a rhetoric com-bining psychiatric science and clinical acumen, governmental concern for efficient stewardship, and compassionate care for those unfortunate enough to require admission.

Reading more than a century's annual reports grants one a privileged position of observing continuity and discontinuity over the long arc of orga-nizational development. Beyond the first decade, BSH annual reports rarely report events in an historical context, being content to list "what hap-pened" in almost ahistorical terms rarely linked to earlier events. By con-trast, historians can discuss long-term change from that privileged position of seeing the entire series laid out on a chart, with the data from 1881 just a few inches from the data for a century later. This is privileged observation in several senses: we can see "events" across much more than a human life-time; we know how the story "turns out," and we can correlate changes in one series of events (say, the unemployment rate or population growth) with events inside the institution.

The most important trend over time was the increasing size of the state hospital. Table 5.4 presents a picture of the enormous size to which New York's state hospital system grew. (New York State 1993: Table H–14). Large by any standard even in its first days, by mid–twentieth century the state hospital system became even larger, measured in terms of the absolute

Table 5.4 Trends in Inpatient Workload, New York State, 1869–1991

Inpatient Census, Additions, Discharges and Deaths with Annual Change, Percent Change, Readmission Index for Year. All Programs Including Mental Health and Alcoholism

1 Year	2 Residents			3 Additions							4 Discharges			5 Deaths					
					Admissions											Rate Per 1000			
																Clients[8]		Avg Resi	
	End of Year	Yearly Change	Percent Change	Total Addit'ns	Total Admits.	First Admits	Re-Admits.	% Re 61	Index 71	Other Addit'ns	Total	Direct	Other	All Ages	Age 65+	All	65	All	65
1993	12,538	-1,454	-10.4%	24,112	24,112	9,764	14,348	60%				23,191		425					
1992	13,992	-1,652	-10.6%	31,357	25,836	10,184	15,652	61%	163	5,521	27,075	24,958	2,117	505	384	13	88	34	97
1991	15,644	-1,539	-8.9%	34,176	28,204	10,970	17,234	61%	170	5,972	29,201	26,962	2,239	583	430	13	69	36	89
1990	17,183	-1,758	-9.3%	37,284	30,822	11,780	19,042	62%	185	6,462	31,957	29,380	2,577	685	525	14	71	38	92
1989	18,941	-2,099	-10.0%	41,043	33,439	13,043	20,396	61%	203	7,604	34,716	31,773	2,943	843	655	15	78	42	99
1988	21,040	-1,128	-5.1%	42,909	34,373	13,569	20,804	61%	213	8,536	34,592	31,654	2,938	983	795	19	86	46	106
1987	22,168	-160	-0.7%	44,185	34,645	14,099	20,546	59%	216	9,540	33,679	30,806	2,873	1,089	881	19	90	49	108
1986	22,328	-601	-2.6%	40,630	32,495	13,115	19,380	60%	203	8,135	32,024	29,345	2,679	1,197	972	22	95	53	113
1985	22,929	-402	-1.7%	40,165	32,563	12,991	19,572	60%	205	7,602	31,871	29,138	2,733	1,252	1,011	22	94	54	112
1984	23,331	-324	-1.4%	40,794	32,276	12,675	19,601	61%	205	8,518	31,360	28,571	2,789	1,311	1,060	23	96	56	112
1983	23,655	-720	-3.0%	42,675	32,897	12,123	20,774	63%	218	9,778	32,099	28,981	3,118	1,353	1,088	24	92	56	109
1982	24,375	-457	01.8%	41,990	33,211	11,772	21,439	65%	228	8,779	31,871	28,997	2,874	1,376	1,090	24	88	56	104

Table 5.4 Continued

1 Year	2 Residents			3 Additions								4 Discharges					5 Deaths			
					Admissions												Rate Per 1000			
																	Clients[8]		Avg Resi	
	End of Year	Yearly Change	Percent Change	Total Addit'ns	Total Admits.	First Admits	Re-Admits.	% Re-61	Index 71	Other Addit'ns	Total	Direct	Other	All Ages	Age 65+	All	65	All	65
1981	24,832	-699	-2.7%	40,824	32,471	11,165	21,306	66%	225	8,353	31,656	28,743	2,913	1,646	1,341	28	103	65	122
1980	25,531	-1,277	-4.8%	42,971	31,592	10,542	21,050	67%	214	11,379	31,897	28,209	3,688	1,721	1,420	30	103	66	122
1979	26,808	-1,058	-3.8%	41,685	31,110	10,833	20,277	65%	193	10,575	30,622	27,087	3,535	1,788	1,455	30	101	65	119
1978	27,866	-1,682	-5.7%	43,123	32,003	11,277	20,726	65%	192	11,120	32,113	28,583	3,530	1,979	1,610	32	105	69	125
1977	29,548	-2,449	-7.7%	45,829	34,981	11,923	23,058	66%	214	10,848	35,633	31,040	4,593	2,264	1,787	34	106	74	129
1976	31,997	-3,225	-9.2%	46,185	35,945	12,614	23,331	65%	218	10,240	37,415	31,929	5,486	2,537	2,000	36	108	76	133
1975	35,222	-4,015	-10.2%	45,496	33,879	12,126	21,753	64%	202	11,617	35,147	29,517	5,630	2,893	2,236	40	110	78	134
1974	39,237	-4,844	-11.0%	43,426	32,516	11,356	21,160	65%	194	10,910	35,011	28,193	6,818	3,549	2,711	46	121	85	145
1973	44,081	-5,509	-11.1%	43,801	32,679	11,684	20,995	64%	189	11,122	36,706	28,394	8,312	4,331	3,362	53	134	93	160
1972	49,590	-8,035	-13.9%	45,083	31,248	12,226	19,022	61%	162	13,835	35,808	25,900	9,908	5,115	4,000	58	—	95	—
1971	57,625	-6,759	-10.5%	48,022	37,177	16,171	21,006	57%	175	10,845	36,838	27,931	8,907	5,822	4,540	57	—	95	—
1970	64,384	-6,381	-9.0%	52,865	37,986	18,259	19,727	52%	163	14,879	38,190	27,032	11,158	7,064	5,549	65	—	105	—
1969	70,765	-7,246	-9.3%	54,820	40,024	21,122	18,902	47%	176	14,796	42,476	27,713	14,763	8,407	6,775	71	—	113	—
1968	78,011	-2,310	-2.9%	54,331	44,183	25,722	18,461	42%	203	10,148	39,632	25,938	13,694	9,706	7,917	78	—	123	—

Year																			
1967	80,321	-2,444	-3.0%	53,302	40,977	24,626	16,351	40%	218	12,325	38,768	22,025	16,743	9,053	7,344	73	195	111	243
1966	82,765	-2,094	-2.5%	51,404	36,442	23,590	12,852	35%	194	14,962	28,738	13,846	14,892	9,065	7,308	75	196	108	247
1965	84,859	-554	-0.6%	49,545	35,254	22,740	12,514	35%	203	14,291	23,674	10,394	13,280	9,567	7,781	79	—	112	264
1964[a]	85,413	-694	-0.8%	46,876	33,255	21,629	11,626	35%	204	13,621	22,663	9,805	12,858	9,014	7,269	76	199	105	248
1963	86,107	-483	-0.6%	43,741	30,919	19,990	10,929	35%	202	12,822	19,951	8,990	10,961	9,412	7,581	80	208	109	260
1962	86,590	-927	-1.1%	39,897	27,922	18,083	9,839	35%	197	11,975	19,050	7,960	11,090	8,901	7,118	77	198	102	244
1961	87,517	-1,251	-1.4%	41,158	29,279	19,799	9,480	32%	210	11,879	18,126	7,683	10,443	8,428	6,737	71	189	96	232
1960	88,768	-1,014	-1.1%	37,168	26,773	18,021	8,752	33%	216	10,395	16,819	6,885	9,934	8,966	7,129	77	199	100	247
1959	89,782	-1,409	-1.5%	34,039	25,252	17,721	7,531	30%	207	8,787	14,962	6,174	8,788	9,198	7,435	79	207	102	256
1958	91,191	-1,218	-1.3%	31,014	23,286	16,972	6,314	27%	194	7,728	13,336	5,286	8,050	9,421	7,529	81	209	103	258
1957	92,409	-453	-0.5%	29,576	21,828	16,014	5,814	27%	188	7,748	12,290	4,268	8,022	8,555	6,869	75	194	92	238
1956	92,862	-452	-0.5%	28,593	21,454	15,849	5,605	26%	183	7,139	10,788	3,958	6,830	8,345	6,588	73	191	90	234
1955	93,314	2,421	2.7%	28,249	21,459	15,643	5,816	27%	182	6,790	9,554	3,093	6,461	8,078	6,321	72	—	88	—
1954	90,893	2,025	2.3%	28,617	21,577	15,734	5,843	27%	182	7,040	10,602	3,257	7,345	8,056	6,044	73	—	90	—
1953	88,868	2,570	3.0%	28,480	21,309	15,592	5,717	27%	178	7,171	10,562	2,981	7,581	8,120	6,089	76	—	93	—
1952	86,298	1,690	2.0%	27,223	20,140	14,667	5,473	27%	177	7,083	10,802	3,028	7,774	7,680	5,632	73	—	90	—
1951	84,608	1,702	2.1%	29,181	20,420	15,114	5,306	26%	180	8,761	10,716	3,177	7,539	7,629	5,602	74	—	91	—
1950	82,906	2,748	3.4%	29,939	20,902	15,597	5,305	25%	194	9,037	10,575	2,969	7,606	7,432	5,288	74	—	91	—
1949	80,158	2,544	3.3%	29,438	20,059	14,968	5,091	25%	193	9,379	9,615	2,934	6,681	6,995	4,803	72	—	89	—
1929	45,319	847	1.9%	13,855	10,750	8,550	2,200	20%	166	3,105	4,605	—	—	4,193	1,803	76	—	93	—

Table 5.4 Continued

1 Year	2 Residents			3 Additions							4 Discharges			5 Deaths					
					Admissions											Rate Per 1000			
																Clients[8]		Avg Resi	
	End of Year	Yearly Change	Percent Change	Total Addit'ns	Total Admits.	First Admits	Re-Admits.	% Re-[6]	Index [7]	Other Addit'ns	Total	Direct	Other	All Ages	Age 65+	All	65	All	65
1909	29,363	1015	3.6%	7,375	6,625	5,222	1,403	21%	133	750	3,246	—	—	2,374	753	68	—	82	—
1889	5,201	248	5.0%	1,739	1,739	1,540	199	11%	—	—	1,141	—	—	350	51	52	—	69	—
1869	745	175	30.7%	605	605	—	—	—	—	—	366	—	—	64	—	62	—	92	—

Source: NYS Office of Mental Health
Bureau of Planning Assistance
Mental Health Information Unit
March 28, 1992.

1/ State fiscal year.
2/ Census includes all leave types.
3/ Additions include admissions, transfers, and returns from care or LWOC
4/ Discharges from all statuses; does not include placements on care or LWOC status.
5/ Deaths on resident or leave status.
6/ Readmissions as percent of total admissions
7/ Number of readmissions per 1,000 patients discharged (from all statues) in the previous three years.
8/ Resident patients at the beginning of the year (end of prior year) plus admissions during the year.
a/ Excludes Syracuse Psychiatric Hospital in 1964 and prior years (71 resident patients and 458 admissions in 1964).
b/ In addition to 5,201 patients in "State Asylums," there were 8,818 in "County Asylums," and 385 in "County Poorhouses" totaling 14,404 patients in public civil institutions.
c/ Includes 603 patients at Utica and 142 at Williard.

size of its inpatient population or relative to the size of the surrounding population. Between 1900 and 1950, the overall admission rates to state mental hospitals in the United States approximately doubled (Center for Mental Health Services 1994b). In New York, 5,201 persons were residents in state hospitals in 1889; at the peak year of 1955, 93,314 were residents. At the Buffalo institution, comparable trends were evident.

MENTAL HOSPITAL ADMISSIONS AND ECONOMIC CHANGE

If the overall trend is clear, what about the shorter-term fluctuations in admissions around that trend? Since its first days, the Buffalo institution's annual reports have frequently commented on the short-term rise or fall in admissions and in overall inpatient population. The hundredth anniversary report in 1980 is different in this respect only in presenting the comment in the form of a graph of the "average daily resident plus leave census" for 1979 through 1981 (AR 1981: 22).

The most important attempt to explain fluctuations in mental hospital populations is a body of research that began with publication in 1973 of a pioneering study by M. Harvey Brenner. Brenner used innovative statistical approaches on data about New York state mental hospitals (including Buffalo), and found evidence for a long-term relationship between "the state of the economy" and mental illness, indicated by first admission to one of the hospitals. Most of the data were for the period 1914–1960, but one remarkable analysis was done for a 127 year period beginning in 1850. Brenner (1973: ix) reached several broad conclusions: economic change was not only the most important factor in explaining fluctuations in admissions, it was virtually the only major factor for some segments of society, and this relationship held stable over a very long period of time (at least 127 years).

The argument is also consistent with a broader assessment of impact of capitalist economic development on social life. Advances in living standards notwithstanding, economic development in nineteenth- and twentieth-century America has also been a series of boom-and-bust cycles with potentially devastating costs for many people. Brenner's research allowed empirical examination of just what costs were borne as the result of economic change. His original work (1973) provoked considerable interest as well as attempts at replication and extension, including a series of studies that used data for the Buffalo area and its state mental hospital.

In a study that criticized and partly replicated Brenner's analysis, Marshall and Funch (1979) used data for all New York state hospitals. When age was examined separately, the association between economic change and mental hospitalization held true only for men and women of working age, but not for the young or the elderly. Marshall and Funch also reported that hospital capacity was a better predictor of first admissions than was the economy, particularly for the young and elderly. Rather than economic change provoking new cases of serious mental disorder, perhaps intolerance of deviant behavior led to greater hospitalization, particularly when facilities for the segregation of disordered individuals became more available.

Ratcliff (1980) pointed to one common weakness in both the Brenner and Marshall and Funch studies: testing the hypothesis against data for only public hospitals meant the data excluded more affluent populations likely to be shielded from the effects of economic downturns. She also suggested that Brenner had tended to choose time periods showing a stronger association with economic downturns as compared to those which showed weak or no association.

The present author and several collaborators examined the Buffalo data very closely in three different time periods: 1881–1891 (Dowdall, Marshall, and Morra 1990), 1914–1955 (Marshall and Dowdall 1982), and 1970–1980 (Dowdall, Kirshstein, Marshall, and Pinchoff 1982). The time periods were mostly dictated by when a particular series of data was available. In the earliest period, for example, we used individual patient data from admissions registers for the three institutions serving the insane in the Buffalo area. The second and third time periods were set by the availability of consistent economic time series. Coincidentally but usefully, the three studies examine the Buffalo institution when it was a state asylum, a state hospital, and a state psychiatric center.

Dowdall, Marshall, and Morra (1990) used the data previously described in this chapter for the three institutions that received the insane in the 1880s in Western New York. Unlike Brenner's original work, these data are about individual patients admitted to each institution, thus avoiding one of the basic complaints leveled at research in this tradition, namely that it is based on highly aggregated information and not about individuals. Only one previous study (Catalano, Dooley, and Jackson 1985) had used data on all individuals in a single area (Rochester NY) using mental health services, and no study had previously examined data of this type for the nineteenth century. Moreover, Dowdall, Marshall, and Morra (1990) used sophisticated statistical methods, which are described in detail in their paper.

The 1880s were a tumultuous economic time, beginning with a period of boom in late 1879 that persisted to the end of 1883. A dramatic depression followed in 1884, but expansion of the railroad industry led to a period of prosperity. By early 1891, the economy was again depressed, but then went into a boom that lasted past the last quarter of 1891. Thus the period of study exhibited just the kind of vigorous and dramatic change that should provide a fair test of the hypothesis.

A rigorous statistical analysis taking into account earlier criticisms of the research literature was explained in detail in the published paper. The conclusion was unambiguous: "the data provide only minimal evidence of any causal relationship between the Business Activity Index and first admissions to the three Buffalo institutions for the insane." (Dowdall, Marshall, and Morra 1990: 145). Tests of the hypothesis that economic downturns provoked first admissions to mental hospitals, the "provocation hypothesis," had produced similar findings on nineteenth-century Buffalo data and on twentieth-century Rochester data; in both instances the data were about all individual admissions in the metropolitan area, and proved clearly superior to the type of aggregated data originally used by Brenner.

Another study (Marshall and Dowdall 1982) used data for the Buffalo State Hospital that spanned the period from 1914 to 1955. Compared to the original Brenner work, the study used somewhat more advanced statistical techniques; it included a variable measuring hospital capacity (to assess whether fluctuations in admissions are associated with increased capacity, as had been argued); and it used a measure of economic change (an adjusted index of manufacturing employment) based on data specifically for the Buffalo metropolitan area. Marshall and Dowdall (1982) concluded that employment was associated with hospitalization, but that the direction of the relationship was positive, just the opposite to that found by Brenner. Moreover, other factors predicted hospitalization, including hospital capacity and the unusual effects of a wartime economy during World War II.

A third study used somewhat different methodological approaches to look at the decade of the 1970s, arriving at similar conclusions to those for the two earlier periods (Dowdall, Kirshtein, Marshall, and Pinchoff 1982). This study examined both inpatient and outpatient admissions.

One of the goals of the present book was to study the asylum's development by connecting it to the larger events of the surrounding society. These several studies take an approach that connects one of the most profound dimensions of social history, the fluctuations in employment and unemployment, to admissions to the asylum. In contrast to Brenner's original finding, careful examination of the data for Buffalo finds no evidence that the two series are correlated in such a way as to connect downturns in the economy with later first admissions. What Brenner had described as the most important explanation for variation over time in admissions fails to explain what happened in Buffalo.

An additional piece of evidence about the long-term performance of the state hospital should be noted. Of all the social identities that might lead an individual to admission into the state asylum or hospital, gender remains the most puzzling. The Buffalo State Asylum was planned from its founding to have equal numbers of male and female patients, though its Annual Reports make clear that equality was rarely the case. In the midst of the patriarchal world of nineteenth-century New York, this planned equality is itself noteworthy. Moreover, as the next chapter describes, the institution's workforce has been since its beginning profoundly shaped by gender.

Studies done before 1980 tend to suggest that women "are more vulnerable to mental illness," at least in highly industrialized societies, and several more recent epidemiological studies identify the ratio of males to females among the seriously mentally ill as between 75 to 84 males per 100 females (Center for Mental Health Services 1994b). But from 1881 to the mid 1960s, for most of the history of the institutional care of the mentally ill, the ratio of males to females admitted to state hospitals remained surprisingly similar, with a ratio of roughly 110 to 120 males per 100 females admitted (Center for Mental Health Services 1994b).

What light do these data shed on the historical development of the state hospital? Until the 1960s, men tended to be admitted to state hospitals somewhat disproportionate to their representation in the population as a whole, perhaps in part because mentally-ill men were perceived to be more of a threat to public order than mentally-ill women. As a later chapter will discuss, since 1965 a growing concern about violence and other antisocial acts (presumably more likely to be committed by men) has led to a dramatic and disproportionate increase in male admissions.

State hospitals until the 1960s were remarkably evenhanded in their admission of women and men, though men were more likely to be admitted than women. This calls into question whether an explanation of the state hospital as solely an instrument of social control is fully warranted.

What larger point do these findings about gender and about unemployment make? One interpretation of the rise and development of state mental hospitals tends to stress their role as part of the apparatus of social control. In one sense, this interpretation is of course correct on the face of it, since we have seen that the primary motivation to build the Buffalo Asylum included providing institutional care for the seriously mentally ill who were either without homes or whose "home" had become incarceration in the Erie County Poorhouse or the county jail.

But there is another sense (perhaps best captured by Erving Goffman, writing about what state hospitals had become by the 1950s) in which social control is used in a much more sinister sense. Goffman's *Asylums* (1961) implied that what leads to incarceration in the huge warehouses of mid–twentieth-century public psychiatry is a string of unfortunate circumstances, not a wise and informed professional diagnosis of a severe or long-term psychiatric disorder.

Were Goffman's argument largely true, we would expect to see some fluctuation over time tied to one of the most profound sources of change in circumstances in our society, the periodic rise and fall of the economy. A broad view of how society shapes health and mental health might argue that this rise and fall produces at least two forms of change that might force hospitalization. On the one hand, profound economic change should be linked to enormous and catastrophic change for some individuals. Some lose not just a job to economic depression but a way of life, an existence: unable to support themselves or their families, losing both the means of living as well as a central identity in American life, they lose everything in both an economic and psychological sense. Swept away by the same economic storm are many of the community resources that can buffer these same stresses, including the use of whatever rudimentary or sophisticated mental health care or its equivalent might be available to them. The state asylum, or the state hospital, or the public psychiatric center, becomes first an unpalatable choice but finally a simple necessity for the afflicted individual or an increasingly desperate family.

As persuasive as this argument appears, there is almost no credible evidence to support it, and the several Buffalo studies summarized above actually argue strongly against it. Periodic fluctuations in the economy were not linked to first admissions to the Buffalo institution, an argument made even the stronger by the differences in historical period, variables measured, and statistical approaches used. Moreover, there is little evidence to suggest that gender, social class or ethnic factors played a role in the length of stay once patients were inside the walls of the nineteenth-century asylum.

This is not meant to be some sort of defense of the late-nineteenth-century or early-twentieth-century state asylum or hospital. There is abundant evidence both for Buffalo and for other institutions that support the view that these were sad and perhaps terrible places to live out one's life. Unfortunately, the lives of the seriously mentally ill have often been so, whether in the meanest state warehouses or the most expensive private hospitals. But we do not serve the cause of understanding what our society can do for the seriously mentally ill by misunderstanding the complex historical path that got us where we are today.

ASYLUM TO STATE HOSPITAL: INNOVATION TO STAGNATION

Taken together, the annual reports of the Buffalo institution shed considerable light on the profound organizational stability that marked so much of its history. One of the most significant indicators of this stability is presented in Figure 5.1, which show the outcome of care at the State Hospital from its earliest days to the mid–1950s. Two issues stand out: very few patients were discharged as recovered or cured, and the percentage so discharged remained very stable over a very long period of time. Unlike an older institution such as the Worcester State Hospital (Bockoven 1956), the Buffalo hospital did not have a long early period of success against

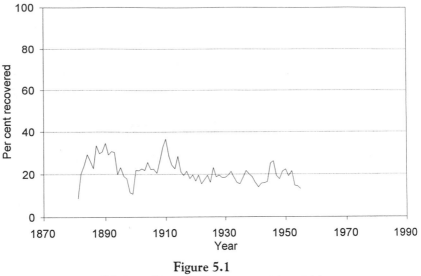

Figure 5.1
Buffalo State Hospital: Recoveries, 1881–1955

which this period of stagnation would be compared. But the relative absence of criticism of its role in the local press also suggests that its transformation into a largely custodial institution was either understood and supported by the larger public, or ignored by the public but supported by the state government.

Figure 5.2 presents another yearly statistical series that helps understand this long period of stagnation. Considering the largesse that helped plan and erect its initial buildings, support for the institution throughout much of its history reverted to a low level—and remained low throughout much of its history—soon after its founding. While Figure 5.2 also shows that funding for the institution did vary somewhat over the long term, it perhaps was never enough to enable the institution to provide more than custodial care to most of its patients. What is also clear from the data is that the post–World War II state hospital began to receive significant increases in support, and that the era usually called deinstitutionalization saw a combination of a reduced residential population combined with a very dramatic increase in funding to unprecedented levels. Later chapters take up the story of the transformation of the state hospital into a psychiatric center, a change made possible by this vast increase in funding combined with far more selective admissions policies and dramatic changes in discharging patients into the community.

In essence, then, a reading of the historical record of the state hospital as well as quantitative analyses of time series over the same period converge

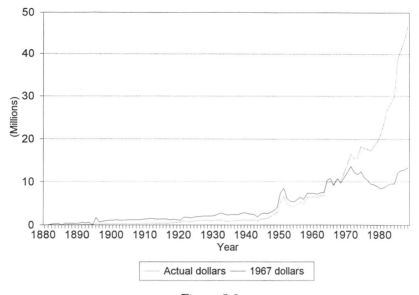

Figure 5.2
Disbursments, Buffalo State Hospital, 1880–1990

on the same conclusion: remarkable institutional inertia marked the period from the institution's opening in 1880 until at least the 1950s. Despite the numerous events reported in detail in the Annual Reports and the occasional news reports in the Buffalo press, little change took place in the overall pattern of organizational life at the Buffalo State Hospital.

More importantly, the same inertia marked the entire population of state hospitals. The Buffalo State Hospital is a very representative example of how a maximalist organization, exposed to relatively little environmental pressure, exhibits both considerable inertia and very low mortality. During much of the twentieth-century, American state mental hospitals had remarkably similar organizational histories to that exhibited in Buffalo.

Chapter 6

"Trying Times of Transition": From State Hospital to Psychiatric Center

The individual state asylums that opened across the United States during the nineteenth century were transformed during the latter decades of that century into state hospitals, largely as the result of expansion in size combined with either flat or even decreasing per capita expenditures. In this respect, as in others, the institution in Buffalo is a representative case of broader trends. Previous chapters have discussed how the character of the Buffalo State Asylum for the Insane, opened in 1880 and renamed the Buffalo State Hospital in 1890, assumed shape during its founding and early years of operation. As the institution grew, the individual care provided by its superintendent and small staff gave way to increasingly custodial care by a large bureaucracy. Through much of the twentieth century, the Buffalo State Hospital changed, but in ways that did not alter its fundamental identity.

This chapter first examines daily life in the long period between its founding and the close of World War II, using two different approaches to visualize what the organization was like during this time. The first method is to use the photographic record left of this period; the second method is to present the results of a survey done by knowledgeable outsiders who systematically inspected the institution and compared it to national standards. The chapter then takes on the task of explaining how the state hospital of the early and middle twentieth century was transformed into the contemporary public psychiatric center. Once again, events in Buffalo prove to be a good representation of what happened in several hundred other institutions.

PHOTOGRAPHS AS DATA: DAILY LIFE IN A STATE HOSPITAL

The first method used here to visualize the daily life of the hospital is to inspect the photographic record left of this period. This chapter uses photographs as data with which to examine the hospital. A full report of this approach to understanding historical change in an institution such as a mental hospital has been published elsewhere (Dowdall and Golden 1989;

see also Appendix A). In this chapter are presented a few of the more than 800 images that we gathered, almost all of them unpublished photographs taken by amateurs. The brief discussion helps understand how each image captures something of the everyday reality of the asylum.

Elsewhere this book makes use of a variety of unpublished data, much of it quantitative, about the population of several hundred state hospitals. As valuable as these data are, they are not a complete record: missing from the tables and numbers generated through this method is the sense of every-day life in a complex institution largely shielded from public scrutiny for over a century. Photographs provide a window into this world.

The photographs came from several sources. The majority were col-lected by the hospital's director of public information. Of these, a number had been discovered in boxes in her office, while others were donated by former staff members; among the latter contributions were several photo-graph albums, one of occupational therapy, the other of the hospital's annual field day.

Our search generated approximately 800 images from the hospital, all but a few unpublished. We selected 343 for special scrutiny. We initially organized the images by content, dividing the photographs displaying insti-tutional life into thirteen subject categories, three of which contained more than half of all the pictures: employees and volunteers (78 images, 23% of the total) men's occupational therapy (60 images, 17% of the total) and close ups of the various buildings and interior views (54 images, 16% of the total). We developed a layered analysis in which we examined the images in continuously greater depth. A first approach, *appraisal*, examined the congruity between the written and visual data. *Inquiry*, a second layer, looked thematically at the collection of images as a whole. The last form, *interpretation*, was based on "thick description" of individual images.

APPRAISAL: COMPARING WRITTEN AND VISUAL DATA

The images presented information conflicting with written reports in three major areas. One is the physical setting of the institution, the second is the sex ratio of patients in occupational therapy and a third is the staff/patient mix. In appraising the photographs we note both the existence of these dis-crepancies and the possible explanations for them.

In a majority of cases the hospital's environment is deceptively pre-sented. Figure 6.1 is a straightforward view of the exterior of the main hos-pital building and of the surrounding grounds. Published in several of the *Annual Reports* in the early years of this century, this photograph (like sev-eral other exteriors) disguises the hospital's urban setting, though whether intentionally or not cannot be determined. Buffalo was already a thriving commercial and industrial city whose urban growth had encompassed the

Figure 6.1
Exterior of main administration building and connected ward buildings,
Buffalo State Hospital, approximately 1900.

hospital's grounds when the institution opened its doors in 1880, and the grounds had been incorporated into Frederick Law Olmsted's overall plan for its parks system.

The founders of the hospital subscribed to the prevailing orthodoxy that stressed removing the insane from disorder and tumult to the calm and repose of rural life, yet they located the institution within the boundaries of a major city. The photographs disingenuously pay homage to the theory of the therapeutic setting, ignoring one of the institution's most salient characteristics. Several of the earliest photographs of the institution offer scenes of the well-landscaped and wooded approaches to the main buildings (see for example, AR 1912: facing page 1), the male patients hard at work gathering hay, and a herd of swine near the institution's barn.

Figure 6.2 (source and date unknown) presents a more accurate depiction of the hospital's relationship to its surroundings. Behind several men (probably patients) loading hay onto a wagon loom the towers of a church in the industrial neighborhood of Black Rock, immediately north of the hospital. Another image shows that the hospital's farmlands immediately adjoined a neighborhood that contained both working class housing, and, visible beyond the houses, the watertowers of factories located on the city's West Side. One other photograph shows trolley tracks running in front of a reception building opened in the early part of this century, linking the hospital with the urban neighborhoods that provided its patients. With

Figure 6.2
*Male patients gathering hay on the farm of the Buffalo State Hospital, with
towers of a church in neighboring Black Rock visible in background.*

these exceptions, virtually all the photographs we viewed ignored the urban
world that surrounded the hospital from its opening day.

The question these images raise is whether the hospital deliberately
presented itself as rural, or whether the photographs reflect the institution's
isolation from the surrounding neighborhoods, an isolation resulting from
the stigma of mental illness as well as from the hospital's own efforts to erect
boundaries between itself and its neighbors.

Sixty photographs show men in "occupational therapy" or what might
be termed institutional labor, as in Figure 6.3, which shows men repairing
shoes. Only 13 images show women engaged in work, for example, Figure
6.4, an early photograph of the institution's laundry. The *Annual Reports*
provide a contradictory view, stating that the rates of patient activity were
higher for women. In a culture in which men are expected to be employed
the photographs may have reflected the normative expectations of the photographers and/or the intended audience. To show patients at work is to
suggest they are regaining health and may be able to resume their expected
social roles. It also supports the prevailing therapeutic model held by hospital superintendents, who believed physical activity would stimulate mental clarity. There was, in short, less need for photographers, viewers, and the
psychiatric authorities to observe women engaged in occupational therapy.

Misrepresentations of gender ratios arise within the collection as a
whole. About 58 percent of the images show male patients or a preponder-

Figure 6.3
Men repairing shoes in the workshops of the Buffalo State Hospital.

Figure 6.4
Women working in the institution's laundry.

ance of male patients, while only 41 percent show exclusively or majority female patients. Viewed without reference to the written evidence, they suggest the institution housed more men than women when, in fact, the opposite was true. Here again, the intentions of the photographers and the audience may have had greater salience than the realities of institutional life.

Quantitative information is also suspect in analyzing the role of the staff. Sixty-six images show patients and staff together. Counting all the patients and staff in all the photographs yields an overall ratio of nine patients for every staffer, close to the hospital's published ratio of 10 to one in the years between 1920 and 1937 (the only period for which this information is provided). Some situations necessarily required larger numbers of workers, such as when there was a greater threat of violence. When patients were passive and well behaved, fewer attendants were needed. Thus the variations in ratios in the photographs, ranging from 1: 1 to 1: 29, stress the variations in types of care and patient/staff encounters, while the *Annual Reports* merely provide an aggregate view of what was clearly a complex interaction.

These few examples illustrate the investigation available at the level of appraisal. We can compare written and visual information, count a variety of activities, and engage in a primitive ethnographic exploration of the institution. On a superficial level appraisal means viewing fragments of a culture. Moving beyond the level of illustration, appraisal elicits questions and tentative answers, thus inviting deeper inquiry.

INQUIRY: THEMES IN THE COLLECTION AS A WHOLE

While appraisal is concerned with assessing different forms of evidence, at the level of inquiry we survey the internal landscape, looking at the photographs as a whole. The themes we unearthed ranged from the mundane (such as changes over time in the institution's physical and therapeutic milieu) to the striking (such as the pervasiveness of a distinct work culture). While few of the photographs can be dated with precision, they can nonetheless be arranged in a rough chronological sequence to shed light on continuities and transformations in the daily life of the institution. Physical changes, due to innovations having nothing to do with mental health, include the substitution of electric lights for gas fixtures, the replacement of billiard matches with bingo parties, and the shift in clothing styles. The most arresting contrast is between the well-furnished, well-lit, and well-staffed hallways (Figure 6.5) of the asylum's first years, presented in several official photographs from the early *Annual Reports* (see for example, AR 1901: following 736) and the shabbily dressed patients jammed against these same walls only a few decades later. Figure 6.6 shows how the spacious hallways served not only as day rooms for idle male patients, but also contained beds to relieve the overcrowding in adjacent bedrooms and dormitories.

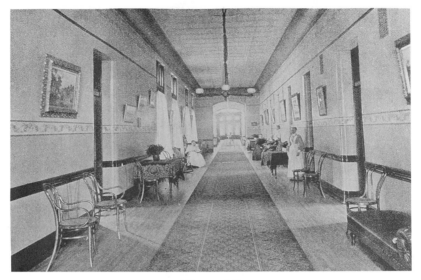

Figure 6.5
A well-furnished, well-lit, and well-staffed hallway in a ward for female patients in the early years of the Buffalo State Hospital.

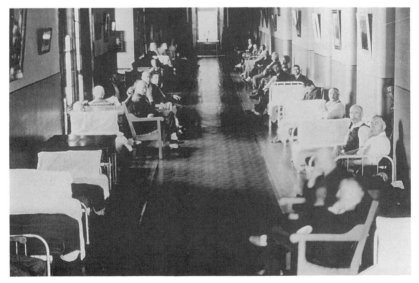

Figure 6.6
Overcrowding at the state hospital meant that male patients used a ward hallway as a dayroom in the early twentieth century.

Figure 6.7
The Buffalo State Hospital staff team won the championship of the Buffalo Industrial League in 1924.

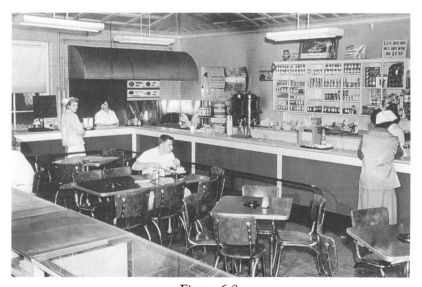

Figure 6.8
Nurses and attendants could relax in a small luncheonette in the mid-twentieth century; a glimpse at the world of work for the hospital's staff.

Little has been written about the lives of state hospital workers and their impact on patient care, other than brief and dramatic exposes of abuse and neglect. Rather than being seen as workers in highly stressful, low-paying positions, laboring in a milieu which is ostensibly therapeutic and in reality, custodial, the hospital nurses, occupational therapists, aides and attendants are typically described only in terms of their numbers or their misdeeds. Their lives, as workers, union members, and community residents, go undocumented, as do their experiences on the wards, their "shop floor."

The photographs identify the hospital's staff as members of the city's working class. As Figure 6.7 shows, they fielded a team in the city's industrial baseball league, and, within the hospital, maintained a distinct identity and culture in terms of their dress, demeanor, and the maintenance of segregated rest areas. Photographs record the workers looking at ease in dining rooms and luncheonettes (see Figure 6.8). While several of the softball team members smile warmly at the camera, images depicting their coworkers with patients show them looking stiff and outnumbered. Several photographs document the graduation of workers from "remotivation classes," a not-so-subtle hint that the hospital had to maintain a conscious, on going effort to boost morale and skills. The *Annual Reports* record the high level of turnover, attributing it to low wages as well as to difficult living and working conditions and the availability of other types of employment. The photographs clarify what the *Annual Reports* cannot, just what those working conditions were actually like. Images such as Figure 6.9, 6.10, and 6.11

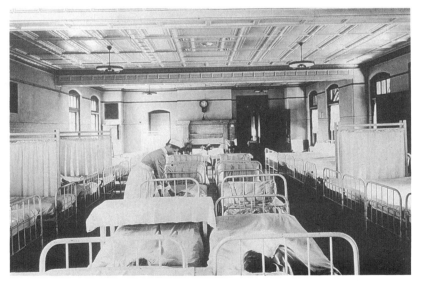

Figure 6.9
A nurse attended to a bedridden patient in an overcrowded ward for the elderly.

Figure 6.10
Male staff and patients played billiards, part of life in the sex-segregated world of the Buffalo State Hospital.

Figure 6.11
Women patients and staff shared domestic tasks like sewing, depicted in this early photograph from the Buffalo State Hospital.

Figure 6.12
Two generations of nurses at the state hospital.

Figure 6.13
This snapshot of two young nurses tells of the lighter side of caring for the insane at the huge state institution.

Figure 6.14
The state hospital's superintendent posed with its nursing staff.

allow us to see patients and staff not just in the wards, the most common worksite of the institution, but in the billiard and sewing rooms, where typical gender-specific roles of domestic life were reproduced by both patients and staff throughout the history of the institution.

Viewing the collection in its entirety, we uncover themes not accessible either in the printed sources or by a comparison of the written and visual material. The work culture of an institution rarely receives validation in the *Annual Reports* or professional literature. Photographs make it visible and allow us to see its various dimensions, including the attempts by workers to establish points of separation between themselves and their patients.

Photographs convey emotion and sentiment, not just neutral information. Consider the meaning of Figures 6.12 and 6.13, which show two sets of women wearing the hospital's nursing or nurse's aide uniforms. For much of its history, the institution operated a training school for nurses and aides, the first to be opened in a public mental hospital in the United States. Whatever else it may have been, the training school offered women a chance to build a career that included advancement to supervisory roles generally unavailable to women in Buffalo's other industries. The pride and happiness that we read from these images reflect how women could build a "little world of our own" within the walls of the massive state hospital (Tomes 1978). As Figure 6.14 documents, however, that world ultimately revolved around the orders of the institution's head, who, until just a few years ago, was always a male.

Figure 6.15
*Enforced idleness at the Buffalo State Hospital: male patients crowded
onto a locked porch.*

INTERPRETATION: UNDERSTANDING INDIVIDUAL IMAGES

Probing individual images presents the most difficult challenge and offers
the greatest rewards in terms of comprehending the texture and nuances of
institutional life. There is a trade-off, however; as we focus on the abundance of detail, the larger history and context may be obscured. Any one
method of studying an institution proves inevitably limited when contrasted with the use of multiple methods. Two concepts, "compelled activity" and "enforced idleness," grounded in our close reading of a select group
of images, show what careful interpretation, as part of a layered analysis, can
yield.

Enforced idleness is visible in a number of the pictures in which the
patients literally do nothing more than sit. Whether their physical or mental condition dictates this behavior, or whether it results from a regimen
imposed by the institution as a means of dealing with a large clientele, is
uncertain. Idleness pervades images taken in the early years of the institution as well as in more recent photographs, suggesting a relatively static
quality to asylum life despite the introduction of new therapies and bureaucratic policies.

Figure 6.15, a picture of the men on the porch, one of three similar
images, points to the irony of the institution's setting. Earlier, we discussed
how the architectural images falsely conveyed that the hospital existed

within a bucolic pastoral setting, when in fact it was surrounded by a bustling, industrial city. The porch scene is misleading in the opposite way; it suggests a lack of access to the outdoors. Although the hospital was part of the urban world it was surrounded by almost 200 acres of grounds. Nevertheless, screened porches filled with park benches were added to all three floors of the building, whose original design included "pleasure grounds" immediately adjacent to the wards. Caging the patients may have been the result of staff shortages, patient frailty or fractiousness, the desire to prevent escapes, or some combination of these and other factors.

The porch scene raises other questions. Clearly we are viewing a group of men similarly dressed and with similar demeanors, but why have they come together? The patients' clothing is little different than the attire worn by other working-class men. There is no immediate suggestion that the group is marked collectively by mental illness. We would be willing to accept that these are union members at a meeting, or a group of unemployed workers waiting in a hallway for the opening of a soup kitchen. In this particular image the screen is not shown prominently and thus there is little evidence that the men are purposefully confined. Nor do their postures and faces necessarily give this away. While some sit in a slumped posture, others, clearly aware of the camera, face the photographer. Were there attendants shown standing and observing the group, we might begin to suspect that the men had not congregated by choice. By contrast, Figure 6.16 shows how screened porches had been added to the original design of the building sometime after the turn of the century (compare with Figure 6.1, which shows the original construction).

The density of the group is perhaps the most overwhelming feature of Figure 6.16. The dry statistics on hospital overcrowding, highlighted in nearly every annual report, are unable to convey the degree to which patients lived literally inches away from one another. They slept in beds parked side by side, ate at crowded tables, and congregated on the porch benches, day after day. Yet, population density was a feature of working-class life. Buffalo was one of America's most crowded industrial cities, with poorer families packed into one floor or less of a small row house and industrial laborers working side by side in factories. Institutional crowding, certainly much greater than desired by the hospital's administrators, staff, and patients, was merely an extension and an exaggeration of the crowding experienced by those who lived and worked in the surrounding city.

Crowded conditions in the hospital were the theme of local newspaper articles published in 1929 and 1930. Written by a member of the hospital board of managers, the articles explained why the hospital required an increase in state appropriations. The crowding made visible in Figure 6.17 cries out for reform. Yet, the article and the photographs are in no way reminiscent of later revelations of hospital "snake pits" in which patients were

Figure 6.16
An exterior view of porches added to the original Richardson buildings
to accommodate overcrowding.

exposed to abuse and neglect. The message conveyed by the images and the text is simply one of an institution unable to provide adequate care.

The photograph of the women crowded into a "corner of a disturbed ward where the most troublesome types are encountered" shows them clearly to be inmates of an institution. In many cases their dress is shabby, their hair is unkempt, their posture is poor, and their expressions indicate agitation. Like the men on the porch, the women seem to range in age from those in their twenties to those who are elderly. Unlike the photograph of the men, whose reason for being together is somewhat vague, we are clearly aware that the women are incarcerated.

Standing amidst the patients are three workers, one who looks at them, another who faces the camera, and a third who gazes at a coworker. The ratio of workers to patients in this image is actually higher than the ratio listed for the institution as a whole in this same year. The image suggests that the role of the staff was largely to keep order, rather than to provide any form of therapy.

Idleness is a recurring message in the photographs. Other pictures of the dining room, of occupational therapy occurring in the hallways, of beds lining the halls, express the relentlessness of the overcrowding problem and the inability of the institution to lower its occupancy rates.

Figure 6.17
This newspaper photograph depicted a "corner of a disturbed ward where the most troublesome types are encountered." It accompanied an article discussing overcrowding at the state hospital and arguing for a new bond issue to expand the state hospital system.

The inevitable counterpart to enforced idleness is compelled activity, in which workers and patients engage in physical activities mandated by their superiors. In the case of workers, we see the feigned smiles of those graduating from "remotivation classes." For patients, posed in workshops, craftwork in hand, activity seems similarly imposed. Congregate institutions by definition must schedule daily life: meals, sleep, showers, and work are all arranged for the convenience of those responsible for the inmates. In a mental hospital, however, activity is deemed therapeutic, hence the occupational and physical therapy sessions displayed in so many of the images. When mental illness is implicitly and sometimes explicitly defined as the inability to manage thought and emotions, the imposition of order is critical.

Figure 6.18, which shows men seated in groups around tables filled with beads, epitomizes the effort to coax activity from an unwilling group. Only a few are engaged in work; the majority sit in slumped postures, ignoring the task and the camera. Two of the men appear to be without shoes and badly dressed. They have no beads in front of them, suggesting that the attendant may have recognized the futility of trying to induce them to work. The attendant, clearly differentiated by his dress and appearance, busies himself overseeing the rear of this crowded ward corridor. The picture is clearly posed because there is a sign indicating to the viewer the location of the activity, "Ward 9" and yet reveals, as do the photographs of idle patients, the essential torpor of asylum life.

Figure 6.18
Some of the men on Ward 9 were supervised by staff in the compelled activity of stringing beads; some merely sit by.

Other photographs validate this interpretation. Figure 6.19, in which patients display the fruits of their labor, is marked not by the pride of workmanship, but by the sullen passivity of the psychiatric inmate. Even photographs of more useful work, such as men repairing shoes in a small workshop, shows the labor to be induced, not welcomed. Recreational scenes, such as bingo parties held around the same crowded tables in the same narrow corridors as the bead-stringing work, also reveal the grudging compliance of participants. Only a few images of women in physical therapy classes show a busy and seemingly contented group of patients. But these pictures, apparently taken by but not published in the local newspaper, are posed, and stand in contradistinction to the message delivered by the other, more candid images.

Emotionally equidistant between the images of the happy women exercising outside and the bead stringers in their compact corner are the photographs of women in the occupational therapy center. They have space to work, good lighting, the attentions of young female occupational therapists, and productive work to do. Many of the women seem to be engaged in their work, and so ignore the camera. Nevertheless, the surroundings, specifically the large flowers painted on the wall, give away the ultimately coercive character of the setting, which conveys a sense that these women are being infantilized like children in a schoolroom. This is an institutional workshop. The behavior is coaxed but it is also engaging, approaching the ideal of occupational therapy in which labor yields its own rewards.

Figure 6.19
Sullen passivity, not pride of workmanship, marked this gathering of state hospital patients displaying their craft.

Only through close analysis of individual images does the narrow range of institutional behavior from idle to active become apparent. Much sociological literature on mental hospitals stresses the interactions of patients and staff; the photographs suggest these interactions were perhaps more episodic and infrequent than presumed. Seeking to observe and explain social activity, sociologists may have unwittingly exaggerated its significance and ignored the long periods of institutional torpor and individual lethargy that the photographs reveal.

Figure 6.20 shows a striking image of elderly patients confined to their beds in a crowded infirmary, revealing a form of care that had become increasingly important during the early twentieth century. Whatever the intentions of its founders, this institution, like many another American mental hospital, was transformed by the large numbers of elderly and infirm patients who spent their last years in its care. This photograph contrasts sharply with comparable images of general hospitals of the period, where even in the most overcrowded hospitals beds were rarely crammed together as they are in Figure 6.20. For these patients, the institution struggled to provide basic custodial care, diverting its scarce resources of funds and staff time toward their survival.

Missing from all but a few of the images in the collection are the physicians who ruled over the massive institution. A few posed ceremonies show them standing with the graduates of the nursing school, introducing Governor Rockefeller at the opening of a new building, grouped together

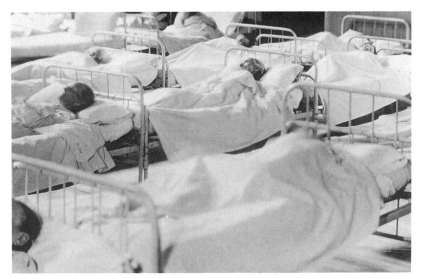

Figure 6.20
For the infirm elderly, custodial care often meant confinement to beds crowded together on a ward.

at a meeting of the medical staff, or throwing out the opening pitch at a ball game. There are no pictures of anything resembling the professional practice of medicine or psychiatry, and only a few pictures of distinctly medical culture, such as an image of the pharmacy, a new piece of operating room equipment, and a teaching amphitheater. In striking contrast to what students of medical photography (Fox and Terry 1978) have found—images that increasingly document the spread and dominance of a distinctly medical culture during the early part of this century—this collection demonstrates that almost the opposite was true for a mental hospital. The only therapies the images show were provided by occupational and recreational therapists and nurses.

These images of daily life at the state hospital help expand the understanding of the institution based on its published and unpublished documents. What is particularly striking is that analysis of over 800 photographs shows so little evidence for much change in everyday life over the course of more than a half century. The state hospital as a maximalist organization clearly changed very little over much of its history.

SURVEYING THE STATE HOSPITAL: 1942

Another approach to understanding everyday life at the state hospital is to view it through the eyes of knowledgeable observers. The hospital was formally inspected in 1943 by Samuel Hamilton, M.D., an experienced psychiatrist who also was among the very few people to attempt a complete survey of state hospitals in the country (Hamilton, Kempf, Scholz, and Caswell 1941). Because Hamilton attempted to assess how well the Buffalo State Hospital matched existing American Psychiatric Association standards and also fashioned a survey data set that directly compares it quantitatively to the entire population of state hospitals, his view of the institution allows us both a quantitative and qualitative way to assess its performance.

To see the Buffalo State Hospital (BSH) in this way is to view both the hospital and the norms and values held by doctors and nurses. A 60–page unpublished typescript found in the files of the BPC Director's office offers this opportunity (Hamilton and Corcoran n.d.).

The survey was one of many carried out beginning in 1936 by the Mental Hospital Survey Committee, composed of representatives of the U.S. Public Health Service, five American and Canadian medical organizations, and the National Committees for Mental Hygiene of the two nations. The survey was carried out at the invitation of New York Governor Herbert H. Lehman, though at the suggestion of the committee, which wanted to add more information about New York institutions.

The survey team—Dr. Samuel W. Hamilton, M.D., Miss Mary E. Corcoran, R.N., and (by special arrangement) Dr. David Slight, M.D.—visited the BSH for several days, and based their report on their observations, "conversations with officers and employees," the "wealth of information" in New York's printed reports, and tabulations of the Bureau of the Census (which, until NIMH took over in the late 1940s, collected and published data on American mental institutions). In addition, Dr. Hamilton claimed the advantage of occasional prior visits to BSH, and "personal acquaintance with many who have served on its medical staff."

The team's report begins with a brief history of the hospital, noting the architectural achievements of Richardson and even some of the early controversy about controlling its construction. It also notes that a substantial reception building was added in 1897 and later torn down and replaced with a new building in 1933; expansion of the original main building and construction of several detached structures are also discussed.

Control over the institution was, according to the report, exercised by the Department of Mental Hygiene (DMH) and its commissioner. In addition to divisions over special activities, the DMH had "a strong bureau of inspection with a staff that at times includes four medical inspectors." BSH had a seven-member board of visitors, at least two of whom had to be women.

The hospital served the two counties of Erie and Niagara, though it shared admissions from the former with Gowanda State Hospital, and (by comparison with the large state institutions near New York City) was one of the smaller state institutions. USPHS data enumerated 2,699 patients on the books at the beginning of 1942, with 690 admissions (530 first admissions, 145 readmissions, and 15 transfers). 548 patients were separated from the institutions—262 discharges, 246 deaths, and 40 transfers.

According to the report, "The hospital shows both the advantages and difficulties that belong to an urban institution." Its well-kept grounds included only 89 acres, yet shrubs and grass grew well and it had "beautiful big trees, spacious lawn, pleasant walks, and a few seats distributed here and there." The main building is described as an "imposing structure" of many connected blocks of three- and four-story buildings. Other structures included the new (1933) reception building, a cottage housing 40 workers, and a "substantial" powerhouse. While the structures had some walls in need of paint and a few worn-out floors, they were "evidently well maintained." Heating and lighting appeared "generally good." Water and sewage were described briefly. Plumbing was satisfactory in form but not in numbers, with as few as five toilets for 120 patients; and privacy was provided "in some wards by partitions between the stools." Both the laundry and storage facilities bordered on inadequate. An ice plant and maintenance shops appeared good to poor. There were no farm buildings at the time of the visit.

Details about patient areas were few, and tended to report adequate if threadbare furnishings. Sitting room space was reported to be good but not "cozy," and dormitories were "quite drab." Single rooms were few, because many rooms that were planned for the occupancy of one person had "for a long time housed two." Furniture was said to be "generally comfortable and adequate in amount," although more pictures could have been found for the walls. "In most regards the wards are well equipped." Metal bars covered the windows of the main building, and screening against flies was "still incomplete." The report also noted the existence of a "pleasant" chapel and assembly hall dating back to 1904, but added that it seated only 500 and was inadequate to present needs. The main building was not "highly fire resistant" but firefighting equipment and a sprinkler system had been installed, and a fire drill was held every week.

The hospital's organization is sketched in Figure 6.21, developed from the details presented in the BSH Annual Report, and comparable to those in the USPHS survey.

The report's Section IV (Medical Organization and Staff) described several features of BSH. Consultants numbered 23; the University of Buffalo had a medical school, and "practice in this city is on a high plane."

At the time of the USPHS visit, Dr. Christopher Fletcher was about to assume the superintendency. Four of the 14 resident medical staff were on leave for military service. The APA standard of 1940 called for a physician for every two hundred resident patients, plus another physician for every one hundred annual admissions. Against this standard BSH was down four, or 22 percent; a table compared BSH with five other institutions: two (New

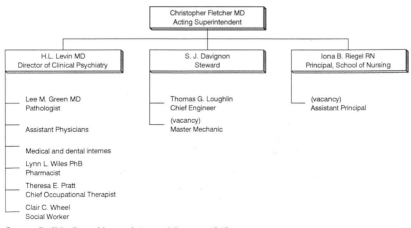

Source: Buffalo State Hospital Annual Report, 1942

Figure 6.21
Buffalo State Hospital Organization, 1942

Jersey State Hospital and Warren (PA) State Hospital) had more favorable ratios, while three others (Longview (OH) State Hospital, Peoria (IL) State Hospital, and Worcester (MA) State Hospital had poorer ones. (As with many other comparisons, then and now, BSH tended toward the middle of the distribution.)

Physicians' salaries ranged from $1800 to the superintendent's $6,000 per year, with added allowances. The superintendent and his first assistant had their own houses on the grounds, most others lived in apartments in the staff house, and a few commuted and were given stipends.

Working conditions for the physicians included a separate office and examining room on his service. Three services—men's, women's, and reception—were staffed. Most physicians took turns each week as night officer, making an "extensive" tour of the hospital and answering calls. During a physician's first two years, he or she would work on each service as well as in the laboratory, in occupational therapy, or in outpatient service. The clinical director "follows such lines as he prefers" in the supervision of new physicians. Twice-weekly diagnostic conferences chaired by the clinical director, as well as monthly administrative conferences run by the superintendent, were usually scheduled. Case records were described as "well prepared," with admissions, physical and mental examinations, and laboratory records kept on each patient; progress notes were kept, "though they say little about treatment." Nurses' notes were reported to be "fairly full", conference notes "very full" and summaries "usually good."

A special building housed the laboratory and morgue; though "suitable to its purpose," it was hot in summer and dusty the whole year. Autopsies were performed on 15.2 percent of the deaths, just barely above the AMA standard for "proper hospital activity." The surveyors commented that "since physicians constantly need valuable light thrown on their procedure by a study of tissues after death, it would seem desirable to raise this percentage."

Other health specialists were also on the staff. BSH had a resident dentist (whom each patient saw yearly) and a dental hygienist (whom each patient saw twice a year. X-rays were taken by a technician (also the hospital's photographer), with each film read by the first assistant physician and some referred to a consultant, at that time the President of the Board of Visitors. While there was no psychologist, two social workers occasionally gave Binet examinations. As for neurology, the surveyors commented that "The mental hospitals are becoming medical treasure houses of neurological material." One BSH physician was noted to have had "especially good training" in this specialty. Surgery made use of a "good operating suite," and elective surgery was thought to be "approximately up to date." While there were few urological cases, gynecology was fairly active, an opthamologist visited twice a month, and a laryngologist and otologist were on call.

The report claimed substantial professional support for the medical staff. A medical library of 500 volumes was maintained at the hospital. The superintendent attended quarterly conferences of the State Department of Mental Hygiene, and he and his colleagues attended an annual interhospital conference and maintained memberships at and gave occasional addresses to local medical societies. While several physicians planned further study, no current research was being done at the institution.

BSH DURING WORLD WAR II:
UP TO STANDARDS?

The conclusions of the USPHS report consist of two parts, a comparison of the hospital to the current national standards, and a set of recommendations for improvement. The first listed the twenty standards of the American Psychiatric Association, and then compared BSH to them (see Appendix B). For the most part, BSH met the standards, at least on paper. The staffing standard of one physician for every 200 residents was met by BSH's ratio of 1: 162.2, when all positions were filled. But because of the war, the actual ratios were much poorer. The standard for mechanical restraint and seclusion was met, but the surveyors noted: that "Probably the amount of mechanical restraint can be reduced through instituting a more active program for the disturbed patients." The standard for food was largely met, but it was noted: "Kitchens are adequately equipped. The hospital does not have a graduate dietitian. The dining room equipment should be improved. Food is good but should be more varied."

Thus almost all of the standards were fully or largely met on paper. The most serious deficiencies were the actual staffing patterns, which, due in large part to the war, were difficult to achieve. But since these standards defined the most critical factor in the quality of care for patients, it is likely that the hospital, despite being "up to standards," provided not much more than basic custodial care for most of them.

The surveyors' recommendations for change offer additional insight into the actual quality of daily life at the hospital. When the surveyors turned to their recommendations, they first provided a context: because New York hospital standards were considered to be high, they noted that "any sweeping criticism is likely to prove incorrect." A few points, however, showed that the "organization and activities" of the hospital could be improved. While acknowledging that some "may have to wait for the end of the war," the surveyors advised that some could "perhaps be undertaken now" and that "all can be planned."

The 13 items listed under the "treatment" section of the recommendations make clear how low an actual level of treatment the hospital provided. The surveyors called for: a "great increase in the amount of outdoor activity"; indoor exercise in bad weather; the resumption and extension of physical training; the strengthening of "habit training for untidy patients;" expansion of occupational therapy; full use of hydrotherapy; reduction in mechanical restraint; expansion of music; ways to "break the dulness (sic) of long evenings in the wards." The surveyors also recommended that "amusement schedules should be restudied to ensure working patients their relaxation"; Protestant chapel services made "more worthy and more attractive"; and books and magazines made available to those who could not go to the library. Finally, the report also recommended that "the traditional methods of mass bathing should be restudied in order that shy and even ordinarily modest women patients may enjoy greater privacy in attendant to their bodily needs." (Hamilton and Corcoran n.d.: 58–59).

The surveyors made four recommendations about diet: meals should be conducted on a "better professional basis"; greater variety of food was needed, including "much more" fruit and fresh vegetables; heated carts should replace the unheated ones that take food to dining rooms; and the last meal should be later in the day.

Four comments were made about nursing. Better organization, recruitment on a continuous basis, an increased number of authorized positions (so they can be filled "when economic conditions become more normal"), and more extensive physical training for pupil nurses were called for.

Seven observations concerned medical work. The first was that "four more medical positions should be established so that promptly upon demobilization a standard ratio of physicians to patients can be put into effect." Given the shortage at the time, it was suggested that nonphysicians take over certain of their duties such as the inspection of housekeeping and administration of personnel. It was also recommended that a change in organization be made so as to permit fewer interruptions in interviews with patients, and that more psychologists should be added to the staff "for the time being" to handle some of the responsibilities of physicians. It was also recommended that, after the resumption of normal activity in schools of medicine, a few senior students be recruited to be in residence at BSH. Finally, the surveyors recommended that the medical library be enlarged, and that charts showing dental treatment, weight, and menstruation be included in the patients' case histories.

A further set of eight recommendations was made about buildings and grounds. Four recommendations covered improvements in fire resistance, fly screening, the amount of "attractive adornment" on the wards, and plantings to screen parts of the campus to allow use by groups of patients. Three more suggested a new assembly hall, laboratory, and cottages for senior physicians. Finally, "in view of the increasing numbers of old, feeble, and sick patients," it was suggested that the Hospital make better provision for their treatment.

The overall tone of the documents contrasts sharply with what it actually reports about conditions at the hospital. In 1942, the Buffalo State Hospital was almost certainly among the better state hospitals in the United States, and almost certainly was a "snakepit." The latter term would come into widespread use in American culture just after the end of World War II, with publication of the novel *The Snake Pit* by Mary Jane Ward (1946). Later serialized in the *Reader's Digest*, it was made into a very popular film starring Olivia De Haviland and nominated for an Academy Award in 1948. The novel's title comes from a quote opposite its title page: "Long ago they lowered insane persons into snake pits; they thought that an experience that might drive a sane person out of his wits might send an insane person back into sanity."

Ward had been a patient at Rockland State Hospital, another of New York's massive institutions and one that probably resembles the Buffalo State Hospital fairly closely in this period.

How can the report be approving in tone yet the Buffalo State Hospital be labelled a snakepit? The phrase "snakepit," whatever meanings it may have acquired since the 1940s, is probably most accurately translated into "overcrowded custodial institution." Given the times, and the cultural assumption that most serious mental illness was either incurable or only partially treatable, custodial care in a large state hospital did not have the deeply negative image it has since acquired (or, more accurately, since been given by a new generation of community-oriented reformers). After all, in Ward's novel, Virginia, the main character, is given very humane care by Dr. Kik, despite the generally shabby living conditions and mass treatment she experiences while an inmate at "Juniper Hill." It is perhaps surprising to find almost no hostile criticism in the Buffalo newspapers of the time about the Buffalo State Hospital; instead, one finds pleas for more state appropriations to relieve overcrowding at the huge institution. A particularly telling image is reproduced as Figure 6.17, which appeared in a newspaper story titled "Our Overcrowded State Institutions."

THE 1950s: THE BEGINNINGS OF CHANGE FROM STATE HOSPITAL
TO STATE PSYCHIATRIC CENTER

How was one reasonably representative state hospital transformed into a contemporary public psychiatric center? Perhaps because of the stigma still associated with the seriously mentally ill (or even more precisely, with those treated in public hospitals), there has been little written about this transformation, and so this account tries to present a detailed portrait of change, drawn mostly from the hospital's Annual Reports (cited as AR and the year of publication). (The hospital's Monthly Reports, cited as MR and the month and year, are the primary source beginning in 1985.) Most writing on public mental health ignores the state hospital or gives the impression that little has changed (except perhaps overall size) since deinstitutionalization began in the 1960s; in fact, as the following account makes clear, it is actually the case that little has remained the same at state hospitals since the 1960s, and that such organizations were transformed through a combination of external pressure and internal development, often involving great conflict and tension. The result was a different organizational form, as the next chapter will discuss in detail.

The term "state mental hospital" contains the three most significant sources of change in this organizational form: state policy and funding; mental health care practices and procedures; and hospital organization and leadership. All three factors changed dramatically during the period from 1955. State policies (lumped under the title of "deinstitutionalization") favored community services over hospital-based care, while overall funding expanded during the 1960s and 70s and then contracted sharply during the 1980s. Morrissey (1982) has suggested that deinstitutionalization occurred in two broad phases: an early period of "opening the back door," when for a variety of reasons hospital patients were released more quickly than before and both admissions and readmissions accelerated; and a later period of "closing the front door" when admission policies became more restrictive as alternative settings for treatment became more competitive. Mental health practices turned toward a combination of drug therapies and more active treatment, using a variety of behavioral techniques, with increasing emphasis on avoiding prolonged hospitalization. Finally, the acute-care hospital became the most powerful organization in general health care and increasingly both the site and the model for psychiatric care, with profound and largely uncharted implications for the state mental hospital; a new generation of leaders tried to shape organizational change toward more active treatment of much smaller inpatient censuses. In the next chapter I examine how accreditation became one of the most important issues in managing the state hospital during the past twenty years.

Together, these broad factors transformed the state mental hospital into a different organization, even as continuities with its past persisted.

OPENING THE BACK DOOR: DEINSTITUTIONALIZATION BEGINS

Organizational turning points rarely can be fixed with certainty, but the mid–1950s marks the beginning of fundamental change in the character of the Buffalo State Hospital. In New York, an important policy shift began in 1954 with passage of the Community Mental Health Services Act which encouraged the development of local mental health services outside the immense state hospital system (Grob 1991: 171–73).

Figure 6.22 shows how the more or less steady growth in the inpatient census had led, by 1955, to making the Buffalo State Hospital an immense institution. It also shows how dramatic change would be in the coming years. Better physical facilities improved the ability to recruit personnel and "heightened employee morale and feelings of usefulness" (AR 1955: 8). The medical staff of 21 full-time members was now using the new Medical and Surgical Building (called "M&S"), with an accompanying increase in activity of the visiting, consulting, and attending staffs. Some of the changes were narrowly medical, attempting to enhance the physical health of the institution's huge residential population. Among the most important was a routine gynecological exam on all female patients during admission (AR 1955: 13); in this one respect, at least, the institution's female patients received more advanced medical care than most New Yorkers were accustomed to having.

But the most dramatic change came in psychiatry itself that year. Very soon after their first appearance on the market, new psychoactive drugs were used in several New York state hospitals, including Buffalo:

> The new drugs, chlorpromazine and reserpine, were available in trial quantities during the early part of the fiscal year and a very small number of cases were treated up to the time these were reported at the conference on drugs at Creedmoor State Hospital in December 1954. Following this, the drugs were administered to a larger number of patients, and they were first made part of the official monthly report in January 1955. In the

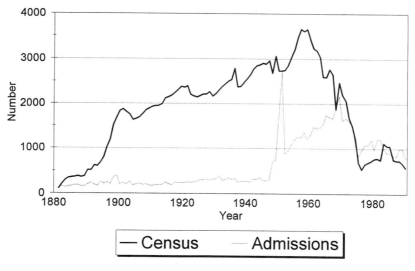

Figure 6.22
Inpatient Admissions and Census, Buffalo State Hospital, 1880–1990

remaining three months of the fiscal year, 177 patients received chlorpro-
mazine and 167 received reserpine. Following this, the use of these drugs
was markedly increased and evaluation will be made in the next annual
report. It may be said, at this time, however, that the use of the new drugs
is encouraging. It has not been found that they can entirely replace con-
ventional shock therapies, but the use of shock therapy has diminished
with the expansion of the drug program and a number of people who failed
to improve with electric shock and insulin therapy showed gratifying
improvement with the new drugs. (AR 1955: 15)

Appearing at a time when morale and staff performance seemed to be
rising for other reasons, the drugs' introduction into clinical practice helped
to strengthen the feeling that major improvements in care were possible.
Older therapies (including a few lobotomies) continued, however, and
newer approaches such as psychology were expanded modestly (AR 1955:
19–20). Full-time Catholic and Protestant chaplains and a part-time
"Hebrew" chaplain began work, with "a profound effect upon the hospital,
its patients and its community relationship." Another 39 staff positions
were added, chiefly in ward service, bringing the total to 881 employees.
The medical staff was allocated 23 positions, with 20 actually filled (AR
1955: 32). Certified capacity increased to 2,503, but the hospital had on its
books 1131 more patients, making overcrowding 41 percent overall.

By 1956, the Director observed that the increased staffing, recruitment, new M&S building, and the new drugs had led to "an increase in the
total rehabilitative efforts." Indeed, "The combination has resulted in an
increase in the number of patients released from the hospital or allowed
increasing privileges within the hospital. This has further resulted in an
increasing feeling of therapeutic importance on the part of the ward service
personnel" (AR 1956: 8). Morale also rose among the staff because of the
planning and funding for a new 940-bed building for infirm and disturbed
patients, an 150-bed addition to the reception building, and rehabilitation
of five of the main building series (AR 1956: 9). The hospital also began a
geriatric rehabilitation unit on an experimental basis. A large minority of
the resident patients, a total of 1,127, received drugs alone or with other
somatic therapies, an astonishing increase in some type of active therapy
over just a few years.

Clearly, major changes were sweeping through what had been only a
few years before a largely stagnant institution. Because the drugs were the
most striking innovation, observers credited them with most of the
changes:

The results roughly parallel those obtained in the other areas and reported
in the literature. The general movement of patients was considered gratifying and significant beyond any statistical evaluation of the results. The
general improvement in patient behavior, the appearance of the wards,

the morale of the personnel, all of which could be attributed to the increasing use of the tranquilizing drugs, was observed here as it had been in many other institutions. (AR 1956: 14)

The Director saw tranquilizing drugs replacing other forms of organic therapy, with release rates roughly the same at about 23 percent: "It should be stated again, however, that the release rate does not measure the entire benefit of such therapy to either the hospital or the patient since the improvement of those patients who do not respond sufficiently to warrant release but who do show a degree of improvement which renders them more accessible and reduces the behavior problem is very important" (AR 1956: 15).

Unlike other writers at the time, who saw the drugs as revolutionary in their impact on state hospitals, the BSH Director saw them as helping to make his hospital more manageable and therapeutic, but hardly as eliminating the necessity of its other programs. One such program, the Recreation Therapy (RT) program, was designed to reach patients on the active wards at least twice a week for one hour. In 1958, the Director aired his belief that personnel, not physical facilities, determined patient care, but that nonetheless "morale and motivation" improved when the latter improved (AR 1957: 9). But he also argued that without more facilities and reduced overcrowding, BSH would not attain American Psychiatric Association standards (AR 1958: 7–8).

The character of admissions had not changed: conditions associated with advanced age made up 47.6 percent of admissions in 1957. A table showed those treated and released with different therapies (AR 1957: 13); while not "biostatistically valid," it does show gratifying results. Group psychotherapy was described as a major activity, involving a total of 245 patients, 104 at one time; individual psychotherapy was given to 21 patients, a recent activity due to increased number of physicians. (AR 1957: 13–14). By 1958, the other somatic therapies had been reduced by a reliance on drugs, which had greatly overshadowed any other form of therapy.

The 1959 Annual Report contains items that show the increasingly contradictory character of the organization: in some ways a traditional custodial hospital, in other ways an increasingly dynamic institution adapting innovations from the national movement toward community psychiatry. Aided by a transfer of patients to Marcy State Hospital, the decline in patient census continued. But perhaps more significant for the hospital's character was an important change in the character of inpatient care. Patients with grounds privileges increased to 800, with more "open wards" replacing the traditional locked wards (AR 1959: 8). Among the changes was the first year of activity of the Department of Volunteers and an outpatient clinic at the convalescent hospital for Erie County. Outside accreditors gave only conditional and partial approvals, which were due to "overcrowding and the inadequate physical facilities," despite the fact that new laundry, storehouse and bakery buildings had been opened (AR 1959: 8–9). Perhaps most significant of all were changes in the plans for a new patient building; originally intended for 940, the building was now stripped back to 520 beds; no longer mentioned was the planned 150-bed addition to the reception building. While building plans were cut back, the medical staff was increased from 24 to 29 by the end of the fiscal year, and overcrowding decreased to 32 percent.

The next year saw several other signs of a shifting philosophy of care. Patients with grounds privileges increased from 800 to 1500. The psychiatric staff ran a series of conferences on admission, diagnosis, and release, "intensifying the training program and bringing more clearly into focus the needs of the individual patient." The treatment effort was "advancing consistently with the application of improved methodology" (AR 1960: 9).

During 1961, patients on open wards increased from 1500 to 2266, and in that year made up 71 percent of the incare population (AR 1961: 8). Representatives of the New York State Citizens Advisory Group for Mental Hospitals and Schools visited, as did Dr. Ralph Goldsmith of the Joint Commission on the Accreditation of Hospitals. The former registered their concern with "overcrowding, the non-fire-resistant character of the majority of the patient buildings, and the inadequate toilet, wash, and bathing facilities in the same area." The latter claimed these problems had to be corrected for full accreditation (AR 1961: 9). The Annual Report noted a second year of shift toward younger admissions, though once again no reason was advanced for this important shift.

1963 saw a major shift in leadership, as Dr. Duncan Whitehead retired and was replaced by Dr. Henry Haines as acting director. The psychiatric character of the institution was reemphasized. A new Narcotics Addiction Unit opened in January 1963 on the fifth floor of the M&S building (AR 1963: 6, 14). The overwhelming majority of inpatients—2151 in all—received psychiatric drugs during the year; by contrast, only 139 patients were involved in psychotherapy. "The Open Ward Policy" could not be expanded this year, with 65 percent of the patients living on them. "The nature of the institution makes it impossible to open certain wards, such as those caring for narcotic addicts, court cases, acutely disturbed patients, and senile individuals on upper floors" (AR 1963: 9).

During 1964, overcrowding had fallen to 10.7 percent. A 50-bed unit for children opened on the second floor of the M&S building (also called Building 52; like other large state institutions, BSH used numbers as names for its many buildings). Recreation Therapy was described as "plagued" by a shortage of personnel. Dr. Joseph Sconzo was named director, as Dr. Haines returned to the full-time medical staff after his months as acting director.

In 1965, the transformation from custodial to active treatment continued, though again at a pace that must have frustrated those looking for more rapid reform. Overcrowding was reduced to 9.4 percent (AR 1965: 7). A new 100-bed intensive treatment unit opened to rehabilitate patients hospitalized continuously more than two years.

During the late 1960s, major changes took place in both the hospital's physical plant and the character of care. On Oct 21, 1965, Governor Nelson Rockefeller dedicated the new 544-bed Reception and Intensive Treatment Building (named the Strozzi Building, after a former board member). This almost eliminated overcrowding, now down to only 3.4 percent (AR 1966: 8). A number of attendants were trained in the remotivation of long-stay patients, while an experiment had 58 patients working at a canning factory for three months at minimum wage.

During the next year, the Board worked hard to get accreditation for the care of Medicare patients in Strozzi and on the third floor of the M&S building. The Board also paid more attention to community relations, forming a new group, "The Friends of the Buffalo State Hospital." The Intensive Treatment Unit (ITU) moved from CTS (Continued Treatment Services, a phrase used at this time to indicate the back ward units with many long stay patients located in the original Richardson complex) to the third floor of Strozzi, the new Reception Building. The ITU was credited with its success in returning back to the community many patients hospitalized for years (AR 1967: 9). The institution's tradition of nursing education continued, with 455 nursing students completing a psychiatric nursing experience at BSH during the year.

CHANGING ADMISSIONS: CLOSING THE FRONT DOOR

Another physical change indicative of important organizational shifts occurred in 1968. The state demolished Buildings 6, 7, and 8 of the original Richardson complex to prepare the site for a new recreation building more consistent with contemporary trends in community psychiatry. The institution also achieved full accreditation by the Joint Commission on the Accreditation of Hospitals (JCAH) (AR 1968: 7).

But perhaps the most significant change of the entire decade occurred during 1968, when a new statewide policy to control admissions of elderly patients began to change operations at the institution. A "Geriatric Screening Team" became operational in August, 1968. This team, made up of a psychiatrist, a social worker and a community mental health nurse, began to screen all patients age 65 and over, resulting in a significant decrease in the number of elderly patients admitted (AR 1968: 9). Readers of the annual report would not learn that this represented a major savings by the state; those elderly formerly admitted to care at full state expense would now be diverted to nursing homes, where the costs of care would be paid for by federal dollars.

By itself, the dramatic decline in census well underway at the state hospital would have brought considerable change. In part because of increased federal spending but also in part because of a great increase in state spending, the mid–1960s saw a very dramatic increase in spending at the hospital, as demonstrated in Figure 6.23.

The end of the 1960s also saw other efforts to shift care away from traditional inpatient modes. One of the most important was family care, in which patients (often older and more stable) were placed in private homes but with mental health services provided by the institution (see Erie Alliance for the Mentally Ill 1989: 62). In 1969, "considerable effort" was reported to create additional family care homes and eliminate poor ones (AR 1969: 9). The institution was once again given a full three-year accreditation by JCAH. Noted briefly in the pages of the annual report was a strike by 250 staff members affiliated with American Federation of State, County, and Municipal Employees (AFSCME) on November 25–27, 1968.

The beginning of the 1970s saw evidence of continued change, but also some of the turmoil created by change. The Board announced itself "gratified with the excellent strides the hospital has made in moving toward a fully unitized hospital and [becoming] an active community-oriented treatment center" (AR 1970: 6). But the Director reported it was far from

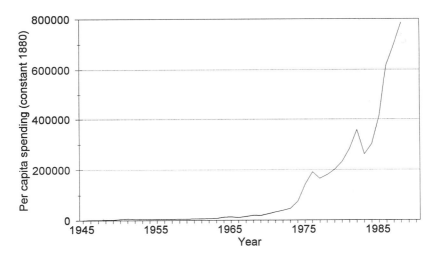

Figure 6.23
Per Capita Spending, Buffalo State Hospital, 1945–1988

smooth, with both quantitative and qualitative shortages, a significant morale problem, and security problems in the old main buildings.

The following year saw the Board concerned about the deterioration of the quality of housekeeping on the wards, a hiring freeze imposed in December of 1970, and a series of major fires in July, 1970 that demonstrated the need for additional security (AR 1971: 6–7). The East and West Units were further subdivided. The geographic units functioned well, internally screening admissions with alternatives such as day care and outpatient care, and then referring rejected candidates to community agencies. The Director noted that chronic patients had been involved more intensively with treatment teams and with intensified resocialization programs (AR 1971: 8–9).

During 1972, the economic problems of the institution became paramount to the board, or at least to those of its members who regularly attended its meetings; poor attendance by some was significant enough to be mentioned in the annual report. Those who did attend worried about the two strike threats in 1972, one of which ended in a two-day strike. Budget cuts and staff shortages once again disrupted the daily operation of the institution, so that even though the new Rehabilitation Center was completed, it couldn't actually be opened (AR 1972: 6). The Board also discussed the Buffalo General Hospital Community Mental Health Center, soon to be opened to serve Buffalo's East Side; this is one of the first times the Annual Report mentions another mental health organization, perhaps because of a shared-staffing plan that would link the two organizations (AR 1972: 6). Dr. Sconzo retired as director, replaced by Dr. Haines, who once again assumed the acting directorship.

The next year, 1973, represented another crest in the waves of community care that swept across American mental institutions in the era of community psychiatry. In part, the occasion was the installation of a new director, Stanley Platman, M.D., who would continue to serve as director of the Buffalo General Community Mental Health Center. Tied to this appointment was a real shift in emphasis on community care. By discharging patients outright rather than placing them on convalescent care, and by implementing an expanded family-care program, a steep decline in census of 24.6 percent was recorded for 1973 alone, by far the sharpest decline in the history of the institution. Admissions were also transformed by screening potential patients even more scrupulously, "in line with the philosophy that it is better not to be in a hospital than in one." A mobile geriatric screening team handled 400 cases, admitting only 137, whereas it was entirely possible that all 400 cases might have been admitted to the institution just a few years previously, before statewide policy and institutional practice changed so dramatically. "It is apparent that the community is beginning to realize that the State Hospital was inappropriately utilized for the care of the aged in years past" (AR 1973: 9). Platman stated his philosophy as one of greater community involvement and unit independence, with decreased priority on involuntary admission and better relationships with the community mental health system. Another sign of how rapidly the old ways of state hospital care were disappearing followed a Supreme Court decision that ended unpaid patient labor, with an immediate impact most directly on the Grounds Department.

Even more change marked 1974 as another real turning point in the history of the institution. Only months after he had been appointed director, Platman resigned to take a new position in another state, with Desmond Moleski, M.D., named acting director. During his brief tenure, Platman had shifted the institution from "primarily hospital based programming to a much wider involvement in community based psychiatric service." With its 25 percent drop in census in just a single year, BSH had the fastest census decline in the entire state. What had once been clinical units entirely focused on inpatient care had become units actively involved in communities across Western New York. As if to underscore what was happening organizationally, the last patients finally moved out of the original Richardson buildings. In another event that underscored how deep a change was actually taking place, Dr. Salaban, the long-time Clinical Director, retired. Concerns in the community were addressed indirectly, but centered, the Annual Report observed, on the "presence of some odd-looking people in the community who were not there before" and also about the possible loss of jobs and contracts from the once larger institution (AR 1974: 6). The Board acknowledged that "several unfortunate incidents were widely publicized to support resistance to reform of the institution" (AR 1974: 6). The Board took obvious pride in assisting in reform (AR 1974: 7). Major surgery was phased out at the institution, now to take place at the county hospital, Meyer Memorial. The Board took note of "elements of organizational turbulence" (AR 1974: 9). Many more visitors showed "the growing diversity of the involvement of the institution with academic, community, political, and State administrative constituency." The director thanked the staff for their dedication "in these especially trying times of transition" (AR 1974: 10).

ORGANIZATIONAL TRANSITION:
FROM STATE HOSPITAL TO PSYCHIATRIC CENTER

Not coincidentally, the institution known as the Buffalo State Hospital since 1890 was renamed, in 1974, the "Buffalo Psychiatric Center" (BPC), with the other New York state hospitals also changing their names during this year. New York's Commissioner of Mental Health claimed this change reflected the many new functions that these institutions now performed, beyond the traditional ones of custody and care. In this case, the name change stemmed not merely from organizational public relations, even if one of the consequences of the change was to lessen the connection with a stigmatized past. New York was one of the very few states that attempted to transform its old state hospitals into centers for non-inpatient treatment, so in a real sense the name accurately reflected a profound change in function. It also most certainly reflected the extraordinarily negative image that "state hospital" conjured up in both professional and lay circles.

The next year, the newly renamed institution was reaccredited for a full two years by JCAH (AR 1975: 3). For the first time, the General Statement at the end of the annual report announced that 33 percent of expenditures for personal service and maintenance and operation were for other than inpatients (AR 1975: 9).

With a new name and well-defined mission, BPC might have moved into its future with stability and confidence, but almost the exact opposite ensued. 1975 was one of the most troubled years in its long history. First, open conflict between its administrative and medical staffs broke out, with a special meeting called on June 4, 1975 to discuss the problems. Next, the Board's composition was changed by the Legislature. The Board was required to include "at least three individuals who are parents or relatives of patients or former patients" and to prove "that the remainder includes only those persons who shall have expressed an active interest in, or shall have obtained professional knowledge in the care of the mentally disabled or in mental hygiene endeavors generally" (AR 1976: 4). Adding to the turmoil was change in leadership: Dr. Moleski resigned on July 2, 1975, with Platman (now serving as Regional Director of OMH) taking on the added responsibility of Acting Director until the appointment of W. Ralph Michener, J.D., as Director in November. Michener was the first non-physician appointed head of the institution, a fact that did not endear him to the medical staff.

Two layoffs added to already existing stresses. The Physician and Medical Staff were concerned about the unfilled position of Deputy Director, Clinical, and the hospital medical staff by-laws (AR 1976: 7). Added to these difficulties were several cases of friction between BPC and local mental health services corporations about staffing and treatment responsibilities.

The following year began with some indications of increasing stability at the institution. James Minteer was appointed Deputy Director, Administration (AR 1977: 1). JCAH continued its accreditation after the Medical Staff rewrote its by-laws in conformity with national norms (AR 1977: 10). But after years of little local media coverage of other than a positive or routine nature, BPC became the subject of much attention, usually very negative in tone. A special grand jury began investigating Erie County's mental

health care system. Fall and early winter stories in newspapers and TV criticized the Center, and the Board countered with its own position, as the
administration and state authorities met with the Editorial Board of the
Buffalo Evening News. The Board's statement confirmed the existence of
considerable conflict at the Center, with the medical and dental staff fight-
ing with the administration about professional autonomy and the union
employees concerned about job security. As if local matters were not
enough, Governor Carey issued an executive order limiting the amount of
private practice time of state physicians, causing at least one resignation
and much unhappiness among the medical staff. Two years before, BPC had
34 full-time physicians and seven residents, but now it had only 25 and
three, respectively. Conflicts about community care developed into "an
out-and-out vendetta" against the administration, the Board contended
(AR 1977: 4). "The physicians and union leadership have collaboratively
aided and abetted each other in their endeavors to oppose administration.
In a highly unprofessional manner they have drawn in clients, relatives, and
a hostile community surrounding the center, as well as the local press and
politicians" (AR 1977: 5). Erie County cut its mental health funding when
BPC lost 90 positions, resulting in major loss of service and greater anxiety
about job security. But with all of this, the Board endorsed community
mental health as a concept: "mental health problems must not be confined
behind thick walls" (AR 1977: 6). The Director reported some of the continuing problems of realigning services after the consolidation of catchment areas (AR 1977: 8).

Far from abating, the troubles continued well into the next year,
despite the Board's claim of much better management-staff relations (AR
1978: 1). The Board was involved in defeating a proposal for county take-
over of BPC, recommending instead a tightening up of inspection (AR
1978: 2). On Oct 13, 1977, the Board took the extraordinary step of send-
ing Governor Carey a telegram (whose text was then made public) express-
ing its "grave concern" about the "totally inadequate" and "dangerous
understaffing."

Internal reorganization also advanced when BPC shifted toward a
"matrix organization," with appointment of Nancy Lyons as nursing coordinator and Dorothy Pappas as social service director. Line supervision of
nurses and social workers still took place through the Deputy Director Clinical and the Unit Chiefs; but these new roles were responsible for assessing
the quality of professional practice. A new unit designed for violent
patients called the Intensive Treatment Unit was established, but only at
the cost of the reduction of staffing on the geriatric and geographic units.
The Alcohol Rehabilitation Unit was moved to a separate building. Meanwhile, Buffalo's only community mental health center, operated by Buffalo
General Hospital in an inner city neighborhood, closed temporarily,

returning a BPC unit of 17 patients and some staff back to the facility (AR 1978: 4).

"Sobering" was the word chosen to characterize the following year at BPC (AR 1979: 1). The new Intensive Treatment Unit opened as planned, but other initiatives developed by BPC staff for new programs and more staff were rejected by the state. As expected, the Erie County Grand Jury concluded its investigation with no indictments, but with twenty-five specific recommendations (AR 1979: 5).

In an important shift in direction after the period of deinstitutionalization, the Office of Mental Health (OMH, one of three offices that comprised the New York State Department of Mental Hygiene) announced in April a new program of community support systems. "All state facilities and all counties were asked to rearrange their scheduled administrative activities and to immediately, and cooperatively, identify the gaps in community services for discharged patients and develop program proposals for meeting those needs" (AR 1979: 5). By July, BPC submitted to the Regional Office of OMH about a dozen proposals, but met with no approvals by year's end. While the patient census increased, the overall staff fell: an attrition of 17 percent of the workforce took place during 1978–79 (AR 1979: 7). Funding in other areas was also problematic, as other-than-personal-service funding was described as "tumultuous" due to the deteriorating fiscal conditions statewide (AR 1979: 10). These policy and funding shifts led to organizational changes. A detailed report from the Board of Visitors discussed formation of an Operations Council involving the major administrators of mental health organizations of Erie County. The Council forced BPC to accept referrals from the Erie County Medical Center (formerly Meyer Memorial Hospital), the largest public acute-care hospital, on a "non-decline basis," resulting in overcrowding at BPC (AR 1979: 18).

Another sign that policy had shifted was found in the views of the President of the Board of Visitors, Googie Butler, herself a former patient at BPC. She discussed deinstitutionalization, which she had once believed in but found had been "misused and abused" and was now widely viewed as synonymous with "dumping" and "playing the numbers game." According to Butler, "The pendulum has swung too far" (AR 1979: 25).

CHANGING DIRECTORS AND CHANGING DIRECTIONS

Yet another indicator that, for better or worse, the era of deinstitutionalization had ended was the changing cast of characters in major leadership roles at the institution. During 1980, three different men played the role of director: James Michener, J.D., who resigned early in the year, Augustine Diji, M.D., a Unit Chief appointed as acting director for several months, and Mahmud Mirza, M.D., named director later in the year. Mirza arrived with high expectations about his own ability to transform BPC, and by the end of the following year, was able to list several major accomplishments of his new administration, including the formulation of eight new goals for BPC, a two-year JCAH accreditation, a new functional reorganization, and the Centennial celebration. A Crisis Residence program, part of an admission diversion program, was opened in the newly renamed Cudmore Building. Pre-discharge patients lived in a new Homeward Bound program.

Perhaps the most extensive changes were in a newly organized Quality Assurance Program, made up of Medical Records, Utilization Review, Program Evaluation, Education and Training, the Discipline Heads, and Compliance and Certification (AR 1981: 12). In part, these new departments brought staff trained in various disciplines and management innovations (see Dowdall and Pinchoff 1994 for the case of the Program Evaluation Unit, founded and directed by Diane Pinchoff) and show the impact of external organizational standards on BPC's internal operations. Combined with some earlier and more incremental organizational changes, the result was a very different organizational structure than that of the old state hospital. Figure 6.24 presents the organizational chart of BPC in 1982. It is a striking example of how external environmental pressures are mapped onto the organizational structure. The reformatted Annual Report, now a buff-colored 24–page pamphlet with photographs and charts, was part of an expanded public relations effort, and contained paragraph descriptions of the major departments of the facility; its slogan, "100 Years of Caring," echoed the Centennial celebration.

The theme of 1982—"planning, preparing, upgrading"—did not include completion of the long-planned functional reorganization of inpatient services, but Mirza was able to report that "our progress toward upgrading the quality of our services has been marked" (AR 1982: 2). The "extensive" efforts to prepare for JCAH accreditation was the lead story. A measure of how much BPC had changed was that the most substantial changes of the year affected community services, which now served over 1200 persons. The 11 facility-wide goals included several new emphases including tighter internal management, patient care and treatment, research, and perhaps most importantly, increased attention to outside agencies that could "develop and implement a plan of corrective action in response to OMH preaccreditation site surveys, JCAH accreditation services, HHS allegation surveys, Commission on Quality of Care reports, Regional Office program reviews and management audits" (AR 1982: back cover). The planning for JCAH clearly paid off, since the highlight of the next year's annual report was receiving full three-year accreditation by JCAH. This came during a year described as "sobering" due to the state's fiscal problems, shrinking resources, hiring freezes, and the threat of layoffs.

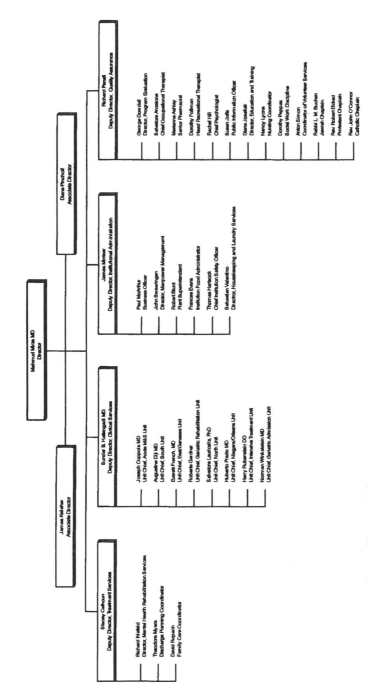

Mahmud Mirza MD
Director

James Kelleher
Associate Director

Diane Pinchof
Associate Director

Stacey Calhoun
Deputy Director, Treatment Services

- Richard Hatfield
  Director, Mental Health Rehabilitation Services
- Theodore Myers
  Discharge Planning Coordinator
- David Pegvach
  Family Care Coordinator

Sundar B. Hallangadi MD
Deputy Director, Clinical Services

- Joseph Coppola MD
  Unit Chief, Acute M&S Unit
- Augustine Dji MD
  Unit Chief, South Unit
- Everett French, MD
  Unit Chief, East/Genesee Unit
- Roberts Gardner
  Unit Chief, Geriatric Rehabilitation Unit
- Salvatore Leurisotto, PhD
  Unit Chief, North Unit
- Huberto Prado MD
  Unit Chief, Niagara/Orleans Unit
- Henry Rubenstein DO
  Unit Chief, Intensive Treatment Unit
- Norman Winkelstein MD
  Unit Chief, Geriatric Admission Unit

James Minhas
Deputy Director, Institutional Administration

- Paul McArthur
  Business Officer
- John Swearingen
  Director, Manpower Management
- Robert Blunt
  Plant Superintendent
- Frances Evans
  Institution Food Administrator
- Thomas Hartsock
  Chief Institution Safety Officer
- Sebastian Valentino
  Director, Housekeeping and Laundry Services

Richard Persall
Deputy Director, Quality Assurance

- George Dawidal
  Director, Program Evaluation
- Salvatore Anzalone
  Chief Occupational Therapist
- Marianne Ashley
  Senior Pharmacist
- Dorothy Follman
  Head Recreational Therapist
- Rachel Hill
  Chief Psychologist
- Susan Joffe
  Public Information Officer
- Diana Josefak
  Director, Education and Training
- Nancy Lyons
  Nursing Coordinator
- Dorothy Peppas
  Social Work Discipline
- Anton Simon
  Coordinator of Volunteer Services
- Rabbi L.M. Buchen
  Jewish Chaplain
- Rev. Robert Bidried
  Protestant Chaplain
- Rev. John O'Connor
  Catholic Chaplain

Figure 6.24

Buffalo Psychiatric Center Organization, 1982

Source: Buffalo State Hospital Annual Report, 1982.

Cast in a role as provider of last resort for the Western New York psychiatric care system, BPC's inpatient census rose in 1984 from a low of 730 to more than 800. The functional reorganization of the adult (or non-geriatric) inpatient units was completed, allowing patients "to be better grouped according to their psychiatric needs, and [permitting] staffing to also be allocated on the basis of patient needs" (AR 1984: 2). Mirza could claim that after almost five years, BPC had been reorganized almost completely.

Several internal organizational issues defined the key issues of 1985 at BPC. Early in the year, Patricia Oulton was appointed director, the first woman to be appointed to that role and the second non-physician. A little later in the year, patients responding to a survey about their satisfaction with treatment identified three problems, that "they were not given copies of patient rights on admission, that the facility was too restrictive, and that there were insufficient activities" (MR March 1985: 2). A federal Health and Human Services survey found BPC out of compliance. Because BPC was accredited by JCAH, HHS looked only at two areas, staffing and medical records. The former was found out of compliance, in part because of deficiencies in nursing and psychology, in part because of deployment in social work, physical therapy, and activities therapies (MR May 1985: 2).

External audits led to internal changes in 1986. In addition to adding more staff and redistributing existing staff, BPC responded to the HHS survey by rescheduling staff on evenings and weekends to provide additional programs, which had been identified as a major problem area (MR June 1986: 2).

THE CHANGING ROLE OF THE STATE PSYCHIATRIC CENTER

A series of events in the summer of 1986 allow an assessment of what BPC's top administration saw as its major internal problems (MR August 1986: 2). Several task forces were set up to deal with "areas of major concern." The first was to examine establishing a centralized admitting unit to shorten length of stay and divert admissions. A second task force looked at setting up a residential care center for adults (RCCA), since BPC was designated for an 80–bed facility of this type during the next fiscal year. A third examined inpatient staff scheduling. A fourth investigated "intensive treatment services for females and the functioning of the Secure Ward on the Erie County Male Unit." A fifth was appointed to look at the Uniform Case Record, an attempt to make more comparable and thereby improve psychiatric record-keeping and documentation.

Several items mentioned in the unpublished monthly reports of BPC during 1985 help define how changed the role of the state psychiatric center had become compared to that of the state hospital. They show the limited and very definite tasks set as BPC became treatment of last resort in an increasingly complex public psychiatric system.

A September, 1985 report reveals how its managers defined the role of the state psychiatric center:

> More than any other factor, the patient census affects the quality of care we are able to provide. In recent weeks, the census has begun to rise again, putting a strain on staff, causing crowding, and creating problems in maintaining a therapeutic environment. Added to this, the opening of the proposed RCCA (Residential Care Center for Adults) in fiscal 1986–1987 and other OMH program initiatives designed to reduce the inpatient census statewide in the next year makes it imperative that we take more aggressive actions to keep the census at the level for which we are budgeted (743 currently; 677 by the fall of 1986). As a result, we have set census goals for each of the inpatient units and we are encouraging the unit staff to become more aggressive in their discharge and community placement efforts. Initially, the units will be monitored on a weekly basis to determine how close they are to their occupancy goal and what problems are being encountered in reaching these goals. In addition, the units have been asked to prepare a list of discharge ready patients, the staff member responsible for placing each patient, and whether there are problems in placement. Staff are being encouraged to explore more than one possible placement for each patient to speed up the discharge process. We will be expecting staff to refer patients to more than one placement resource so that if there is a long waiting list for one, another may be able to accommodate the patient in a shorter amount of time. After January 1, we expect to further reduce the occupancy goal for each unit as we move to stay within the census for which we are budgeted. We are hopeful these actions will give us a measure of control over the patient census and will enable us to do a better job with those patients remaining in the facility. (MR September 1985: 1–2)

By the next month, increased admissions into BPC's three major feeders—Buffalo General Hospital, Erie County Medical Center, and Niagara Falls Community Mental Health Center—had increased so much that pressure was being put on BPC to accept their overflow. "At this point, our staff is pursuing all possible discharge options, but with limited beds in the community and the difficulty in placing our patients with voluntary providers, many of the solutions will have to be long term and will not alleviate our immediate situation" (MR October 1985).

A generation before, Buffalo State Hospital had offered virtually no services other than long-term incare. How profoundly the institution had changed is indicated by the fact that, by 1985, BPC's noninpatient programs seriously vied with inpatient care for the attention of its administrators (MR November 1985: 2). In addition to its outpatient programs, BPC ran an 80–bed RCCA on campus and two 12-bed community residences off-campus; moreover, it was beginning to build a 24-bed community residence on campus. That BPC would soon be running 128 outpatient beds was a "major change," allowing "us to maintain more people in community settings for longer periods of time."

BPC also participated in efforts to restructure the mental health system of Western New York (MR June 1986: 1). But many decisions were still made for BPC, not by it. The state Court of Appeals ruled that a court must determine that involuntary medication take place, except in emergencies. This threatened to lengthen stay, even though only one patient currently received antipsychotic drugs over his objection (MR June 1986: 3).

Once again, BPC reorganized its staff, who were given the chance to state their first three choices of job assignment. The reorganization was designed to provide better staff coverage and reduce overtime, though it is likely that it had little impact (MR September 1986: 1).

By early 1987, the census, well above normal for the fourth straight month, remained of great concern (MR February 1987: 1). For the first time, the county commissioners of mental health joined an annual census meeting for BPC at the OMH Regional Office, with a discussion of such topics as length of stay, census, and current admissions:

> The data on current admissions shows that 33 percent of admissions are minorities, two-thirds are under the age of 40; 75 percent of black males are under the age of 40, and many of our current admissions have serious social problems in addition to mental health problems. Our analysis of our pre-RCCA patients indicates that this group is more dysfunctional than the original profile developed by OMH. Many of them are younger than anticipated and have shorter lengths of stay. (MR March 1987: 2)

As the census crisis deepened, BPC tried to control its admissions. Though BPC had to accept admissions from its feeder institutions on a non-decline basis, its management decided in April, 1987 to accept new admissions only during the day shift on weekdays, with hopes of doing a better job. "A first admission to BPC can be a frightening experience for individuals and families who have never been here before. We need to be able to offer additional care and attention to these people, and this is best done on the regular day shift" (MR April 1987: 1). A veteran administrator later recalled that the Regional Office of OMH had ordered the BPC Director to rescind this policy, thought to be out of compliance with its certification as a 9.39 (emergency) facility.

To deal with the soaring increase in admissions (MR May 1987: 1), BPC opened a new ward, closed admissions to Erie County residents to facilitate discharge of inpatients, and began negotiating an agreement for a ceiling on admissions from Erie County hospitals and the Holding Center. In another major indicator of how much the state's policy about inpatient care had changed, the Office of Mental Health mandated a minimum of 20 hours of program activities per week for each patient.

These changes helped almost immediately, and it was hoped that the RCCA's scheduled opening would also help (MR June 1987: 1). Nonetheless, the continuing overcrowding led to a nine-point plan to reduce the census (MR July 1987: 1). Two new initiatives sought to increase the number of psychiatrists on the BPC staff. The first made use of consultants from the SUNY at Buffalo School of Medicine as part-time staff. The second was to be far more controversial, a contract with a for-profit out-of-state firm, Liberty Health Care Management, to recruit psychiatrists (MR July 1987: 2). BPC also sought to change management of the clinical units by establishing a new model for unit management with both a medical director and a non-medical administrator (MR August 1987: 1).

By the end of 1987, the census had finally been reduced to below the target of 572, allowing the closure of four wards and better coverage on the remaining 19. The year ended with a visit for the first time by OMH Commissioner Surles; members of the New York State Assembly and their staffs had visited a few months earlier. Also noted was increased patient programming, and a detailed list of all the groups being run on different units, appended with a statement that the expectation was now that every professional would run at least one group. The new RCCA had almost all of its 101 beds occupied. "Overall the environment of the RCCA is excellent, far superior to what is available on incare. The new residents are very happy to be there and are enjoying their new surroundings" (MR December 1987: 4).

1988 began with one of the relatively few contributions by staff members to national psychiatric publications, a paper published in the January, 1988 issue of *Hospital and Community Psychiatry* about the BPC family support project. But 1988 saw several major problems continue. Most serious was the census, which had once again become elevated (MR March 1988: 1). The 24-bed State Operated Community Residence opened on the last day of March.

A CHANGING INSTITUTION: IMAGE AND REALITY

After years of effort, the original Richardson buildings were designated a National Historic Landmark, one of only 15 hospitals so distinguished in the United States and one of only eight buildings in Western New York. This event was covered by all local media, but showed how fragile good news could be. "The 6 p.m. news barely mentioned the ceremonies and went right into film clips of 'The Snake Pit' and 'One Flew Over the Cuckoo's Nest' and indicated there was 'trouble behind the facade' at BPC." A representative of the Erie Alliance for the Mentally Ill said she'd seen patients "poorly clothed, without bras and dirty." The Monthly Report claimed this coverage was "totally inappropriate and unfair . . . it was television news at its worst." (MR April 1988: 2)

During 1988 BPC's ties were strengthened with the Boston University Center for Psychiatric Rehabilitation. In April, BU ran a third day-long retreat to help improve planning for 20 hours of programming per week for each patient; this year was proclaimed to be the "year of groups" at BPC (MR April 1988: 1).

BPC's Cabinet met with BU personnel to develop a new mission statement:

To promote the dignity and autonomy of individuals we serve so that:

- Disabling symptoms are decreased
- Functioning skills are increased
- Independence in (sic) maximized, and
- Quality of life is improved. (MR May 1988: 2)

The mission statement and several organizational changes showed how much BPC's top management had come to accept a treatment philosophy that blended a highly medicalized psychiatry with elements drawn from the psychiatric rehabilitation movement. After BPC had gone several years without a chief psychiatrist, Dr. Jeffrey Grace accepted the position of director of psychiatry (MR June 1988: 1), also involving himself in clinical research at the institution. In conformity with a new OMH policy, BPC identified 120 individual patients for a new intensive case management program, with 12 new personnel to be hired (MR August 1988: 3). Two new positions with the title Deputy for Program Operations (DPO) were created, each reporting to the Clinical Director. The director for community services was to become DPO—Rehabilitation; and a new DPO—Acute was to be appointed (MR October 1988).

But whatever the ideology or language used, older problems continued. Overcrowding brought about environmental problems, particularly worn furniture and draperies. Allegations of neglect once again were raised after Wayne Vernor, a 30-year-old patient, committed suicide on January 27, 1989, the first suicide at BPC in nine years. An extensive investigation was begun (MR January 1989: 1). Finally, a new outpatient program moved 20 male residents to the "Y" on North Street, with BPC staff giving on-site support. But the Erie Alliance for the Mentally Ill didn't like the plan and put out incorrect information about it, according to BPC (MR January 1989: 4–5).

The Board of Visitors held a brunch in February, 1989 for area legislators, with very good attendance, and included an overview of 1988 that might stand for an overall report on the Center's operations and plans for the future. In addition to those mentioned above, several major clinical projects were under way, including a Clozaril Research Project (about a powerful new drug said to be effective in treating previously "treatment-resistant" schizophrenia); a MICA (mental illness chemical abuser) program; an effort to reduce the number of escapes; the Buffalo State College Education Intervention Program, modeled after a Boston University program; and the Justice Department suit (treated in the following chapter) were discussed. A new pilot program for restricted Intensive Treatment Patients resulted in 90 percent receiving 20 hours of programming per week (MR February 1989: 20).

But even with these new programs came old problems, as a hiring freeze intensified staffing problems. The Vernor suicide investigation was completed, with BPC seeking one termination, two demotions, two five-month suspensions, and one one-month suspension. One of BPC's initiatives was ended when the state Department of Social Services disapproved its YMCA plan. In the midst of these changes, Patricia Oulton resigned as director, and was replaced by Richard Panell as acting director (MR April 1989).

A new patient advisory committee held its first monthly meeting in May, 1989, with patient representatives from each of the units, Outpatient Services, and on-grounds residential programs. Concerns included "discharge planning, staff attitude, patient education, privileges, on-ward activities and Sunday evening activities, and counseling. The group also discussed what they viewed as positive achievements at BPC. Acknowledged were the increased opportunities for residential placements . . . and certain staff who have made special efforts to reach out to patients."

During the next month an executive committee retreat focused on insuring that all patients receive "at least 20 hours of active treatment each week," with a current focus on restricted and unmotivated patients. But the worsening financial situation of the state made these initiatives problematic; shortages in direct care staff made management even more difficult, and the state announced that BPC must reduce its staff from 1230 to 1172 by attrition. Within a month further staff cuts were announced, with a laundry consolidation resulting in 24 more staff lost. Dramatic increases in overtime resulted from attrition of positions. Some lab work was shifted to a nearby health center, Roswell Park, with more staff losses. Several outpatient programs were "transitioned" out of service (July 1989: 4).

The summer of 1989 brought more bad news. After several nurses were attacked, security at BPC was tightened; patients were eliminated as suspects. The media picked this up after an employee union representing white collar workers (the Professional Employees Federation) staged an informational picket line. A reporter printed a critical story about the Liberty contract to recruit psychiatrists (August 1989: 3). Yet another clinic was "transitioned."

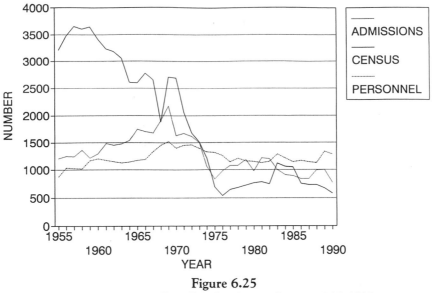

Figure 6.25
Patients and Staff, Buffalo Psychiatric Center, 1955–1990

During 1989 and 1990, budget problems continued to plague not only BPC but many other state agencies. By mid–1990, delay in approving the state budget had caused serious budgetary problems, with some vendors refusing to accept BPC purchase orders, and BPC lost more than 100 positions from its staff. Several revitalization projects had already been cut because of the fiscal crisis (MR November 1990).

Even with the dramatically negative fiscal news, other business was conducted that showed continuity with BPC's long past. In June, 1990, the Dean of SUNYAB Medical School visited BPC, the first visit by its dean since the mid–1970s, and perhaps an indication of the modest rise in stature that a former state hospital enjoyed as psychiatry 'remedicalized' and as the job market tightened. In July, 1990, the Medical-Geriatric Open House succeeded in attracting 15 outside providers.

Finally, the holiday activities that closed 1990 were probably not greatly different from those reported in the institution's annual reports from more than a century earlier. The institution was very different in size (especially of staff), character and even name, but it continued in its mission of providing inpatient care to mentally ill Western New Yorkers. At the end of 1990, only 415 people were on inpatient census with 35 on short-term leave. 1014 were in various outpatient and residential programs, with 175 in Family Care.

Figure 6.25 presents a graphic summary of how much change had taken place at BPC over the course of several decades. It also suggests that in a sense BPC had experienced "inertia as reform": staffing stayed about at the same level during a period of time when the incare population fell rapidly and outpatient services expanded in the community. Along with the several hundred other public mental hospitals, BPC offered its patients the promise of asylum and the reality of public psychiatric care, for better or for worse greatly different in character than the snakepits of several generations before. The next chapter examines the contemporary state mental hospital as an organizational form powerfully shaped by the national standards against which it is accredited.

Once again, the events in Buffalo are representative of the changes that affected the several hundred other state hospitals around the country. Almost all of them underwent the same journey from relatively stable state hospital for much of the first half of the twentieth century to a somewhat more rapidly changing institution during deinstitutionalization. In the latter phase, the state hospital itself became stigmatized as the place of last resort for the seriously mental ill and the employer of last resort in public psychiatry. As its stigma increased, the state hospital went into eclipse, and the very real changes that took place in its daily life became largely invisible not only to the public but even to those concerned with mental health policy.

Chapter 7

The Contemporary
State Psychiatric Center:
Up to Standards?

Has the state mental hospital changed into a different kind of institution for the far smaller number of patients now resident in its wards? Or is it an embarrassing anachronism that has failed to keep up with current standards of care?

Between the end of World War II and the beginning of the 1960s, a new myth of community care for the seriously mentally ill rapidly began to replace the myth of the asylum. The new myth held that state mental hospitals were purely custodial, harmed their inmates rather than helped them, retarded the advancement of psychiatry rather than supported it, cost much more than better care in the community, and should be closed. Over time, the myth took hold and became orthodoxy: to argue otherwise meant professional marginality. Like many myths, considerable support existed for this one, much of it the results of failed reform from the previous century to the present; some support came as well from the historical and contemporary study of the state hospital and its predecessor, the state asylum.

Two central parts of the myth held that state mental hospitals could not be changed, and that they inevitably fell far below national standards of care. The latter was of course largely true, as has been demonstrated here and elsewhere. But was the former true? Were these institutions beyond change, thoroughly bankrupt, incapable of being transformed from custodial to therapeutic organizations? Was it (is it?) impossible to bring the state hospital up to contemporary standards of care? In order to answer that question, we turn once again to a detailed analysis of one representative state hospital.

By 1955, the year that marks the onset of deinstitutionalization, the Buffalo State Hospital was at the end of the second stage of its organizational career. Opened in 1880 as a state asylum, it had evolved within 10 years into a state hospital. A comparison with all other state hospitals demonstrates that BSH was a fairly typical example. A relatively small staff of physicians led what had become largely a custodial institution, with little active therapy for the thousands of long-term patients who resided in its wards.

Recent organizational theory (both population ecology and neo-institutional approaches) has renewed research interest in basic questions of organizational survival and change (Hannan and Freeman 1989; DiMaggio and Powell 1983; Meyer and Scott 1983). A previous chapter explored the founding, persistence, and closing of state hospitals. Despite deinstitutionalization, which was among the most profound transformations of American social policy, a minority of state hospitals actually closed. Instead, patient censuses fell sharply from the mid–1950s to the present, levelling off at roughly a fifth of their historic highs. Public mental health care shifted dramatically away from confinement in institutions toward various forms of treatment in the community (or no treatment at all). Did these dramatic shifts in size and market share transform the state hospital, or is it still the same type of institution, practicing, as one critic (Fowlkes 1975) put it, "business as usual?"

Recent organizational studies suggest that a strategic place to look at these issues is to examine the development and application of standards by which certain agencies (mental hospitals among them) are judged fit for public use and trust, as well as governmental or private funding. In the case of the state mental hospital, this is particularly intriguing, since standards have played an important part (though a changing one) over such a long period of history. On the level of public understanding, state hospitals have been eclipsed, with little recent public discussion of how they operate at present. (Perhaps this lack of current attention permits the increasing call for reinsitutionalization of the chronic mentally ill, which assumes nostalgic images of care far from any reality.) But regardless of this lack of public discourse—and although they are much smaller absolutely and relatively—state mental hospitals remain crucial to the care of the seriously mentally ill (Gronfein 1985).

Aside from size and market share, has the state mental hospital changed? Thirty years ago, the Joint Commission on Mental Illness and Health's *Action for Mental Health* (1961) discussed the lag between support and interest for physical and mental health, stating it was "nowhere more evident" than in a comparison of state hospitals with community hospitals. The report goes on to compare three indicators: daily patient costs, ratio of employees to patients, and accreditation.

We can roughly assess the amount of change by comparing these three indicators: costs, patient/staff ratios, and accreditation over the recent past. One of the few researchers to examine the change empirically, David Mechanic observes that the public mental hospital was transformed from custodial care to active treatment, in part because staff-patient ratios "improved enormously." Mechanic claims "little resemblance" between state hospitals then and now (1989: 479).

On the question of accreditation, the Joint Commission reported that, in 1960, 29 percent of state mental hospitals were accredited, while 67 percent of community hospitals were. Hadley and McGurrin (1988) report 1983 data on accreditation of 216 state psychiatric hospitals: 63.4 percent were accredited, more than double the rate of 30 years before.

One of the unexamined changes in the history of the state hospital concerns outside scrutiny. This chapter examines three different forms of scrutiny, respectively accreditation, inspection, and investigation of the state mental hospital. *Accreditation* is a formal process involving a scheduled visit by a team who judge whether an institution meets a set of standards. *Inspection* is based on a visit, usually unannounced, by outsiders who assess conditions inside an institution. *Investigation* is an inquiry by a governing agency to establish whether allegations made about the institution are true.

In this chapter I first discuss briefly the evolution of accreditation for psychiatric hospitals. Next, I present a case study of how BPC experienced accreditation, inspection, and investigation in a brief and very traumatic period of time during the past decade. A final section draws some conclusions about whether the state mental hospital has changed.

ACCREDITATION: THE DEVELOPMENT OF NATIONAL STANDARDS

Minimum standards for mental hospitals grew out of two traditions, one dealing with institutional psychiatry and the other with the American community hospital.

Earlier, we discussed efforts to establish "propositions" about the construction and operation of mental asylums that date back to before the Civil War (Grob 1973). Like many other institutions, the Buffalo Asylum was built to these detailed specifications, differing only in its location near the center of a large and growing industrial city. By 1924, a committee of the American Psychiatric Association had published a set of minimum standards for mental hospitals (see Appendix B). The 17 statements tended to be fairly general, though specific doctor-patient and nurse-patient ratios were included as well as specific structural features prescribed. Few state hospitals ever met the staffing standards; but even in 1942, with great staff shortages due to wartime, the Buffalo State Hospital met many of the non-staff standards (Hamilton and Corcoran n.d.). Overall, the APA standards were treated as desirable goals but hardly realistic expectations, given the . low level of funding most state hospitals experienced.

A second line of development grew out of efforts to construct a system of standardization of hospitals first begun in 1912 by the Clinical Congress of Surgeons, an organization later merged with the American Congress of

Surgeons (Ginsberg 1974; Stevens 1989). That organization, along with the American Congress of Physicians, the American Hospital Association, and the American Medical Association, formed the Joint Commission for the Accreditation of Hospitals (JCAH) in 1951; the name was modified in the 1980s from "Hospitals" to "Healthcare Organizations" (JCAHO).

Separate standards for psychiatric hospitals were published by the APA in 1971, and, along with those for psychiatric facilities for children and adolescents and for general hospitals, provided the basis for the first JCAH *Accreditation Manual for Psychiatric Facilities*, published the following year. By the beginning of 1974, the Accreditation Council for Psychiatric Facilities had completed surveys on 272 facilities: 63 percent received two-year accreditations; another 32 percent were accredited for one year; and only 5 percent were not accredited (Ginsberg 1974: 91).

Observers differ on the utility of these standards. On the more positive side, one of the few extended examinations of the transformation of a state hospital into a psychiatric center used a JCAH report as a source of information about the quality of its inpatient care (Levine 1980: 9, 15, 17, 87). Levine portrays JCAH accreditation as a major challenge facing the hospital, and its attainment as a major accomplishment. Another observer (Torrey 1988: 176) advises that "a measure of hospital quality which has become increasingly useful in recent year is accreditation by ... JCAH ... The survey is very thorough ... Full accreditation by JCAH probably means that the hospital is a good one although, since the accreditation is for the hospital as a whole, there may be individual wards in an accredited hospital which are below standard." Finally, in trying to answer the question, "what do good mental health services look like?," a group of mental health activists (Torrey et al. 1990: 27; 182) lists accreditation standards first in their list of sources (see Appendix B). On the other hand, these same authors also point to limitations with these standards. They note that: accreditation is voluntary, so states probably self-select only those facilities that meet the standards; most attention is focused on records and administration, less on treatment and quality of care; accreditation is almost automatic, with few hospitals losing accreditation.

In a more critical vein, Johnson (1990: 243–47) argues that the 1979 JCAH *Standards* (well after Wyatt v. Stickney, discussed below) have been attacked as "overspecific, redundant, plagued with omissions, and given to setting controversial standards." Johnson contrasts what the JCAH accreditors assess—the measurable—with what clinicians do—the ineffable; and contrasts the bureaucratic with clinical perspective. But she also argues that the outside audit

is the one place in the whole system at which policy and practice intersect, the one moment where practice can inform policy and policy can reflect practice—but no one wants the information . . . In short, they see a picture of facility life that is in no way representative and may well be deceptive. They see precisely what we want them to see, and we cannot wait to get rid of them. (Johnson 1990: 242)

A pivotal force in pushing states to spend more money on their state hospitals was a 1972 Supreme Court decision, *Wyatt v. Stickney*, that forced states to meet minimum staffing, treatment, and physical care standards. The standards, presented in Appendix B, almost surely played an indispensable role in making JCAH and other professional standards into actual norms against which individual hospitals would be held accountable, rather than merely ideal goals that few would meet.

Since Wyatt versus Stickney, accreditation of state hospitals has become a much more important issue, in that it is tied to both federal and private insurance reimbursement and to state policy. Thus, in New York State

it is the policy of the Office of Mental Health, that all State operated psychiatric centers seek and achieve accreditation from the Joint Commission on Accreditation of Hospitals. Thus, in effect, the Office of Mental Health has adopted the nationally recognized Joint Commission on Accreditation of Hospitals' Consolidated Standards as the minimum standards of care. The comprehensive JCAH criteria encompass four broad categories: program management, patient management, patient services and physical plant management, and are generally accepted national professional standards. The JCAH is a highly respected organization of psychiatric and medical professionals and the value of its comprehensive accreditation program has been recognized by Congress and the courts. In fact, several courts have cited the JCAH accreditation criteria as a valid measure of adequate care. (New York State Commission on the Quality of Care (CQC hereafter) 1984: OMH appendix 2)

Appendix B contains a list of the chapters included in the 1981 JCAH standards used in accrediting psychiatric hospitals. After applying to JCAH, a hospital is visited for several days by a team usually made up of physicians, nurses, and administrators. The team inspects sites, reads manuals developed to show how the hospital is organized to comply with standards, and interviews selected staff; each standard is evaluated to judge whether the hospital complies.

ACCREDITATION AT THE BUFFALO PSYCHIATRIC CENTER (BPC)

To examine accreditation, a case study of the experience of one more or less typical state hospital is presented. Except for a brief period in the 1960s, BPC was always accredited by JCAH, which might imply that this constant feature of its organizational life was of less importance than those that varied considerably over time. In fact, however, preparing for one accreditation visit (which occurred through this period every one to three years), or removing the deficiencies from the last one, was a central question, perhaps among the most important ones occupying the administration. For example, in reviewing the monthly reports of BPC's director to its Board of Visitors (cited as "MR"), accreditation and other outside reviews are mentioned in almost all of them; during the period from 1970 to 1990, accreditation and other reviews are discussed in almost every annual report (cited as "AR"). By contrast, while BPC was the subject of more than 100 stories in the *Buffalo News* (cited as "BN") during the 1980s, only a few mentioned accreditation outside of the context of the scandal discussed below. Accreditation became one of the most crucial questions in understanding the state mental hospital in the 1980s, as well as a key to understanding its capacity for change in the future, but neither popular media or even scholarly literature published much about it. This is an intriguing change in itself, since one of the themes of earlier generations of critics of the state hospital was that it was "Out of mind, out of sight" (Wright 1947), "out of range of critical shot" (Mitchell 1894), and generally hidden from public inspection (Deutsch 1948).

The last chapter discussed how the Buffalo State Hospital was surveyed against American Psychiatric Association standards by a team from the US Public Health Service in 1942; though BSH met many standards and failed the staffing standards, nothing much followed as a consequence. Funding for BSH, as for most state hospitals, came directly from the state, and failure to meet standards meant no real change in its operations. Nonetheless, beginning in the late 1950s, accreditation activities are mentioned with increasing frequency (see, for example, AR 1959: 8; AR 1960: 10; AR 1961: 9; AR 1969: 6–7, 12; AR 1975: 3; AR, 1977: 1; AR 1978).

As we have seen, the end of the 1970s marked a major turning point in the institution's history, with the most substantial structural reorganization in a century. In 1979, with Dr. Mahmud Mirza the newly appointed Director of the Buffalo Psychiatric Center, an upcoming accreditation of the facility became the center of his efforts to reorganize BPC in both administrative and clinical areas (Pinchoff and Mirza 1982).

The JCAH accreditation visit of 1980 bears several formal similarities to earlier ones, including the one carried out during World War II discussed in a previous chapter. Each consisted of a several-day visit by a team that included a physician and nurse. The teams toured the facility; talked with administrators, staff, and even patients; read various documents about its organization; compared the institution to a set of national standards; and issued a written though unpublished report summarizing their findings. Despite these similarities, the qualitative differences between the two visits are striking demonstrations of how changed both the institution and the nature of accreditation had become.

On March 6, 1980, the three surveyors presented a summation of their visit to a BPC staff meeting (unpublished BPC memo, "Minutes of Summation by JCAH March 6, 1980"). The first speaker, Weaver O. Howard, M.D., commented briefly on three areas. Physicians were supposed to "authenticate" patients' histories developed by nonmedical staff members; "I think you aren't doing this in every instance." Restrictions on mail and phone calls by patients on the Intensive Treatment Unit "were not really reviewed at the required interval," at least every seven days. Finally, standards about the therapeutic environment were not met because of problems in a number of areas: inadequate access for handicapped individuals to elevators; waiting areas that lacked privacy; several wards with locked iron grills that restricted patient movements and were "reminiscent of the bars of a jail;" and dorms with 18 beds rather than the maximum of eight. But Dr. Howard also noted more positively that the OMH regional director was constantly present during all four days of the survey: "This represents what we like to see as interest and concern in accreditation matters."

Under the general topic of "functional safety and sanitation," Ruth Mrozek, R.N. presented a variety of points at variance with national standards, though she tended to see most of them as relatively minor variations. Standby electrical power, smoke stop partitions and walls, smoke dampers, vision panels and steel wall doors, and illuminated exit signs were among the physical environmental concerns she raised. Problems of a more serious nature dealt with staff composition, particularly the role of nurses:

> there is a lack of documentation, while you meet the minimum standard which means you have an RN on duty in all buildings and all units there must be evidence that the RN is planning, supervising, assigning and evaluating the nursing care needed in your facility and to assure the administration and governing body that the patients are receiving the nursing care that requires the judgment and skill of a registered nurse. The lack of documentation in relation to meeting the standards makes it difficult to evaluate whether your RNs meet the standard. There are some team meetings with no RN in attendance which would certainly be one way to show supervision. There are some patient charts with no RN notes in a period of over a month which shows lack of supervision of the nursing care plan. The lack of nursing care plans in the multi-disciplinary treatment care plans makes one question the supervisory role of the RN and her contribution on the multi-disciplinary team. The lack of well defined therapeutic psychiatric nursing responsibility defined in your program description makes it questionable of the role of the RN in the facility, so based on all that I ask you to review those components with the seriousness of the standard because these are the only professionals on duty in this facility after

4: 00. There are 16 hours of patient care supervision that must be evidenced in some way through some mechanism in your facility.

Mrozek concluded BPC was in "substantial compliance" in all areas of quality assurance except one. She offered suggestions for change or minor criticisms in several areas—program evaluation, clinical privileges, utilization review, dietetic, pharmacy, infection control, and nutritional assessment. But BPC was out of compliance with the standards of professional growth and development, and needed to create an annual inservice training program for all employees and some mechanism for evaluating its effectiveness.

The final JCAH speaker, Robert Cvetkovic, M.A., raised several points quite critical of the documentation of intake assessments and ongoing treatment at the facility. Intake assessments appeared to lack specific comments on the patient's individual experiences and needs, while treatment planning seemed sketchy:

> There should be documentation of the multi-disciplinary input. In reference to short-term and long-term goals a time frame should be designated. The anticipated reactions or responses to treatment pertaining to each modality should also be documented. Criteria for termination of treatment and aftercare should be included. Involvement of family and/or significant others should also be included and subjective interpretations be documented and be supplemented with descriptions of actual behavior observed. Also that there is documentation of staff effort in helping patient attain stated goals, that the aftercare plan be periodically updated.

Educational services for clients also came in for some very critical comments, with 11 different standards cited as out of compliance.

While BPC would receive a full two-year accreditation as the result of this visit, the transcript of this summation session points to reasonably serious gaps in some critical areas, including the physical environment, nursing, documentation of intake and ongoing treatment, and staff and patient education.

JCAH formally announced BPC's accreditation a few months later (Myrene McAninch to Mahmud Mirza, May 16, 1980). Two issues were highlighted: "1. Safety deficiencies involve rooms, compartments, floor, buildings and exits. 2. The treatment plan does not reflect nurses' input, goals determined by the patients' family, nor criteria for terminating treatment." In addition, eleven broad areas were listed under "recommendations for future compliance" (with the numbers in parentheses indicating specific standards for review): governing body (1); staff composition (2); quality assurance (9); patient records (7); patient management (33); activity services (1); dietetic services (1); pharmacy services (4); building and ground (10); therapeutic environment (6); infection control (1).

JCAH concluded its letter with the following admonition: "THESE AREAS ARE OF CONCERN AND SHOULD RECEIVE PROMPT ATTENTION. IT IS INCUMBENT UPON THE FACILITY TO EFFECT A CONTINUAL UPGRADING OF ITS SERVICES AND PROGRAMS . . . DECISION OF THE ACCREDITATION COMMITTEE OF THE BOARD OF COMMISSIONERS: TWO YEARS" (emphasis in original).

Thus, in 1980, the first year of Director Mirza's administration, the facility received what its director characterized as "the happy news" that JCAH was providing a full two-year accreditation (AR 1981: 3). The next year's annual report featured preparations for the next accreditation ("preparations are extensive") as one of the most decisive activities of the center: "Preparations for a spring 1982 JCAH accreditation survey, important for the Center's continued participation in private, state, and federal reimbursement programs, occupied a significant proportion of staff time throughout the year."

The report goes on list a series of important steps taken to achieve accreditation:

> All aspects of the Center's operations were carefully scrutinized . . . All facility policy and procedures manuals were reviewed, revamped and updated. A comprehensive review of medical records was made . . . A vigorous maintenance and painting schedule was undertaken . . . A total of $55,000 was spent on lounge furniture for visiting areas and dayrooms . . . Shortly before the fiscal year ended, additional temporary cleaners were hired . . . Clinical staff turned their attention toward improving treatment plans and increasing patient involvement in therapeutic programming. (AR. 1982: 3)

In fact, the published annual report probably understates how important and significant accreditation had become. A memo circulated among BPC's senior officers (Richard Panell, "Proposed Accreditation Schedule," April 27, 1981) presents a compelling picture of how JCAH norms had become the de facto standard operating procedures of the institution. The memo listed the following major activities that would lead up to the JCAH visit scheduled in the coming year:

1. Revise 1980 Deficiency Report using 1981 J.C.A.H. Standards.

2. Complete a "Self Assessment" according to the 1981 Standards.

3. Complete an Objective Assessment on the 1981 Standards for Outpatient, Support, Geriatric and M&S Services.

4. Complete Objective Assessment on 1981 Standards for Reorganized Units (Current Adult Geographic).

5. Pre-accreditation Survey by Central Office.

6. Pre-accreditation Tune Up

7. J.C.A.H. Inspection.

Six areas appeared to need special attention: medical records; the environment (including cleanliness of units, a home-like environment, and visiting areas); education and training; unit ward activities; staffing (including rationale and allocation); and safety and construction in outpatient areas. A few days later, a 12-page single-spaced memo presented a list of the standards that were judged to still be deficient, followed by a report on their present status and the administrator responsible for each (Richard Panell, "Accreditation Deficiency Report," May 1, 1981).

In the midst of a year characterized as "sobering" because of the state's fiscal troubles, the news that JCAH was giving a full three-year accreditation came as a "highlight" in 1983. The director noted that "the surveyors were generous in their praise, citing the "exceptionally high" quality of our patient care and noting the progress made in converting to the state's new medical record system" (113th AR 1983: 1). Work to correct structural problems in buildings went ahead, and full compliance with JCAH standards in this area was anticipated within two years.

As of 1984, BPC seemed close to achieving the goals that Dr. Mirza had set almost five years earlier. Patient care was the top priority, the annual report proclaimed. Inpatient services were to be reorganized along functional rather than geographic lines, and community services continued to be perceived as a statewide leader.

INSPECTION: THE COMMISSION ON QUALITY OF CARE (CQC)

Against this rising tone of optimism, the findings of another outside agency must have come as a shock. Individual hospitals apply to JCAH for accreditation, and then JCAH announces its surveys well in advance, giving each facility and its state agency considerable opportunity to prepare for the visit. By contrast, New York State's Commission on the Quality of Care (CQC) for the Mentally Disabled performs unannounced inspections. During 1984, the CQC included BPC in the nine facilities (of the 25 in New York) it studied. Six wards were chosen at random, though specialty services were excluded (CQC 1984). A two-person team spent three days, interviewed staff and patients, and compared living conditions against 133 indicators of quality, many drawn from JCAH.

One basic finding of the CQC study was variability, both within single institutions and across the nine studied—so that it appeared that each facility was free to set its own threshold, with little evidence of some statewide standard. Public mental health care, in the opinion of the commission, faced a basic quandary: "it must meet essentially limitless demand for service with finite and incommensurate resources." Eight of nine institutions studied by the CQC (including Buffalo) had significant overcrowding, adding to the existing challenges of running a public mental hospital "a pervasive impact upon the quality of life for both patients and staff." After enumerating several correlates of overcrowding, the commission noted the "pervasive inactivity" of patients:

> Although this study did not focus on treatment of patients, the Commission staff were struck by the absence of professional staff on the wards and by the infrequent occasions, during the three days of our visits, on which ward staff were observed to be engaged in activity with the patients. Most patients experienced stupefying inactivity, often with insufficient seating space during the day, leading idle patients to pass their days sleeping on floors, window ledges and bathrooms, shuffling aimlessly about dayrooms and corridors, or staring vacantly at the ubiquitous TV screen.

Alongside many conditions that "would violate constitutional standards to which convicted criminals have been found entitled," the CQC found "islands of excellence" that offered encouragement that conditions could improve.

The contrast with the JCAH judgment of the "exceptionally high" quality of patient care is made by the following *verbatim* CQC comments about the Buffalo Psychiatric Center visit:

> severe overcrowding . . . many of the patients interviewed complained of having to borrow toothbrushes . . . missing bed linens on certain wards . . . dayrooms on four wards were very dirty. Urine puddles were noted on dayroom floors of two wards. Other dayrooms were littered with cigarette butts. Dayroom floors on all four wards were badly in need of a thorough cleaning. Toilet and shower areas on all six wards were dirty; cigarette butts littered the floors; cobwebs hung from ceilings; ventilation ducts were filthy; and some shower ceilings were mold-covered . . . problems with vermin on all wards . . . water leaks, peeling paint, or general deterioration . . . Broken windows . . . exposed wires, dangling light fixtures, and holes in ceilings . . . overall unattractiveness of many of the wards . . . The most typical fire safety problem stemmed from overcrowding of beds in dormitories which resulted in the blocking of dormitory doors. Other problems included inadequate means of egress in case of fire, the lack of fire extinguisher, and fire extinguishers which had not been recently inspected . . . In one of Buffalo Psychiatric Center's seclusion rooms, a radiator was shielded with a sharp metal edged cover, curtain rod hooks which could hold substantial weight were securely in place, and the hardware of an inoperable dead bolt lock was left secured on the inside of

the door . . . patient idleness . . . little structured activity for most patients on the wards during their waking hours . . . an absence of privacy.

In its conclusions, the Commission compared living standards in these state hospitals with those in prisons:

> While the Commission encountered islands of quality care for patients, other conditions witnessed by the Commission—including severe overcrowding; serious neglect of basic cleanliness; inadequate clothing; lack of privacy in sleeping, bathing, and toileting; absence of personal hygiene and grooming supplies; restricted access to drinking water and personal belongings; and the endless hours of boredom—would not meet standards which courts have mandated for state and federal prisons. In addition to not meeting court-mandated standards for incarcerated persons, these conditions fundamentally denied the human dignity of patients.

The Commission identified three main problems: overcrowding, which was the result of the absence of limits on admissions, insufficiency of resources, and inadequate management systems. At the time of the inspection the average annual cost of care at these facilities exceeded $41,000 per patient.

THE OMH INVESTIGATION: THE "LAPSES OF 1984"

On August 5, 1984, the *Buffalo News* published a front-page story of an investigation into allegations made by BPC staff members to Governor Mario Cuomo. Among the charges were "regular" patient abuse, including sexual abuse; neglect of patients; administrative irregularities; "widespread overcrowding and understaffing that results in little treatment for the patients"; and misuse of public property and money.

The *Buffalo News* article described the activities of the eight investigators from several state agencies who were expected to stay on the job for at least three or four weeks. "Countless" staff and patients had already been interviewed, and records had been reviewed to verify the charges that "touch on all aspects of its operation" under its director. The article also summarized the CQC surprise visit of May 30th–June 1st as well as a recent scandal that resulted in the resignation of the director at Creedmore Psychiatric Center in the New York City County of Queens. The article ended by citing sources who claimed employees were fearful of reprisal. The Governor's Director of State Operations responded that this fear was unwarranted, since the Governor had just signed into law protection for whistle blowers.

As the summer of 1984 wore on, the investigation deepened. More allegations of physical and sexual abuse of patients surfaced, along with reports of narcotics and alcohol trafficking on the wards. An elderly incontinent patient was left in her soiled clothing for hours, it was claimed, while another was slapped around. Security personnel were alleged to run a system of "harassing employees and controlling patients" (BN: 8/11/84). BPC physicians were alleged to "routinely cheat on their work time." Dr. Mirza himself was accused of misusing his state car and state home, and of giving his wife a full-time job at the Center as a dentist (BN: 8/19/84). The president of the Board of Visitors called the charges "bizarre" and said they came from "disgruntled" employees (BN: 8/10/84), later claiming that state funding cutbacks could explain their unhappiness (BN: 8/17/84).

Earlier in the summer, a young BPC patient, Peter W. Heggs, walked off one of the Center's open wards, where he had been transferred (though apparently still suicidal) because of overcrowding. A day later he died of a drug overdose at a friend's house. The Heggs case was one of those the state's investigators were examining. It led Lynne Shuster, Ph.D., a community college English professor who had become a friend of Peter Heggs', to organize the Erie Alliance for the Mentally Ill (EAMI), a local affiliate of the rapidly growing national movement primarily composed of family members of the mentally ill. EAMI planned to hold its first public meeting in September (BN: 8/17/84).

Toward the end of the summer, both State Assemblyman William B. Hoyt and the editorial staff of the *Buffalo News* were calling for an outside investigation. Questioning whether the same agency that ran BPC could also investigate it, Hoyt argued that the CQC should investigate the center (BN: 8/17/84). The *Buffalo News* editorial quoted him approvingly, and suggested that the CQC review the allegations independently and lend credibility to the current state investigation (BN 8/21/84).

Even more allegations surfaced, such as the case of "Pamela," a 35-year-old women who had been allegedly raped, abused, and misdiagnosed at the Center. During a physical exam, a BPC physician failed to notice that she was four months pregnant; when this was discovered, staff then waited eight weeks to interrogate the staff member who had impregnated her. After giving birth to a girl who was then placed in the custody of county authorities, "Pamela" was admitted to another state hospital, where she choked to death while in a seclusion room (BN: 8/22/84).

By the end of the summer, reports in the *Buffalo News* had moved from allegations of abuse to a detailed discussion of the difficulties of determining what had happened in individual cases (BN: 8/26/84). A number of allegations had been dismissed. No physical evidence supported five of the nine cases of rape, and several of the abuse cases appeared to be due to falls rather than staff assaults. BPC's Board of Visitors had set up a special committee to study the internal system of reporting special incidents.

Five days before the anticipated release of the special investigation's report, Dr. Mirza announced his resignation as director, and an OMH regional deputy director, David Carlini, was appointed in an acting capacity (BN: 11/3/84).

The report concluded that a "breakdown in controls" had been responsible for the "serious situation" at BPC. Investigators had substantiated 24 percent of the 95 allegations. In all, 20 state officials had interviewed 150 patients and 390 employees. In addition to several cases of abuse, poor or untimely medical treatment resulted in serious injury and in a few cases contributed to patient deaths. Treatment plans were "often lacking or not followed." Dr. Mirza's hiring of his wife was judged nepotism, because she had been hired at a time when the institution's dental staff was not in need of another dentist (BN: 11/6/84; 11/8/84).

The new acting director and the Board of Visitors promised a "crackdown" at the center (BN 11/9/84; 11/21/84). The deputy director for institutional administration and a physician who served as chief of a female unit left for other positions (BN 12/8/84). A search for the new director began, with the Erie Alliance for the Mentally Ill protesting the lack of family and staff participation in the search committee and arguing that Carlini be appointed permanently (BN 1/8/85). Meanwhile, Carlini prepared a very detailed "plan of corrective action" (BN 2/15/85). As he prepared to leave after his 90-day term, Carlini felt considerable improvement had already been achieved (BN 2/16/85). The editorial staff of the *Buffalo News* agreed, saying that his tenure "has done much to clarify and address the center's problems, restore community faith in the institution's future and ease the way for the permanent director who will be hired this spring . . . The Psychiatric Center still has a long way to go" (BN: 2/19/85), opinions seconded by community activists and labor leaders (BN 2/24/91). On March 19, 1985, the new permanent director, Patricia Oulton, was appointed, the first woman and only the second nonphysician to serve in that role. With her appointment, the uproar set in motion by the whistleblowers in August of the previous year largely ended.

In fact, the next report of the CQC noted impressive changes, based on an unannounced review in September of 1985:

Notably, in May 1984 Buffalo evidenced significant deficiencies in 76 percent of the areas examined by the Commission, whereas by September 1985 significant deficiencies were noted in only 12 percent of the areas reviewed. Over this time period, Buffalo experienced a change in administration and many new management initiatives to upgrade the quality of living conditions for patients . . . overcrowding at the facility has been largely eliminated and improved maintenance and housekeeping services have dramatically improved the safety, cleanliness, and attractiveness of patient areas. Equally impressive changes have been made to assure patients adequate clothing and hygiene supplies and to safeguard patient privacy in sleeping areas and bathrooms. Finally, during the recent visit

Commission staff witnessed many more patients on and off the wards engaged in leisure time activities and scheduled programs.

Very few areas of continuing deficiency were noted at the center. Some concerns remained about the secure storage of patient belongings . . . additional efforts to make some patient bedrooms more attractive and personalized on some wards visited were needed. The Commission also questioned the facility's routine use of large plastic bags for patients to store dirty laundry, due to the possibility that patients may use these bags in a suicide attempt. (CQC 1985)

In an editorial, "Rebirth of a Hospital" (BN: 2/10/86), the *Buffalo News* assessed BPC's crisis. The paper credits the CQC with finding "shocking deficiencies" at the center, leading to a state investigation that sustained CQC's judgment and led to the resignation of the facility's director and another top manager in 1984. Citing a string of problems, including a few episodes of patient abuse, the editorial commends the new director, Patricia Oulton, for making improvements: "various monitoring agencies report impressive changes." CQC's followup inspection (noted above) is cited. "Equally reassuring" is the conclusion after a weeklong review by JCAH that BPC provides "a quality service." The paper notes, "Thus two independent, outside groups of inspectors, looking at the Buffalo Psychiatric Center at different times, reached similarly favorable conclusions." But problems remain, and the "lapses of 1984" must not be allowed to recur, the editorial concluded.

In fact, outside inspectors have sustained that positive judgment over the past several years, including the JCAH adding the phrase "with distinction" to BPC's most recent accreditation in 1990. But the reputation generated from the "lapses of 1984" caused a several-year suspension of HCFA certification and an investigation by the U.S. Department of Justice into alleged violations of patients' rights. By early 1990, BPC had its HCFA certification restored (MR Feb 1990: 1). By the beginning of the summer of 1991, BPC was still waiting to hear the results of the Department of Justice action. Meanwhile, BPC staff continued planning for the next accreditation visit.

HAS THE STATE MENTAL HOSPITAL CHANGED?

Has the state mental hospital changed? Examining the case of Buffalo might make one answer initially in the negative, for the "lapses of 1984" recall in surprisingly similar detail the ordeal of its first year of operation. In 1880, the Buffalo Asylum opened as the most advanced institution of its type, fully matching the national standards of its day; within two weeks of admitting the first patients, the Asylum was plunged into a scandal built around the allegations of staff that patients had been abused. Until 1984, that early scandal stood as the most serious rupture of public trust the institution had ever faced. Large and complex state institutions providing long-term care for mentally disabled people share problems across even long historical periods. More abstractly, this is an instructive example of how the state mental hospital can be both a largely inert organizational form, yet turn in a changing (not to say volatile) short-run performance.

At the same time, the case study underscores how much the state mental hospital has changed, even since the early 1960s. Scrutiny is more frequent and yields more successful outcomes. Over twice the percentage of state hospitals are now accredited, a testimony to the "transformation" in the quality of care now provided by the typical state hospital (Mechanic 1989). Accreditation (and the parallel process of Medicare certification) has become the foremost part of "coercive isomorphism," pressing state hospitals toward greater organizational similarity. In New York State, additional scrutiny is provided by the Commission on the Quality of Care.

This case illustrates this process clearly, but it also points out how meeting outside demands may unleash inner conflict in unanticipated ways. After taking office, Dr. Mirza's administration made structural changes, including the addition of several major and minor administrators, in order to secure accreditation, given a very high priority by both himself and by OMH. The organizational change played a role (though difficult to specify) in the resulting turmoil. Whether the documented cases of abuse and neglect would have happened absent these changes is impossible to say, but the breakdown in reporting abuse and the whistleblowing were arguably more likely as a result.

If scrutiny tends to push state hospitals toward greater similarity with one another, the case also shows how local and state-level forces (including funding levels, mix of services and populations, and internal management practices) exert pressures toward diversity in return. Thus, New York leads all other states in its reliance on large state hospitals for the care of the seriously mentally ill, and is one of only a few states to make its state hospitals offer outpatient programs. New York mandates that its state hospitals seek accreditation. The unannounced inspections of the CQC are only done in New York, and played a major role in shaping later JCAH and HCFA accreditation and certification of BPC.

The community response (as judged by newspaper coverage) differs as well. Accreditation (like other routine operations of state mental hospitals) is simply not news, but the negative findings of inspection and investigation are. But even scandal has a positive side to it, sometimes bringing new personnel and new resources to an institution. What is striking about this case is how it played a role in the emergence of a community organization that has persisted in pressing for improvements in care.

The case also illustrates how "coercive isomorphism" acts to transform leadership in organizations, bringing to the fore managers who claim experience in meeting standards. Though with quite different outcomes to be sure, the three individuals who acted or were directors during this period all were selected on their previous ability to deal with scrutiny, or their promise of future capacity to do so. Moreover, it shows very clearly how pressure for accreditation translates into internal structural changes, such as the creation of an entire division of "quality assurance," whose primary mission was to gain accreditation. Much of the administrative growth at BPC during the past few decades has been generated by outside scrutiny.

The case also points to the fundamental uncertainty about the quality of care in a large state psychiatric hospital. The three scrutiny processes examined here are quite different in focus and intensity. Accreditation focuses on whether the hospital has the organization and resources to have the potential to provide custody, care and treatment; inspection focuses on a spot check of daily living conditions; and investigation focuses on a finite list of alleged abuses or problems. Accreditation considers a broad range of issues, while inspection and investigation tend to examine largely custodial ones. Announced or unannounced visits by one to three people of a few days' duration contrast with much longer efforts by many more people in investigation; the one presented in the case study is striking in its duration and scope. The three processes occurred at different times, making any inference about their comparability difficult. Moreover, the different processes interact, though often in unpredictable and surprising ways. Failure to meet one set of standards might bring more resources, ut it might also serve to tarnish the reputation of facilities and administrators in later visits. Resources placed in the service of bringing some departments up to standards are gained at the expense of other departments, whose share certainly declines in a relative and perhaps even an absolute fashion. At a minimum, meeting outside standards may strengthen the hands of those skilled at administrative routines, but diminish the standing of those who spend time tending to clinical concerns. JCAH standards powerfully embody a psychiatric model of care, with physicians firmly in control of treatment decisions. But meeting the standards requires preparing extensive documentation, as task physicians do reluctantly.

Finally, these processes of scrutiny deserve more study, for they stand at the intersection of understanding not only how the state mental hospital changed, but how public policy can influence change in a desirable direction. Scrutiny plays an unusual function in mental health care, serving as an alternative to stronger centralized governmental direction of that care. We simply do not know if the financial and programmatic costs of scrutiny are justified by better patient care, improved productivity, or perhaps the enhanced standing and diminished stigma that results from these improvements. Scrutiny takes scarce funds away that might be employed in improving services, and it also paradoxically diverts administrative and staff attention away from direct care issues. Almost certainly, it contributes to the widespread feeling of alienation that seems to permeate staff life in state hospitals, substituting standards imposed from without for objectives that might have evolved out of staff perceptions. At the same time, scrutiny answers the question, "Who cares?" In the world of the state hospital from the late nineteenth century to quite recently, the answer was just about no one, save the occasional muckraking journalist, the small number of reformers within institutional psychiatry who sporadically visited and then left, and a handful of social movement activists periodically engaged in reform.

By the beginning of the 1990s, BPC had evolved into a very different institution than it was before World War II. Some of its changes were physical, as illustrated in Figure 7.1, an aerial view of the BPC campus taken in the mid–1980s. At center are the original Asylum buildings, empty except for the presence of administrative offices in the central building of the complex. To the immediate right are modern structures that include a sprawling Rehabilitation Center, and two large buildings that housed almost all inpatients. The lower left corner of the campus would be the site for a community residence opened in the early 1990s. Other structures on the plot included the old superintendent's mansion, used as the regional office of the state mental health agency, and visible in the lower right quadrant. The upper half of the original Asylum campus, once its farm, is now occupied by the campus of Buffalo State College.

Organizationally, the Buffalo Psychiatric Center has taken on many functions beyond its original purpose of inpatient care, as its entry in the American Hospital Association Guide (1990) shows. BPC now offers the following services:

- Inpatient Care
- Rehabilitation Services
- Day/Continuing Treatment
- Intensive Psychiatric Rehabilitation Training
- Case Management
- Intensive Case Management
- Psychosocial Clubs
- Screening and Evaluation Services
- Family Care

Figure 7.1
Aerial View, Buffalo Psychiatric Center, 1985

- Community Residence

- Residential Care Centers for Adults

- Sheltered Workshop

The state hospital has managed to survive a period of intense activity directed at its abolition. Its continued, and perhaps even its enhanced role, seems assured. Accreditation, inspection, and investigation show that the contemporary state hospital has managed to evolve into an organization that increasingly meets national standards of care. However, the very high cost of care in the state hospital (much of it due to meeting outside standards) is in part paid for with funds that could be used for what many consider more innovative care in the community. This book's final chapter assesses the changing role of the state hospital in public mental health policy.

Chapter 8

Public Policy and the Seriously Mentally Ill: The Future of the State Mental Hospital

The preceding chapters have looked at the state mental hospital as an organizational form. Organizational theory and previous studies of state hospitals led to a two-level analysis, which compared the study of the whole population of state hospitals across its entire history with a detailed analysis of one representative mental hospital, the institution in Buffalo. What implications does this two-level analysis have for understanding public policy?

As a maximalist organization, state hospitals are likely to survive well into the future. Despite a mania for closing them, most survive, albeit with profound changes in their everyday operations and especially in the dramatic increase in expenditures per patient. Future public policy about the seriously mentally ill will turn on whether the improvements in patient care can be balanced against the considerable increase in cost necessary to achieve those gains. One possible outcome is a return to the asylum, in the sense of a modern version of the small, curative institution of mid–nineteenth-century America. At the opposite extreme is a return to the snakepit, in the sense of a modern version of the large, custodial institution of early and mid–twentieth-century America. Neither vision of the future will be a simple repetition of the past; too many changes in the American standard of living, current standards of psychiatric or medical care, and court-imposed minimum standards of care would allow a return to either past institution. But it is conceivable (and in fact likely) that the future will present updated versions of asylum or snakepit.

If funding were to continue to shift toward community care without extensive increases in overall spending for mental health, the result would be a modern version of the snakepit. Large inpatient populations receiving largely psychiatric custodial care (in its late-twentieth-century version) would fit this model. Care currently given at the poorest quarter of existing state hospitals approximates this model. Failure to meet current JCAHO or

HCFA standards defines this type of care. But instead of the present situation, in which most American state mental hospitals are accredited, the "new snakepit" version of the future would most likely fail accreditation, largely because of inadequate staffing. Inadequate staffing, in turn, would imply an overall absence of individualized treatment planning or aftercare planning. The dungeon-like scenes of the 1940s snakepit would probably not reappear, though the patient experience would almost certainly begin to resemble those days.

By contrast, enhanced funding for the overall public psychiatric system would permit a "new asylum" in which inpatient populations would approximate those seen in the pre-Civil War state asylum. Virtually all state psychiatric facilities would meet minimum national standards, and highly individualized treatment and aftercare planning would be given to patients with very short lengths of stay. State hospitals would continue to be institutions of last resort, with care given to the small number of patients who could not be served adequately in the expanded, community-based system of care. But their role might be increasingly valued because of their specialized mission to deal with individuals who simply cannot be served adequately without 24-hour involuntary inpatient care.

The previous chapters show clearly that maximalist organizations like state hospitals do in fact change very slowly, and when they do change, they do so in response to external standards tied to funding decisions. We now have adequate historical experience since the beginning of deinstitutionalization to draw several conclusions about the behavior of state hospitals in the new era of community mental health. State hospitals, whether in eclipse and thus largely out of public view and regardless of their image or of the words used to describe them, are necessary to the functioning of the community-based system of care, doing in effect the "dirty work" of the overall psychiatric system. They can be forced to change, largely in response to external accreditation standards. Some of their most exasperating characteristics—in particular, their sluggish responsiveness to new policy or to new managers—has much less to do with unionization of their staffs or the personal conservativism of their middle managers and much more with their behavior as maximalist organizations.

Whatever their other shortcomings and the often dismal level of everyday life they provided for most of their patients (Sheehan 1982 1995), state hospitals did and largely still do provide a largely secure and stable institutional environment for the seriously mentally ill. The dream of a community-based public system of care that could fully substitute for that environment has proved elusive, as almost all observers of the current mental health care system acknowledge (For a sophisticated view of mental health services in an urban community, see Dorwart and Epstein 1993). Well-funded and rigorously developed attempts at providing such an environment through innovative delivery systems have not really done much better than the existing *de facto* system. A recent comprehensive evaluation of an important attempt at reform—the initiative supported by the Robert Wood Johnson Foundation—proved that the initiative produced little real change in the lives of the seriously mentally ill, even though considerable change took place on an administrative level (for a comprehensive discussion, see the entire issue of *Milbank Quarterly*, vol. 72, 1; 1994). What were hailed as major reforms to the fragmented public psychiatric system, such as the concept of the case manager, have proved on closer examination to produce little real change (Franklin et al. 1987).

This is not, however, an argument for a return to the state hospital, so much as a critique of an ahistorical denial of the necessary functions they once carried out. But this research does argue for a more even-tempered assessment of the role of state hospitals. Even with some real improvements in the community care of the mentally ill, public policy cannot simply assume away the necessity of the state hospital or its functional equivalent. Almost all states will have to fund state hospitals for some time into the future, and they should fund them at a level adequate to achieve accreditation and certification. As cumbersome as these efforts at forcing conformity with outside standards are, they helped to produce a much higher level of care than existed before.

To ignore the role and the history of the state hospital permits policy makers to indulge in some harmful practices. State hospitals, unlike other past or present components of public mental health care, care almost exclusively for seriously mentally ill people, whose needs should be the focus of public policy. Averting the focus of public policy from state hospitals has often had the tragic even if unintended effect of refocusing on the needs of somewhat less disturbed populations.

Who cares about the seriously mentally ill, and about the one organizational form that throughout American history has specialized in their care? The answers to these questions largely determine the future of the state mental hospital. This chapter examines change in the state mental hospital by discussing its organizational diversity, funding, quality, and future. It weaves together a discussion of the unique character of state hospitals as maximalist organizations with an analysis of how present and future public policy about the seriously mentally ill is shaped by that character.

HAVE STATE HOSPITALS BECOME MORE SIMILAR? THE CHANGING DIVERSITY OF THE STATE HOSPITAL

We began this book by examining how recent organizational theory might suggest different ways of approaching the study of state mental hospitals.

Population ecology suggests inquiry into the long-term survival of organizations; our results suggest that although a wave of closings since the 1960s has affected the overall number of mental hospitals, they have remained the central organization in the public mental health care scene. Recent data on their funding (NIMH 1992: 186) show that the average state spends 57 percent of all state mental health agency controlled expenditures on state hospitals. This occurs even though recent data also show that the decline of the state mental hospital inpatient population has continued and even accelerated, and that only a relatively small percentage of the episodes of care now take place within the walls of state hospitals.

Neoinstitutional theory directs attention to how organizations adapt to their institutional environments. But one of the most important issues in this body of theory has never been adequately addressed empirically. Scott notes the considerable consensus about central elements of the theory. But even with that consensus, he is able to contrast the very different predictions that two of the leading exponents of neoinstitutional theory make about the effects of organizational environments on structure. On the one hand, DiMaggio and Powell argue that as those environments become more structured as a result of coercive, mimetic, and normative isomorphism, organizations should become increasingly similar, and the population of a particular organizational species should exhibit increasing structural isomorphism. On the other hand, Scott and Meyer argue that under certain conditions, greater structure might bring more diversity, such as when decision makers in a highly centralized organizational field mandate organizational diversity (In Powell and DiMaggio 1991: 171–72).

American public mental health care represents an unusually clear example of a highly institutionalized organizational field or sector. From virtually its earliest days, the state mental hospital has been defined by standards that both structure and legitimate its existence. Indeed, there are very few organizations whose standards can be explicitly stated over such a long period of time; Appendix B is a particularly striking exhibit in this respect. From a few dozen to more than 200 pages of highly detailed specifications, and from loose agreement among organizational leaders and founders to relatively tight coupling between meeting standards and important funding decisions, standards for state hospitals represent a powerful empirical example of the growing elaboration over time of an organizational model. These data add powerful support to the arguments about structural isomorphism.

The substance of the standards has shifted in dramatically different ways. The delegitimation of the state hospital of the early twentieth century has been so profound as to cause many institutions to change their names; in 1988, more than 60 different phrases were used to describe what in 1950 was uniformly called a state hospital. The standards themselves have changed more or less dialectically: the earlier ones demanded medical rule over a custodial institution, while the present ones push toward a multidisciplinary team of professionals planning individual care.

But in part because of the dramatic increases in funding required to support the contemporary state hospital at or near JCAHO standards, the role of the state hospital in contemporary public mental health care varies far more from state to state than at any time in its history. Until after World War II, state mental health care consisted almost entirely of state hospitals; even the early outpatient clinics that were the precursors of community care were for the most part operated on the grounds and in the buildings of state hospitals.

Anecdotal evidence suggests that state hospitals have become very diverse. Ozarin (1989) comments: "Public hospitals are not all of one pattern." Size, location, staffing, budget, medical leadership all vary, but all are "an integral part" of the mental health care system, according to Ozarin, a psychiatrist who has visited at least one hospital in every state and territory over the past 50 years.

To go beyond anecdotal evidence, a basic test involves taking what were identified earlier as the most critical indicators—size and per capita expenditures—and using measured for the entire population over a very long period of time. Earlier chapters have presented time series about these two variables for the Buffalo Psychiatric Center, where each has changed dramatically over time. Table 8.1 presents data for the population of state hospitals for the years 1880, 1938, and 1990. Three basic statistical measures are presented: the mean, the standard deviation, and the coefficient of variation (the standard deviation divided by the mean). The data are presented for both the entire population of individual institutions and also aggregated at the state level. "Census" is defined almost identically across the years as the average daily census or population under treatment or in residence. By contrast, "per inpatient" is defined somewhat differently in the different years, but generally means the overall expenditures divided by the average daily census. While not strictly comparable in dollar amounts, I include this variable to at least give an indication of variation across the units.

Over the past half century, state mental hospitals have become considerably more diverse. For the critical variables of average daily census and per capita expenditures, the data show clear support for the arguments advanced by Scott and Meyer. Inspection of other data, which I coded but do not present here, show considerable support for the argument.

These findings have implications for both organizational studies and for mental health policy. First, what are the implications for organizational studies? A maximalist organization like a state mental hospital can be brought up to standards through the expenditure of considerable resources. Since deinstitutionalization, the various states have shifted their mental health systems toward much more diverse and complex sets of organiza-

Table 8.1 Organizational Diversity Measures

	Census	Current dollars per Inpatient
Individual State Hospitals		
USPHS (Hamilton) 1938 (N=170)		
Mean	2261	$290
Standard Deviation	1370	$121
Coefficient of variability	0.606	0.417
American Hospital Assoc. 1990 (N=170)		
Mean	454	$83,670
Standard Deviation	372	$60,129
Coefficient of variability	0.819	0.719
States		
USPHS (Hamilton) 1938 (N=48)		
Mean	7838	$255
Standard Deviation	10995	$76
Coefficient of variability	1.403	0.298
NIMH 1986 (N=50)		
Mean	2102	$22,796
Standard Deviation	3252	$12,592
Coefficient of variability	1.547	0.352

tions, with state hospitals changing from being the near-exclusive provider of frontline services toward a role as provider of last resort to a very small population. Spending has increased substantially but with highly variable results. Mental hospitals increasingly come up to national standards, but their roles across the states vary greatly.

As for the debates within neoinstitutional theories of organization, these results provide a very strong case for the position presented by Scott, and raise interesting challenges to the DiMaggio and Powell position. It is difficult to think of an institutional sector that better exemplifies the notion of a highly institutionalized one than mental health. And, as we have seen, over the past two decades mental health has experienced exactly the kinds of isomorphic pressures that should bring about structural isomorphism. Yet, state hospitals have become more diverse.

The mental-health policy implications of these findings are intriguing. Despite powerful forces such as accreditation, similar state and federal laws and fiscal sources, and professional standards for psychiatry, nursing and other fields, all of which might have made state mental hospitals more similar, these findings show how dissimilar state hospitals can in fact be. Unlike the era when huge state hospitals were more similar to one another than not, and in which visiting one state hospital inevitably meant familiarity with the basic features of all, the present situation seems to be close to the one described by Morrissey (1989): no longer the monoliths of the 1940s, state mental hospitals diversify as they try to find ways of adapting to local service delivery systems.

A major challenge to mental health policy is to enhance the quality of services provided by state hospitals to the special populations that require them, while allowing for even more diversity across the states in their roles. For the most part, the history of the development of standards for mental hospitals has been an effort to create uniform national standards. In the future, having succeeded in raising the floor of overall quality, standards that take into account unique local situations may prove more valuable than seeking national uniformity.

Finally, the diversity of state mental hospitals deserves much further study, not only because it should contribute to a better understanding of organizational diversity in general, but also because it has some considerable practical importance for understanding how to better provide mental health services for the seriously mentally ill. Empirical research on state hospitals (Hadley and McGurrin 1988) indicates that objective factors such as expenditures are of only limited value in predicting whether a particular hospital attains accreditation or certification. The present findings show a considerable diversity across what were assumed to be quite similar institutions. There is much to be learned about what accounts for this diversity, and how the diversity can best contribute to better mental health services.

A major source of the organizational diversity that marks the contemporary state mental hospital apparently flows from the greatly increased complexity of funding. So before examining the future of the state hospital, we need to turn to a discussion of its funding—a long-neglected but crucial question only recently subjected to sustained research scrutiny.

BETTER OR MORE EXPENSIVE?
THE CHANGING FUNDING OF THE STATE MENTAL HOSPITAL

During the 1980s, states continued to have very different levels of support for state hospitals. Schinaar et al. (1992) report that the percentage of state spending on state mental health agencies (SMHA's) varied between 3 percent and 17 percent of its overall health and welfare expenditures, and that the state hospital system received between 17 percent and 92 percent of the overall SMHA budget. These data are based on a newly created data base that presumably is the best one available; because of the complexity of funding sources, previous SMHA budget numbers, especially those that make comparisons across the states, are considered suspect.

Schinaar et al. (1992) present by far the most elaborate attempt to explain interstate variation in mental health expenditures with what is probably the best data yet available. They examine two related questions: what determines the proportion of health and welfare funds going to SMHAs, and what determines how much of SMHA spending goes to state hospitals? The former question is presumed to reflect median voter prefer-ence, that is, overall expenditures reflect the preferences of the typical voter. The latter, by contrast, represent the preferences of the state decision makers in the SMHAs as to hospital versus community spending.

The study gathers a large number of variables, including socioeco-nomic/fiscal variables, market characteristics, and organizational/political factors. All SMHA expenditure and revenue data were collected for four different years, 1981, 1983, 1985, and 1987, for all 50 states; the District of Columbia was omitted because of incomplete data. Overall results show higher SMHA share of the health and welfare budget and a bigger share of the SMHA budget for the state hospital in states with the following char-acteristics: a free-standing SMHA; delivery of services through geographic services areas; developmental disability services delivered separately from the SMHA; SMHA director with good access to the governor; and a legis-lature not dominated by either political party.

Schinaar et al. found a positive relationship between state hospital funding and overall SMHA funding, suggesting to them the impact of hos-pital fixed assets and unions. Also, as overall health and welfare budgets increase, SMHA share decreases, perhaps indicating corroboration of Frank's argument that states expend as little as required on state hospitals or, alternatively, that other human service programs aide mentally ill indi-viduals. Their findings show "the importance of organizational factors in setting funding levels" (Schinaar et al. 1992: 248–49).

Deinstitutionalization occurred while the states and the federal gov-ernment were increasing their spending on the mentally ill. This increase was part of a massive shift in spending by units of government at all levels. The 1980s, however, saw a major reversal of the previous trend. The Reagan years reversed federal mental health spending, with federal dollars declining for the first time since the 1940s. Federal categorical spending was replaced with a block grant category, with the overall effect a substan-tial decline. Moreover, other federal programs that impacted on the life of the seriously mentally ill, most notably public housing subsidies and general support for other urban programs, were also slashed. To be sure, some of the living costs of seriously mentally ill individuals were covered by the expansion of a variety of entitlement programs. Like so many other social policies, mental health programs rise and fall in almost cyclical fashion (Goldman and Morrissey 1985).

From 1981 to 1987, SMHA spending increased from $6.1 billion to $9.2 billion in raw dollars. But when inflation is taken into account, an actual decline of 4.9 percent occurred. The relative decline was even sharper, since actual overall state spending after inflation increased by 10.7 percent, and overall state health and welfare spending increased 7.3 percent during the same period. "Overall, these declines appear to reflect a lower priority for mental health services in the states" (Hadley et al. 1992: 215).

New York's experience is actually even more dramatic than this national trend, with mental health spending declining by 4 percent over the period ($1.172 billion versus $1.112 billion) while the overall state budget grew by 19 percent and health and welfare by 28 percent. Spending on New York state hospitals fell even more precipitously than the overall mental health numbers indicate, with a decline from 1981 to 1987 of 13.12 percent for inpatient services. While New York's cut was sharper than the US average of a 7.68 percent real decline in spending for state mental hospitals, most states cut their hospital budgets during the 1980s; only ten states kept them unchanged or increased them (AR, AZ, CT, KS, KY, MA, ME, MN, NC, WA). Many states, including New York, increased their ambulatory mental health expenditures.

Federal cuts in funding to SMHAs were a significant factor in the decline in SMHA funding to state hospitals. But SMHAs responded by "shifting funding for program types *within* organizational settings, rather than [shifting] organizational setting. An apparent expansion of services offered within hospital settings has enabled this relatively greater shifting of funds from inpatient to ambulatory care" (Hadley et al. 1992: 233). This is apparently mirrored in the considerable expansion of "non-inpatient" services at BPC.

In the early 1990s, an economic decline required increased social welfare spending at a time when both federal and state revenues had fallen, so the likelihood is that state mental health spending may have fallen even more sharply, both absolutely and relatively. State hospitals almost certainly were cut even more dramatically. But note how quickly change took place: on Oct. 29, 1992, the *New York Times* ran a story, "Governors Report Grim Fiscal Status"; just a few months later, the same newspaper reported, "National Recovery Fattening Tax Revenue in Many States" (2/17/93: 1). By late 1994, a growing economy once again brought surpluses back to the states, but the political climate mandated these surpluses lead to tax cuts. One estimate suggested that 10 percent of the employees of state governments at the beginning of the downturn ended up losing their jobs. Almost certainly mental health workers were among them. (*New York Times,* "Growing Economy Produces Surplus in State Budgets," 9/6/94).

BETTER FOR FEWER?
THE CHANGING QUALITY OF THE STATE MENTAL HOSPITAL

The only recent published attempts at a comparative assessment of the quality of the contemporary state hospital were ratings generated in 1986, 1988, and 1990 by writers affiliated with the National Alliance for the Mentally Ill (NAMI). (A planned national update for the mid–1990s was cancelled, leaving further evaluation up to the individual state chapters affiliated with NAMI). The rise of NAMI, an organization made up largely of family members of the seriously mentally ill, deserves a thorough study in its own right. Founded in 1979, NAMI claims to be one of the fastest-growing advocacy movements, with 150 new members and two affiliate members added each week (Torrey et al. 1990: 193). NAMI is now composed of over a thousand affiliated state and local groups, representing over 130,000 families.

The 1990 NAMI ratings are based on a very diverse set of sources. Questionnaires of varying length were sent to a wide variety of state and local officials and advocates for the mentally ill across the states; the longest was a forty-page version sent to the state directors of mental health. Among the other data sets used were several surveys of individual state hospitals, including those done by the Health Care Financing Administration and the Joint Commission on Accreditation of Healtcare Organizations. The authors also visited thirty-five states and the District of Columbia, though it is not clear how many state hospitals were actually visited. After collecting all available data, a single member of the survey team read the data for an individual state, compared the state to NAMI's standards (summarized in the Appendix), and assigned a preliminary score from 0 to 5 in the categories of hospitals, outpatient/community support, vocational rehabilitation, housing, and children's services. The scores on each category were finalized after discussion with other team members, and a total number of points was added up across the categories.

The results were, perhaps inevitably, controversial. Like attempts to rank other complex issues, critics have pointed to the difficulty, perhaps the impossibility, of assigning quantities to the quality of mental health care. This criticism was deepened by the failure of NAMI to provide readers with the raw data or the exact method of calculating scores based on them. It is not clear how the scores were arrived at, and readers are forced to question whether the NAMI authors were able to evaluate such complex issues validly and reliably. Given the very strong stands the authors take on contested questions in public policy, their objectivity can be questioned. But even with these criticisms in mind, this is the most sophisticated and data-driven exercise of its type ever done, and sheds considerable light on the variation across the states in the quality of mental health services.

What was the range in quality found by NAMI among the state mental hospitals? The best one, according to the NAMI researchers, is probably New Hampshire's hospital, not coincidentally the newest state hospital, opened in late 1989 (Torrey et al. 1990: 58–59). Among its virtues is a unique arrangement with a private university, Dartmouth, which finds and employs all of the hospital's psychiatrists. The NAMI team also notes that a workable contractual arrangement discourages dumping of patients into the state hospital; instead, treatment often occurs in general hospitals elsewhere, three of which have involuntary admissions.

By contrast, Hawaii State Hospital is labelled the worst. A U.S. Department of Justice investigation concluded patients' civil rights were being violated. A familiar litany of observations are quoted from the federal report: inadequate food and clothing for the patients, puddles of urine on a rehab unit's floor, patients receiving no treatment from psychiatrists, lab tests left unperformed, and improper prescribing patterns. Staffing inadequacies are indicated by high vacancy rates for nurses (42 percent) and for psychiatrists (50 percent). Glaring clinical problems included "grossly inadequate" documentation in charts, the prescribing of antipsychotic drugs for patients without psychoses, and high levels of medications given without a physician's order. The NAMI team concluded that the state hospital in Hawaii had in fact become "a Third World psychiatric facility" (Torrey et al. 1990: 176).

Table 8.2 presents the NAMI rankings of the quality of hospital care across the 50 states against the criteria listed in the Appendix. Few states receive high rankings, with the average state given a ranking of 2. New York receives this ranking, and the state narrative implies that the Buffalo Psychiatric Center is a bit above the state's overall level, in part because New York City area facilities are generally ranked as poor.

What is clear from the ratings is that despite the existence and impact of national standards for care, the quality of the state mental hospital still varies greatly across the states. The data also presents indicators of how different the role of the state hospital is across the states, given the highly variable percentage of state mental health agency (SMHA) spending devoted to the state hospital. Finally, the data show how different per capita spending (relative to the state's population) is on the state hospital.

What accounts for the quality of the state mental health effort? Hudson (1990) goes well beyond the original authors in trying to account statistically for the overall ratings of the states, though he does not attempt to explain the quality of components such as the state hospitals alone. Cred-

Table 8.2 The 1990 State Hospital: Percent of SMHA Budget, Per Capita Spending, and NAMI Ranking

State	PC SMHA	Per capita	NAMI ranking
Alabama	72	27.52	3
Alaska	38	27.63	2
Arizona	31	8.38	2
Arkansas	73	18.83	2
California	31	13.29	2
Colorado	68	22.84	4
Connecticut	59	42.84	3
Delaware	67	36.77	2
Florida	44	16.47	1
Georgia	75	38.41	2
Hawaii	37	13.84	0
Idaho	49	10.07	1
Illinois	56	19.22	2
Indiana	39	18.16	2
Iowa	85	14.51	2
Kansas	82	29.04	1
Kentucky	74	17.20	3
Louisiana	61	17.37	1
Maine	62	41.55	2
Maryland	71	43.81	2
Massachusetts	36	30.02	1
Michigan	54	39.64	2
Minnesota	44	23.64	1
Mississippi	77	26.07	1
Missouri	72	25.70	2
Montana	74	21.06	1
Nebraska	78	22.77	4
Nevada	68	22.62	2
New Hampshire	45	28.49	4

Table 8.2 *Continued*

State	PC SMHA	Per capita	NAMI ranking
New Jersey	62	35.47	2
New Mexico	54	12.34	3
New York	75	88.40	2
North Carolina	57	26.01	3
North Dakota	48	19.47	3
Ohio	58	23.71	2
Oklahoma	53	19.10	2
Oregon	58	23.79	1
Pennsylvania	67	37.99	2
Rhode Island	46	23.26	3
South Carolina	64	32.62	2
South Dakota	46	11.58	1
Tennessee	68	19.51	2
Texas	65	14.66	2
Utah	50	10.37	4
Vermont	33	18.00	2
Virginia	70	31.34	3
Washington	51	21.80	1
West Virginia	43	10.30	1
Wisconsin	26	9.68	3
Wyoming	77	26.54	2

Source: NIMH 1992: 186; Torrey et al. 1990: 39.

iting the Torrey and Wolfe study as the only systematic research that has attempted to rate state mental health performance, Hudson notes that its statistical analysis remained primitive, and presents a much more elaborate analysis of the correlates of the overall state ratings for 1986. (Whether these findings would hold true for the 1990 ratings awaits further research.) There are plenty of qualifications that can be made about this analysis, beginning with the unknown reliability and validity of the state ratings and extending to the measurement of several of the major dependent variables; moreover, his analysis is based on imputing causal interpretations among a set of variables all measured at the same time, one of the usual limitations of path analysis. Nonetheless, this is by far the most complete and interesting attempt to explain statistically variation across the states in their mental health ratings, and its findings should be summarized.

Hudson (1990) concluded that state socioeconomic composition and a broad set of political and policy factors could account for much of the variation in the ratings. But the former are almost impossible to alter, while the latter are at least in principle modifiable, so that he concentrated his analysis on the latter. He found highly-rated mental health systems associated with well-respected administrators; integrated organizations; rational decision making; policies oriented to integrated services; and adequate professional staffing.

Overall spending was not correlated with higher ratings, and may even have a negative impact, reflecting, Hudson conjectures, that "strong institutional interests" hinder the development of less-expensive community services. While his analysis is not definitive, it suggests that the ratings can be explained statistically to some considerable extent, and that state organizational factors are probably more important than simply dollars spent, a finding quite consistent with the original Torrey and Wolfe analysis.

Frank and Kamlet (1986) examine this problem from a different angle. They begin by assuming that a state government desires three conflicting goals: more units of the good, greater quality, and lower levels of total expenditure. The public seeks to "decrease the visibility of the seriously mentally ill and the externalities associated with having such individuals located in the community" (Frank and Kamlet 1986: 29). Using data from the late 1970s, they conclude that quality of care reflects the minimum standard of care rather than the number of patients treated (Frank and Kamlet 1986: 31).

OUT OF SIGHT, OUT OF BUSINESS?
THE CHANGING ROLE OF THE PUBLIC MENTAL HOSPITAL

The most useful account of the current role of the state mental hospital has been provided by Morrissey (1989). Observing that the period from 1950 to 1985 "encompasses one of the most tumultuous and far-reaching periods of change in the history of mental health care in the United States," he draws on his own previous work on that history to sketch its contours. In effect, the state mental hospital has endured, though its market share has declined. As noted earlier, deinstitutionalization occurred in two phases, "opening the back door" and "closing the front door". Morrissey presents a portrait of public mental hospitals in the 1980s that describes capacity and volume; patient characteristics; staffing and treatment; and finances. He then reviews the recurring debate about whether to close or retain the state hospital, the latter based on the enduring multiple functions of these institutions. Noting that "there is a growing recognition that the future role of state mental hospitals will vary greatly from state to state and community to community" (Morrissey 1989: 330), Morrissey reviews three alternative views of its future developed by Pepper and Ryglewicz. Morrissey quotes Goldman and Taube to the effect that the issue "is not 'will they survive?' but 'can they provide quality services?'" until other facilities take up their loads. He highlights the following issues that will influence its future: mental health financing; demographic trends; intrahospital changes; hospital-community integration; and finally, public support and the threat of reinstitutionalization. In this last area, he notes both good news (organizations like NAMI seeking more support) and bad news (support for easier commitments and reinstitutionaliztion). He concludes that contemporary state hospitals are no longer the monoliths of an earlier generation. While some basic functions persist, state hospitals must find their niche within local systems of care. The ones that do will survive "and even flourish" while the others will disappear (Morrissey 1989: 334–35).

RECENT PATTERNS: THE STATE MENTAL HOSPITAL

The decline of the state mental hospital's census continued through the period ending in 1990. An NIMH report announced that both the number of residents at the end of the year and the number of additions during the year "declined sharply in 1990. This followed a period beginning in the early 1980s when these numbers were levelling off. The 1990 figures suggest an acceleration of the deinstitutionalization process." While the decline in residents was not unexpected, the magnitude of the decrease was, with a 9 percent drop in just a single year down to 92059 in 1990. The average decline per year during the previous five years was only 2.5 percent per year. Why?

> The accelerated decrease in number of residents and additions is due in part to a reduction in the number of hospitals from 290 to 281 between 1989 and 1990 . . . A second factor in the decline is that State mental health agencies are using community-based ambulatory care services and private inpatient facilities as alternatives to State mental hospitals. Finally, the State agencies are reducing the size of State mental hospitals in reaction to decreases in State mental health budgets.

The state hospital has gone into eclipse organizationally, overshadowed by the organizations created in community settings. Data from federal sources help draw a picture of the contemporary role of the state hospital.

Table 8.3 paints a picture of the state mental hospital set against the background of contemporary mental health care organizations. State hospitals were virtually the only mental health care organizations before World

Table 8.3 Number and Rate per 100,000 Civilian Population of Inpatient, Outpatient, and Partial Care Episodes in Mental Health Organizations: United States (excluding territories), Selected Years 1955–1990

Year	Total episodes	Inpatient care episodes	Outpatient care episodes	Partial care espisodes
		Number		
1990	8,617,080	2,262,474	5,810,405	544,201
1988	8,344,904	2,229,217	5,627,792	487,895
1986	7,885,618	2,055,571	5,451,538	378,509
1983	7,194,038	1,860,613	5,007,928	325,497
1975	6,857,597	1,817,108	4,810,923	229,566
1971	4,190,913	1,755,816	2,316,754	118,343
1965	2,636,525	1,565,525	1,071,000	—
1955	1,675,352	1,296,352	379,000	—
		Number per 100,000 population		
1990	3,491	917	2,354	220
1988	3,419	914	2,305	200
1986	3,295	859	2,278	158
1983	3,084	799	2,146	139
1975	3,245	860	2,276	109
1971	2,052	860	1,134	58
1965	1,376	817	559	—
1955	1,028	795	233	—

Source: Center for Mental Health Services (1994a: 5).

War II; by 1990, the 273 state hospitals are a small fraction of the more than 5,000 organizations that make up the specialty mental health care sector.

Comparing this sector from 1955 to 1990, the locus of specialty mental health care has shifted dramatically from inpatient to ambulatory care (Center for Mental Health Services 1994a). In 1955, three-quarters of the episodes of care were inpatient; by 1990, three-quarters of the episodes were outpatient and partial care. State hospitals provide only 16 percent of the inpatient care episodes, 2 percent of the outpatient, and less than 4 percent of the partial care episodes.

Table 8.4 Number of Mental Health Organizations and Number and Percent Distribution of Inpatient, Outpatient, and Partial Care Patient Care Episodes within These Organizations, by Type of Organization: United States (excluding territories), 1990

Type of organization	Number of mental health organizations	Patient care episodes							
		Number				Percent distribution by organization			
		Total	Inpatient	Outpatient	Partial Care	Total	Inpatient	Outpatient	Partial Care
All organizations	5,284	8,617,080	2,262,474	5,810,405	544,201	100.0	100.0	100.0	100.0
State and county mental hospitals	273	513,223	371,325	121,543	20,355	6.0	16.4	2.1	3.7
Private psychiatric hospitals	462	683,806	435,539	198,262	50,005	7.9	19.3	3.4	9.2
VA psychiatric organizations	141	704,183	215,583	455,450	33,150	8.2	9.5	7.8	6.1
Nonfederal general hospitals with separate psychiatric sections	1,674	2,044,880	997,602	978,159	69,119	23.7	44.1	16.8	12.7
Residential treatment centers for emotionally disturbed children (RTCs)	501	291,815	68,729	195,826	27,260	3.4	3.0	3.4	5.0
Freestanding psychiatric outpatient clinics	743	891,982	—	891,982	—	10.4	—	15.4	—
Freestanding psychiatric partial care organizations	93	24,097	—	—	24,097	0.3	—	—	4.4
Multiservice mental health organizations	1,397	3,463,094	173,696	2,969,183	320,215	40.1	7.7	51.1	58.9

Source: Center for Mental Health Services (1994a: 5).

Table 8.4 documents the dramatic rise in use of the specialty mental health sector by Americans. Contrary to much received wisdom, more episodes of mental health care actually take place in private and public hospitals, and so the notion that hospitalization has been declining turns out to be a myth (Kiesler and Sibulkin 1987). But length of stay has fallen in psychiatric hospitals as well as general hospitals. And as Table 8.4 shows clearly, the rate of increase in outpatient and partial care episodes has accelerated well beyond the rate for inpatient episodes.

Inpatient care in state hospitals has become a much smaller slice of the rapidly expanding pie of specialty mental health care episodes. Table 8.5 shows that expenditures are quite another matter. The percent of total expenditures going to state hospitals was a majority or almost a majority of expenditures as recently as 1975 (and remains so for most state governments today). But by 1990 that figure had fallen so that roughly one out of every four dollars spent on specialty mental health care in the United States as a whole goes to state hospital care. Given the great shrinkage in the proportion of mental health episodes of care taking place in state hospitals, the decline in expenditures is far less than proportional.

THE FUTURE OF THE STATE HOSPITAL: THE CASE OF NEW YORK

Release of a unique planning document (New York State Office of Mental Health 1992; henceforth cited as NYSOMH 1992)in January 1992 allows examination of how one state agency plans the future of its inpatient facilities, and sheds considerable light on how public maximalist organizations change—or don't change. The document is particularly noteworthy because of the sheer size of the New York system and the clarity with which it demonstrates the connection between mental health decision-making and the institutional environment.

The cover letter from Commissioner Richard Surles claims New York State is at "an important crossroads which will largely determine the future of our public mental health care system." Observing that "we now know that the vast majority of people with psychiatric disabilities do not need long-term hospitalization and can live satisfying lives in the community," Surles argues this won't happen without a substantial investment of resources into community services from state psychiatric centers; but the latter need "extensive renovation to maintain health and safety standards."

The report grounds its comments on a brief but well-wrought history of how New York's mental health care system has reflected "professionals' thinking on what constitutes best practice" (NYSOMH 1992: 1). The document reviews four previous periods of state policy: the earliest period in which there were no state asylums; a second period with asylums that pro-

Table 8.5 Total Expenditures in Current and in Constant Dollars (1969=100), by Type of Mental Organization: United States, 1969–1990

Type of organization	1969	1975	1979	1983	1986	1988	1990
	Total expenditures in thousands of current dollars						
All organizations	$3,292,563	$6,564,312	$8,713,795	$14,431,943	$18,457,741	$23,029,203	$28,449,187
Selected types, total	$2,606,838	$4,639,746	$5,784,506	$9,092,490	$11,270,412	$14,161,587	$17,324,910
State and county mental	$1,814,101	$3,185,049	$3,756,754	$5,491,473	$6,325,844	$6,978,391	$7,774,482
Private psychiatric hospital	$220,026	$466,720	$743,037	$1,711,907	$2,629,009	$4,588,316	$6,101,063
Residential treatment centers for emotionally disturbed children	$122,711	$278,950	$436,246	$572,983	$977,616	$1,305,337	$1,969,283
VA medical centers	$450,000	$699,027	$848,469	$1,316,127	$1,337,943	$1,289,543	$1,480,082
	Total expenditures in thousands of constant dollars						
All organizations	$3,292,563	$4,414,465	$4,145,598	$4,580,116	$4,828,079	$5,300,162	$5,573,900
Selected types, total	$2,606,838	$3,313,480	$2,736,554	$2,885,589	$2,948,055	$3,259,284	$3,394,379
State and county mental	$1,814,101	$2,141,929	$1,777,083	$1,742,772	$1,654,681	$1,606,074	$1,523,214
Private psychiatric hospital	$220,026	$313,867	$351,484	$543,290	$687,682	$1,055,999	$1,195,349
Residential treatment centers for emotionally disturbed children	$122,711	$187,592	$206,630	$181,841	$255,720	$300,423	$385,831
VA medical centers	$450,000	$470,092	$401,357	$417,686	$349,972	$296,788	$289,985

All organizations						
				Percent of total, selected types		
Selected types, total	79.2	70.5	66.1	63	61.1	61.5	60.8
State and county mental	55.1	48.5	42.9	38	34.3	30.3	27.3
Private psychiatric hospital	6.7	7.1	8.5	11.9	14.2	19.9	21.4
Residential treatment centers for emotionally disturbed children	3.7	4.3	5	4	5.3	5.7	6.9
VA medical centers	13.7	10.6	9.7	9.1	7.3	5.6	5.2

(Each of the seven data columns begins with 100 for "All organizations.")

Source: Center for Mental Health Services (1994a: 4).

vided moral therapy; a third with state hospitals that provided custodial care; and the current era of deinstitutionalization. The report argues:

> one reason that what came to be called "deinstitutionalization" was unsuccessful was that needed services were not made widely available to people who were discharged into the community. It is clear that the development of a comprehensive, community-based system of care is crucial to the success of our current proposal for consolidation and closure of State facilities. If resources are not strategically reinvested in community services, we can expect a recurrence of many of the problems which resulted from deinstitutionalization in the 1960s and 1970s. (NYSOMH 1992: 4)

Of particular interest is the report's comments about the mission and values that should shape the "restructuring" of New York's public mental health system:

> the system must be integrated, comprehensive, and responsive to the individual needs and desires of the people it serves. The system must assure the accessibility and availability of effective services for all individuals who are unable to acquire needed services without the assistance of government. It should provide emergency access, treatment and rehabilitation within a comprehensive, coordinated system to people diagnosed with severe mental illness. This mission must be accomplished in an environment which respects the dignity of each person and offers each person and their family hope.
>
> Recognizing that most people diagnosed with long-term mental illness can live successfully in the community with appropriate support services, the system must assure access to these services. Mental health services for these individuals need to be integrated with health, social services, and other local community services. The system should also have the capacity to treat the vast majority of people with diagnoses of acute mental illness in their home communities.
>
> Individuals recovering from mental illness and their families should have options within a flexible system. Service recipients must have access to services and opportunities for growth within a structure that promotes their participation, is responsive to their individual needs, and protects their personal and civil rights. Families of recipients must have access to services and opportunities for education within a system that promotes their participation. Members of multicultural groups, children, elderly people, and those with multiple disabilities should have access to community services and supports responsive to their individual needs, and consistent with their culture . . . Activities are guided by the basic principle that the citizens of New York State are entitled to be served in their local communities within the least restrictive treatment setting available. (NYSOMH 1992: 4)

As the report shows, the key values of the deinstitutionalization period—community care, least restrictive environment, civil rights, equal access, and participation—were joined in OMH's planning by more contemporary additions, such as multiculturalism and the participation of families.

OMH planned for services in four categories: emergency programs, inpatient programs, outpatient programs, and community support programs. In contrast to state policy only a decade or so earlier, OMH was planning for a future in which its psychiatric centers would have diverse roles:

> In the short term, some State psychiatric centers continue to have a primary mission in acute care, psychiatric rehabilitation, and extended care. In the long term, State psychiatric centers are more appropriately used for intermediate-term care and intensive psychiatric rehabilitation, with general hospitals providing acute hospitalization. Acute hospitalization is best provided in general hospital settings, close to the individual's home community. (NYSOMH 1992: 5)

In its planning, OMH used several approaches to encourage general hospitals to participate more in acute psychiatric care, including reimbursement mechanisms and a newly legislated requirement for psychiatric units seeking certification or recertification to admit emergency and involuntary psychiatric patients.

The document also reveals how OMH sought to define a new role for its psychiatric centers. Where they had once attempted to be "all things to all people"—including providing acute care for seriously mentally ill persons, long-term psychiatric care, geriatric care, and even rehabilitative services and intermediate-length care—psychiatric centers were to become, in OMH's plans, intermediate- and long-term rehabilitation hospitals (NYSOMH 1992: 7).

A comparison with the rest of the US shows New York to be seriously "overbedded," with almost four times the rate of geriatric hospitalization as the rest of the country. Using data from its regular Level of Care Survey, OMH estimates which of three possible treatment settings—nursing facility, community setting, and psychiatric inpatient—are best suited to the 13,652 adults in residence in March 1991 in its psychiatric centers. Only 47 percent require inpatient care, with 40 percent better served in community care, "if appropriate treatment, residential options, and supports were available" (NYSOMH 1992: 9). The remainder should live in some form of residential care facility such as a nursing facility or an assisted community living program. (The report also notes that improvements in technology or medications might even increase the percentage appropriate for community placement.)

These plans for the future were based in part on recent declines in the statewide census of state psychiatric centers, for the most part driven by a decline in admissions and also by an increase in discharge rates of long-stay (longer than three months) patients, primarily elderly patients. Curiously, length of stay had not played a role in the recent census decline. OMH's analysis of these data showed how the changing institutional scene influenced the psychiatric center's performance. The report credited the 37 percent increase in general hospital psychiatric beds during the 1980s, as well as the requirement of emergency and involuntary admissions by general hospitals, with diverting substantial numbers of patients from state psychiatric centers. Added to that were reimbursement mechanisms that encouraged community outpatient providers to give priority access to recently discharged inpatients and that gave outpatient providers incentives to treat individuals diagnosed with serious and persistent mental illness (NYSOMH 1992: 11).

These program initiatives could be characterized as ways of responding to some of the perceived problems of the deinstitutionalization period, when patients were discharged into communities with few psychiatric services for seriously mentally ill people, and almost no individual-level case management after discharge.

OMH's report claims that it has "aggressively" opened several forms of alternatives to inpatient care. Over the decade of the 1980s community residence beds increased from only 308 to close to 8,000. Residential Care Centers for Adults (RCCAs) began in 1985 to provide "extended-stay residential services" for individuals diagnosed with severe and persistent mental illness; by 1991 there were 778 RCCA beds across the state. In the same year, 2,369 individuals were living in Family Care homes, which provided 24-hour supervised residences. These programs housed over 11,000 people, almost all of whom might have been living inside state psychiatric centers.

Finally, the OMH report finds that the largest decreases in the inpatient census has been among the elderly, chiefly by discharges to residential health care facilities.

Estimates by the OMH planners of the state hospitals' future censuses suggested that by the year 2000, probably between 6,000 and 8,000 inpatients will be in residence at the state psychiatric centers, though OMH planners were careful to qualify that number in their search for a figure on which to base capital planning (NYSOMH 1992: 14–16). Compared to the highest inpatient census of the 1950s—93,000—and the 1992 census of 12,500, this represented a real measure of the success of deinstitutionalization in its core goal of decreasing the inpatient population.

That state hospitals are maximalist organizations is evidenced by the details of OMH's capital planning. At the time the planning document was written, the OMH infrastructure included 79 residential buildings at the 22 adult centers it operates—only 6 percent of the total of over 1,300 buildings, the largest inpatient system by far in the United States and "probably in the world." Since many of the buildings are deteriorating, it was noted that per-patient costs of maintenance were increasing, taking resources away from community-based expansion. The 1993 costs of renovating or constructing an inpatient bed were estimated at a staggering $145,000, with added fixed maintenance costs whether filled or not. Moreover, beds built under state bonding authority can't usually be put to alternative uses.

These constraints led OMH planners to proceed with considerable caution in capital planning, using a strategy that grouped beds into those needed just for the next five years (Level I, Short-term Occupancy); those needed for more than five years (Level II, Intermediate-term Occupancy); and those for the long haul, that must be in full compliance with all state and JCAHO standards (Level III, Long-term Occupancy). OMH followed five principles in planning beds for the future:

1. A facility must be large enough to serve the estimated need in its assigned catchment area.

2. Whenever possible, OMH should make use of the available space, in order to reduce the costs of new capital construction, renovation, and long-range operating costs.

3. Newly renovated buildings and buildings under construction should be incorporated into the future capital plan.

4. Each community in the State must have reasonable geographic access to a facility providing State inpatient care.

5. To the greatest extent possible, OMH must take advantage of economies of scale by reducing the per-bed fixed costs associated with facility administration and maintenance. (NYSOMH 1992: 23–24)

Applied to the OMH Western New York Region of 19 counties with a population approaching three million people, these principles led OMH planners to project consolidating Gowanda PC with Buffalo, planning for 306 Level III beds to accommodate a projected low census of 361 to a high census of 483. The 306 beds were to be available after the completion of major construction on Building 62 (Strozzi) by 1993; the construction costs were estimated at $106,000 per bed. Another building (#52, the "M&S," Medical and Surgical Building) was to be partially renovated to provide 94 Level II beds at $30,000 per bed, and other beds were to be used in Building 4 (Cudmore, currently housing the RCCA); the Rehab Center was also to be used. OMH was working with several other agencies on alternative uses for other buildings, but added, "Although the adaptive re-use of some buildings within the Richardson Complex is a possibility, there are only limited areas available for surplus on this compact urban campus." (NYSOMH 1992: A–3)

The physical infrastructure of the maximalist organization is one dimension. What of the organizational environment? OMH anticipated a three-level process that, when examined, begins to spell out how complex that environment is, involving several layers of both state and local governments; employees and unions; consumers, family, and ex-consumers; the media; local providers; and finally "interested parties" (NYSOMH 1992: 31).

For the OMH planners, then, a key to the future is the sensitive question of what they called "work force planning." The implications of the plan were termed "substantial." By the year 2000, the then-current OMH direct care staff of 13,000 was projected to fall to between 7,000 and 9,000, and support staff from 8,000 to 4,400–5,600 persons. Because attrition over the number of years needed to implement the plan would not, it was predicted, be enough, the plan included designation of staff at each facility as "Agency Reemployment Representatives" who would help those impacted by any reduction-in-force (RIF). A concluding paragraph noted that OMH "hopes to continue to upgrade and expand its ability to provide service and support to employees who lose their jobs due to census-driven reductions-in-force." The statement then noted that this depends on the "continued support" of several government agencies and public-employee unions. Whether this support was forthcoming, or whether these same agencies would use their considerable power and influence in other directions, remains to be seen.

The sometimes contradictory pressures that push toward the expansion or contraction of the role of the state hospital can be seen clearly in New York in the 1990s. In the 1994 meeting of the state legislature, a bill passed that made it somewhat easier to compel care for the mentally ill, including involuntary hospitalization (*New York Times*, "Bill Compels Care for the Mentally Ill," 6/31/94; see also *New York Times*, "Mental Hospitals for the Unwilling Gain Support in New York State," 6/17/94). Thus New York joined a growing number of states that have begun to emphasize the rights of the community to remove the mentally ill from its streets in contrast to the earlier emphasis on the rights of the mentally ill to resist involuntary treatment (La Fond and Durham 1992). Should such a shift continue or even accelerate, the role of the state hospital might well expand substantially.

But the same legislative session featured a dramatic conflict between Governor Cuomo and the legislators over a bill that tied the closing of state hospitals (and consequent budget savings) to increases in funding of community care for the mentally ill. In essence, the bill, passed unanimously by both houses of the Legislature, requires that a minimum of $208 million dollars be set aside for community services. As state hospitals were downsized or closed, $70,000 for each bed no longer used would be funneled into community mental health care. Unlike much of the experience of deinstitutionalization, in which state hospital decreases were not matched by increases in community care, the bill would require some balance across the spectrum of spending for state mental health care (*New York Times*, "Paying for Mental Health," 7/14/94).

One of the broadest reforms sought during the 1990s on behalf of the mentally ill attempted to seek parity in the treatment of mental and physical illness. Some reformers sought this goal in the drive for national health care reform led by the Clinton administration. In fact, full parity was apparently not even part of the major proposals before Congress during the debate about reform in 1994. The major bills would have expanded, and perhaps expanded greatly, mental health care coverage (For a review of what national health reform might have done for the mentally ill, see the series of papers collected in the September 1994 issue of *Hospital and Community Psychiatry*). It is perhaps not an exaggeration to say that passage of national health reform might have been the single most important change in the availability of mental health services for Americans. But by September 1994, the drive for national health care reform ended, at least for this year.

On the state level, however, the push for parity led to votes in at least five states—Missouri, New Hampshire, Ohio, Rhode Island, and Virginia. Two states, New Hampshire and Rhode Island, actually passed legislation mandating parity, and each state's governor signed it into law (*NAMI Advocate*, July/August 1994). The implications for the state mental hospital are far from clear, though parity legislation at a minimum might lead to increased use of inpatient care, including state hospitals.

THE FUTURE OF THE STATE MENTAL HOSPITAL

It is fair to say, as a recent federal report observed, that policy makers face truly "momentous" decisions about state hospitals:

> At the one extreme, some argue that these hospitals have contracted in size to such an extent that persons with severe mental illness are being denied admission, and therefore, further downsizing is unwise. By contrast, others argue that all persons, regardless of the severity of their mental illness, can be cared for in the community and that the State mental hospitals should be phased out entirely. Confounding the option of the policy makers are economic pressures brought by communities and labor unions to keep the State mental hospitals open and to increase their size. (Center for Mental Health Services 1994a: 3)

Other forces such as the National Alliance for the Mentally Ill and newspaper and media editorialists are also aligned against the state hospital, and many, perhaps most, mental health professionals trained during the recent era of community mental health would also support downsizing or elimination of state hospitals. The same report notes the paradox that both state-level agencies and federal legislation both favor community-based services over the state hospitals, yet state hospitals still command nearly 58 percent of total State mental health expenditures.

Much of this book has presented the state hospital as a maximalist organization, whose continued persistence and remarkable ability to secure funding should not be surprising. Whether one argues about the several hundred state hospitals or the one in Buffalo, continued endurance with modest change seems the most likely outcome. For the foreseeable future, then, the institution that James Platt White founded, Richardson built, and Olmsted planned will continue to provide care for the mentally ill, though in circumstances far different than it was conceived.

More than two centuries after the Virginia Colony began the long history of American mental institutions, and more than a century after the first patients were received by the Buffalo Asylum for the Insane, the state hospital endures, though in a form that would surprise its former patients and staff. Its short-term future seems secure, despite extraordinary attempts to close it down. But as the dramatic lurches in funding of the 1980s and 1990s make clear, considerable turbulence will probably be a part of that short-term future. Some states will probably emulate the experience of Massachusetts via another wave of hospital closings. More likely will be a continuation of the trend we have noted in New York, with the closing of a few hospitals, the downsizing of many more, and the continued transformation of the state hospital toward a more active treatment center.

At this writing, the future of the entire American health care system appears to be at a strategic turning point, poised on the brink of a fundamental and unprecedented reorganization of the entire health care system, but with remarkable pressure brought to bear in favor of avoiding that change. While health care reform seems less likely, the 1994 Congressional election may lead to a realignment in federal-state responsibilities and funding. What this means for the care of the seriously mentally ill, and more specifically for the organization most directly concerned with their care, the state mental hospital, is far from clear.

But several indications already allow some informed speculation. First, overall spending on the seriously mentally ill will not rise to the level initially offered from inside the Clinton administration of as much as $6 billion dollars (*New York Times* 3/16/93). This figure would have constituted the single largest increase in mental health care in American history, exceeding even the levels that marked the shift toward community care in the late 1950s and early 1960s. Second, the state hospital will remain as caregiver of last resort, as states shift their resources toward community care. Third, the shift will turn out to be far less dramatic than advocates of community care might hope for. This reflects several complex and largely independent developments, including a new clinical turn toward hospital-based care for some serious illnesses; renewed interest in improving care for hospitalized patients; increased success in political advocacy on behalf of the seriously mentally ill; greater emphasis on accreditation and other forms of emulation of the general hospital with its ever-growing costs; and renewed pressure toward inpatient care for those perceived to pose a danger to themselves or their communities (La Fond and Durham 1992). Fourth, state hospitals may well be transformed as state and federal officials adopt theories of their roles that move them away from the actual running of healthcare enterprises toward their regulation; the phrase "steer, don't row" and the broader goal of "reinventing government" implies a retreat from providing direct care at a time when the broader healthcare industry is seeking an expanded role in psychiatric care. Fifth, privatization of mental health services, a substantial development in New York but nowhere near as advanced as in other states such as Massachusetts, may continue to push the state hospital further into a role that restricts its use to only those patients who combine serious, long-term mental illness with almost no financial resources (for a comprehensive discussion of privatization in mental health care, see Dorwart and Epstein 1993).

The state hospital has proved to be the most enduring organization in all of American health care for a very basic reason. No other organizational form has been able to replace its role as caregiver of last resort. As a maximalist organization, it has already managed to survive in the face of sustained and deliberate efforts to close it.

But does it have to be the institution that the late nineteenth century bequeathed to us? Even with the considerable internal inertia we have documented, it is also clear that determined effort, considerable conflict, and enhanced resources did change the state hospital. Its future cannot be determined with certainty, since it depends on decisions Americans and their state officials will make in the future about a maximalist organization unusually resistant to change. Over its long history, political decisions have made the state hospital variously play the role of asylum or of snakepit; the present period is unusual in that their great diversity across the states provide contemporary examples of both.

At one representative state hospital, the Buffalo Psychiatric Center, physical changes provide a clue to a possible future. By mid-1994, all of the remaining administrative staff had moved out of the immense original buildings to new quarters in recently renovated twentieth-century buildings, and a search for some new uses of the original buildings began. But the organization that had begun its life in those building continued to operate, 125 years after Dr. James Platt White and a few reformers began their efforts to provide a home for the seriously mentally ill. While the state hospital they founded might have been eclipsed by the contemporary network of community care, the maximalist organization that White and others created more than a century ago endures.

The state hospital is now in an eclipse, its past forgotten, its present obscure, and its future uncertain. Stigma has obscured its essential role in mental health policy. Barring extraordinary therapeutic breakthroughs, the well-being of many of the most seriously mentally ill is tied to the state hospital. As this book has discussed, long-term constraints limit policy about state hospitals, and those concerned with public policy must be aware of these constraints. But there is also evidence that, even in this maximalist organization, change in the direction of improved patient care is possible.

Appendix A
Data Sources and Methods

This appendix contains brief comments about primary data sources and several key methodological issues. The bibliography contains most of the important secondary sources, and the notes cite important primary textual sources.

PRIMARY SOURCES

Important primary sources about the Buffalo State Hospital include its *Annual Reports* and those of the New York State Department of Mental Hygiene (known earlier as the Commissioner in Lunacy, Commission in Lunacy, and State Hospital Commission).

The Annual Reports run in a continuous series from 1872 to 1984, and are the basic origin of accounts of events that make up the institution's history. The reports are an invaluable source of information about the institution. Even the briefest of them present basic statistical data about such important issues as the number of admissions, residents, discharges, and expenditures. Most present information about the staff, including the names of board members, officers, physicians, and key administrators. In addition, many present detailed charts about such diverse questions as the diagnoses of first admissions, the number of staff for specific job titles, the percentage of patients receiving specific therapies or employed at different tasks, or the specifics of the diet provided to residents. Some were embellished with photographs of patients and staff.

The last of the annual reports was published in 1984. From 1985 to 1990, the monthly report of the Director to the Board of Visitors served the same function, somewhat more informative about events but less descriptive of the structure of the institution than the annual reports. But several key statistical items were published in other state reports or in the AHA Guide to the Health Care Field, making it possible to continue statistics in an unbroken series.

In all, the annual and monthly reports run to more than 5,550 pages of material. I used copies of the annual reports bound and kept in the Director's Office of the Buffalo Psychiatric Center. Photocopies of the monthly reports were provided to me by BPC; I wish to thank again Sue Joffe, BPC's Director of Public Information. I read each of the annual reports or monthly reports several times before making up an index listing each event, and then finally a much shorter listing of events that appeared of unusual significance. I later coded events into classifications that helped explain the institution's history, using categories drawn from organizational studies or from the history of mental hospitals. The main text explains as necessary how statistical series were created from my coding of these reports.

(N.B.: Unless otherwise qualified, "AR" refers to the annual reports of the Buffalo State Hospital. I follow Grob (1973) in citing the year to which an annual report refers, not its date of publication. Thus "AR 36 (1906)" refers to the "Thirty-Sixth Annual Report of the Buffalo State Hospital to the State Commission In Lunacy For the Year Ending September 30, 1906.")

Similar to the use of photographs (Dowdall and Golden 1989), I pursued a layered analysis of the annual reports. After photocopying each of the reports, I read and reread them, creating an index of entries for each report, and then noting which of the entries seemed particularly revealing of continuity or change in the institution's life. I then used the resulting list of items and a shorter list of notable items to build a chronology of the institution's history with a thematic analysis of its most important dimensions of change. I also coded several important pieces of information over the full hundred years from 1880 to 1990, particularly about the patients, staff, and funding of the institution. An assistant combed through the names of members of the Board of Managers (later, Visitors), the officers, and the members of the medical/dental staff and administration to assemble a list of staff (complete except for the period from 1960 to 1975, when the ARs didn't include this information).

The statistical series in the annual reports are of special interest, for they are both important sources of quantitative data about the institution as well as meaningful symbols of the values and myths that shaped its life.

An alternative way of measuring change is inductive, and involves gathering as much data as possible on many institutions over time, and arranging them to assess the degree to which change has occurred. I once again pursued both a local and a national strategy. To assess the role of the hospital in the community, we collected all available newspaper stories about it, made a bit simpler by the regular publication of an index to the only surviving Buffalo newspaper, the *Buffalo News*, and the hiring of a full-time public relations officer by the institution in 1980. The national data we collected came from the only published data on individual (as opposed to aggregate) mental hospital data, the American Hospital Association's *Guide to the Healthcare Field*. Data about the mental health sector come from the work of other scholars, and from published and unpublished data from NIMH.

The AHA presents a relatively consistent set of data from 1955 (the beginning of deinstitutionalization) to the present. Quantitative data include number of beds, admissions, average daily census, expenses (including total and payroll), and personnel (paid, and in the early years, student). Also noted are approvals, including accreditation by the Joint Commission on the Accreditation of Hospitals (JCAH), and certification by the Health Care Financing Administration (HCFA). Finally, a reasonably detailed set of codes for facilities and services are presented.

Other primary sources included the reports of various outside visitors or agencies. Of particular significance were documents that present the reactions of inspectors or accreditors to the institution. Most helpful were the transcript of the 1882 hearing conducted by the Commissioner in Lunacy to investigate charges of abuse of the asylum's patients; the inspection of the hospital in 1942 by Samuel Hamilton, M.D., for the U.S. Public Health Service; and finally the recent inspections of the psychiatric center by the Joint Commission on the Accreditation of Hospitals, the U.S. Health Care Financing Administration, the New York State Commission on the Quality of Care, and the U.S. Department of Justice. Others are cited elsewhere in the body of the text.

An important resource was a virtually complete file of copies of newspaper stories about the Buffalo institution. This was assembled by Jean Richardson and Gretchen Knapp, who started with the bibliography on the institution (Cohen 1981; Cohen and McMahon 1981) and the nineteenth-century scrapbooks provided by Sue Joffe, Public Information Officer at BPC. We used the Western New York Newspaper Index, published by the Buffalo and Erie County Public Library, to add recent news stories to the file. In addition, I used the *New York Times Index*, particularly entries under the topic "Mental Health and Disorders," to assess national attention to similar issues. Newspaper accounts of the asylum are invaluable. Gretchen Knapp assembled and copied hundreds from Buffalo papers, including a virtually complete run of articles about the institution that have appeared in the *Buffalo News* (formerly the *Buffalo Evening News*) and the *Courier-Express* before its demise. I read these many times, and finally constructed an index of my own devising.

Data also come from the annual *American Hospital Association Guide to the Health Care Field*, particularly the entry for the Buffalo State Hospital or Buffalo Psychiatric Center. The AHA's entry for total disbursements for the years 1986–1989 were used to fill in the annual series on "total disbursements" reported in the text for the earlier calendar year. "Constant dollars" that express the buying power of a dollar in 1987 were calculated by multiplying "actual year" dollars by 100 divided by the Consumer Price Index.

An indispensable source about state mental health is the *American Journal of Insanity*, continued as the *American Journal of Psychiatry*. The post–World War II era is discussed in *Hospitals* and *Hospital and Community Psychiatry*.

Much of my data about the population of state mental hospitals was coded from the U.S. Census special reports of 1880, 1890, 1904, and 1910, and from special statistical publications of the National Institute of Mental Health, and are discussed below or in the notes. Special studies by Grimes (1934), Hamilton (1938), and the Council of State Governments (1950) were of special value, since they provide so much detail on the full set of individual institutions. For 1990, I constructed a data set from the AHA Guide on individual hospitals.

POPULATION OF STATE HOSPITALS

After extensive research revealed that, like other organizations, no complete list of the openings and closings of these institutions existed, I set about constructing one. For the most part I used lists of the institutions that were enumerated at points in time, usually about ten years apart. The lists were published sporadically by the U.S. Bureau of the Census in special studies for 1880, 1904, 1923, or by NIMH in 1962, 1963, 1975, 1985, and 1987/88. Though there is a wealth of information about mental health services in the nation as a whole or in the various states published by these two agencies, often on a year-by-year basis (NIMH 1986), there were only a few full listings of the entire set of individual institutions at a single point in time. These federal lists were augmented with the work of other contemporary researchers (Anon. 1848; Wilkins 1872; Toner 1873; Hurd 1914; Grimes 1934; Hamilton 1944; Council of State Governments 1950; and Torrey et al. 1990) who enumerated the state hospitals; historians, both amateur (Brussell 1954) and professional (Grob 1966; 1973; 1983; 1991), who examined their establishment retrospectively; and observers who noted their closings (for example, Brown 1985: 88; Nelson, Vipond, Reese, and McKenna 1983: 1160). Because of the relatively large number of points in time for which lists are available, I am reasonably satisfied that virtually every state mental hospital has been captured in my master list, and that their opening and closing dates are largely accurate.

For most institutions, several of the sources agreed on the opening date. When the sources disagree (and usually it was only about a year or two apart), I used the date most frequently cited; in the very few cases where all the sources disagreed, I favored the most contemporary source (usually Hurd 1914). Hamilton (1944), who usually cited the earlier sources for his own estimate of opening date, was used only for those cases later than Grimes (1934).

A demographic history must discuss the accuracy and completeness of the data. As noted below, the date of the founding of a maximalist institution such as a mental hospital provokes some intriguing sociological and historical questions. At a minimum, however, the existence of several historical sources allows confirmation of at least the basic dates when the institution was opened for patients. Since several of the sources overlap, it has been possible to check the completeness of my set. As Hannan and Freeman (1989) note about their attempts to build organizational population data sets, one cannot always be sure of the completeness of one's count. But in the case of maximalist organizations such as mental hospitals, which carry relatively large founding and start-up costs and in many cases licensing or certifying by state and federal governments, the count at many points in time is almost certainly complete. I am virtually certain that I have enumerated fully the public mental hospitals, and I have counted almost all of the private institutions of any size. As discussed later in the text, the one category that might not be fully enumerated are the very small private sanitoria and rest homes of the early and mid-nineteenth century. But these contained only a very small fraction (perhaps less than one percent overall) of the hospitalized insane. For all practical purposes, then, the findings of this chapter are about the entire population of mental hospitals through 1988.

In almost all cases, the year in which a particular institution opened could be established. The year of closing usually has been inferred, however, using the midpoint of the interval between when a listing last showed the institution still operating and its disappearance from a subsequent list. Given the very large overall time scale of this project (spanning over 200 years, even longer than that used in the Hannan and Freeman (1989) study of unions), the amount of measurement error in estimating a closing date is fairly modest. The opening or closing date was imputed by using the midpoint of the interval between the last known appearance on a reliable list and the first absence.

ADMISSIONS DATA SETS

Several sets of conclusions are based on the analysis of data coded from the original admissions registers of the Buffalo State Asylum for the Insane, the Erie County Almshouse, and the Providence Retreat. I had hoped to be able to perform parallel analyses on these three institutions, and build elaborate comparisons among their inmate populations at admission, during treatment, and at outcome. But the three institutions had such different habits of collecting statistics that a detailed quantitative analysis will only be presented for the State Asylum.

The relative absence of statistics for the Poorhouse and the Retreat, and the wealth of them for the Asylum, states something much more that just the presence or absence of numbers. From the day it opened, the Asylum was intended to be a curative institution. The statistical accounts of its inmates would document for both administrative and research purposes how it had helped in the cure or at least improvement of the cases committed to it for treatment. In sharp contrast, the custodial character of the two other Buffalo institutions is reflected in the very simple tally of a patient's stay at the Poorhouse or at the Retreat. The Asylum's curative intentions did not always succeed, for in fact only a minority were discharged as cured even in its first years of operation.

The data for the Poorhouse were coded from the microfilmed copy made by Michael Katz from the original records. Sister Mary Paul provided me with photocopies of the admissions register pages for the Retreat. My assistants and I coded the Asylum data directly from the original pages of the BSA admissions register. We coded all of the data possible on the first decade of patients to enter the Asylum, omitting only the patient's name and original identification number to preserve even from our coded data any way of identifying an individual patient. Following standard research practice, we coded, as much as possible, with the same categories as were employed by Dr. Andrews and his staff, and thus we are able to reproduce the information with the same detail as the original register. In coding occupation, we used the detailed scheme developed by the Pennsylvania Social History Project to code data from the same era in its Philadelphia research, and then recoded when useful into either the occupational prestige codes preferred by sociological researchers or the class and status categories used by historians.

Why spend the many weeks to code these original data sources when the published *Annual Reports* contain such voluminous data? Some important and interesting questions can be addressed by the published data. But the data are 'highly aggregated', and do not allow access to the specifics of each case. For the statistical analyses presented in the text, individual-level data were necessary, and so this project coded the original sources.

EVENT HISTORY ANALYSIS

The statistical models reported in several of the chapters use an approach that has come to be called "event history analysis." While this family of techniques is both recent to the social science literature and somewhat complex, not to say daunting, it can be interpreted in a relatively simple way. In the text, I present the results of analyses rather than their details, which are reported in this appendix or in the notes that follow each chapter. Since I intend this book to be accessible to any interested reader, I felt that I should keep statistical discussions out of the main body of the text, but that I had to present enough details elsewhere to allow full assessment of the statistical analysis that supports the text's conclusions.

Since relatively brief and accessible introductions to event history analysis are now widely available (Allison 1984; Sutton 1989) and several examples (Halliday et al. 1987; Pavalko 1989) are in major journals, I will present only the most basic ideas here. Event history analysis can be likened to multiple regression analysis, a widely used statistical approach in which the specific values some quantitative variable takes on are explained as the result of some linear combination of the values of several other variables. The former variable is called the dependent variable, since its values are assumed to depend upon those of the other variables; since no explanation is offered for the latter, they are termed independent variables. In multiple regression analysis, the dependent variable is regressed on (its values are examined as the products of) the independent variables, usually using a statistical approach that seeks to find the best possible combination of the variables by seeking a solution that minimizes the error in predicting the dependent variable's values. This solution, usually called "ordinary least squares" because it comes up with the smallest square of the distance between the average value and its prediction, is often taken in studying the behavior of quantitative dependent variables.

The time it takes to found a particular institution, or the amount of time it takes for a patient to be discharged as cured, would seem very much like the kind of quantitative variables that multiple regression could help study. However, two major problems occur when multiple regressions (or similar multivariate techniques) are used for these kinds of issues. First, many of the individual values are censored, that is, individual cases lack an outcome before the data collection period ends. Second, the independent variables themselves change their value over time (in the language of this field, they are "time dependent covariates"). To use an example from the study of the founding of the institutions discussed in chapter 2, a state's urbanization is theorized to be an important predictor of the founding of institutions. But in the period of enormous social change after the American Civil War, few states could pass the ten years between each census without considerable and often dramatic change in the percentage of their populations who lived in cities. Thus, use of standard multiple regression would ignore one of the most dramatic parts of the social changes we are trying to understand.

Event history analysis provides a convenient solution for dealing with both censored cases and time dependent covariates, though at a considerable cost with regard to the computational complexity of the analysis and the ease with which results can be presented. Fortunately, the first issue has now been eased with the appearance of statistical software for microcomputers. The final statistical work and the graphics for this book were done entirely with the statistical package SYSTAT or the spreadsheet Quattro Pro. Discrete-time analysis, used for the examination of the founding of state hospitals in chapter 2, is lucidly discussed in Allison (1984). A very clear example of its use is found in Pavalko (1989). As for the problem of presenting the results, the reader can judge whether the main text does an adequate job of reducing into relatively simple words what was learned through the statistical analysis.

TIME SERIES ANALYSIS

Another statistical technique used to reach conclusions presented in words and in graphics in the text is time series analysis, the study of how two or more quantitative statistical series are associated over time. At several points I refer to time series analyses of admission data. In this case, research papers published or presented elsewhere (Marshall and Dowdall 1982; Dowdall, Marshall, and Morra 1990; Dowdall, Kirshstein, Marshall, and Pinchoff 1985) contain full explanations for particular analyses.

ANALYSIS OF PHOTOGRAPHS AS DATA

In a very different vein than these statistical approaches, Janet Golden and I (1989) located and studied over 800 photographs about daily life at the Buffalo State Hospital. We developed a strategy for the qualitative analysis of these photographs and reported our methodology and results in a paper published in a journal that specialized in qualitative research methods in sociology. Just as with the quantitative analyses discussed above, I have reported the conclusions of this research in the text, without any elaborate discussion of the methods by which we arrived at these ideas.

OBSERVATION

The text of this book is based virtually entirely on the primary and second-ary sources listed in this appendix, the bibliography, and the notes. But per-haps the richest source for my own understanding was the time I spent as a member of the administration of the Buffalo Psychiatric Center from 1980 to 1982 (Dowdall and Pinchoff 1994). When I accepted my position there I decided not to engage in participant observation in the strict sense; if I had, this might have been a very different book, but I certainly would have been a less effective member of the administration. While I therefore have no field notes in the strict sense to draw on, I have several years of very rich experience that shaped this book.

Appendix B
Standards for State Mental Hospitals

ASSOCIATION OF MEDICAL SUPERINTENDENTS OF AMERICAN
INSTITUTIONS FOR THE INSANE (AMSAII): PROPOSITIONS ON THE
CONSTRUCTION OF HOSPITALS FOR THE INSANE (1851)[*]

I. Every Hospital for the Insane should be in the country, not within less than two miles of a large town, and easily accessible at all seasons.

II. No Hospital for the Insane, however limited its capacity, should have less than fifty acres of land, devoted to gardens and pleasure grounds for its patients. At least one hundred acres should be possessed by every State Hospital, or other Institution for 200 patients, to which number these propositions apply, unless otherwise mentioned.

III. Means should be provided to raise ten thousand gallons of water daily, to reservoirs that will supply the highest parts of the building.

IV. No Hospital for the Insane should be built, without the plan having been first submitted to some physician or physicians, who have had charge of a similar establishment, or are practically acquainted with all the details of their arrangements, and received his or their full approbation.

V. The highest number that can with propriety be treated in one building is two hundred and fifty, while two hundred is a preferred maximum.

VI. All such buildings should be constructed of stone or brick, have slate or metallic roofs, and as far as possible be made secure from accidents by fire.

VII. Every Hospital, having provision for two hundred or more patients, should have in it at least eight distinct wards for each sex—making sixteen classes in the entire establishment.

VIII. Each ward should have in it a parlor, a corridor, single lodging rooms for patients, an associated dormitory, communicating with a chamber for two attendants; a clothes room, a bath room, a water closet, a dining room, a dumb waiter, and a speaking tube leading to the kitchen or other central part of the building.

---

*Source: American Journal of Insanity, July 1851: 74–76.

IX. No apartments should ever be provided for the confinement of patients, or as their lodging rooms, that are not entirely above ground.

X. No class of rooms should ever be constructed, without some kind of window in each, communicating directly with the external atmosphere.

XI. No chamber for the use of a single patient should ever be less than eight by ten feet, nor should the ceiling of any story occupied by patients be less than twelve feet in height.

XII. The floors of patients' apartments should always be of wood.

XIII. The stairways should always be of iron, stone, or other indestructible material, ample in size and number, and easy of ascent, to afford convenient egress in case of accident from fire.

XIV. A large Hospital should consist of a main central building with wings.

XV. The main central building should contain the offices, receiving rooms for company, and apartments entirely private, for the Superintending Physician and his family, in case that officer resides in the Hospital Building.

XVI. The wings should be so arranged, that if rooms are placed on both sides of a corridor, the corridors should be furnished at both ends with moveable glazed sashes for the free admission of both light and air.

XVII. The lighting should be of gas, on account of its convenience, cleanliness, safety and economy.

XVIII. The apartments for washing clothing, &c., should be detached from the hospital building.

XIX. The drainage should be under ground, and all the inlets to the sewers should be properly secured to prevent offensive emanations.

XX. All Hospitals should be warmed by passing an abundance of pure fresh air from the external atmosphere, over pipes or plates, containing steam under low pressure, or hot water, the temperature of which at the boiler does not exceed 212 degrees F., and placed in the basement or cellar of the building to be heated.

XXI. A complete system of forced ventilation, in connection with the heating is indispensable to give purity to the air of a Hospital for the Insane, and no expense that is required to effect this object thoroughly, can be deemed either misplaced or injudicious.

XXII. The boilers for generating steam for warming the building should be in a detached structure, connected with which may be the engine for pumping water, driving the washing apparatus, and other machinery.

XXIII. All water closets should, as far as possible, be made of indestructible materials—be simple in their arrangement, and have a strong downward ventilation connected with them.

XXIV. The floors of bath rooms, water closets, and basement stories, should as far as possible, be made of materials that will not absorb moisture.

XXV. The wards for the most excited class should be constructed with rooms on but one side of a corridor, not less than ten feet wide, the external windows of which should be large, and have pleasant views from them.

XXVI. Wherever practicable, the pleasure grounds of a Hospital for the Insane should be surrounded by a substantial wall, so placed as not to be unpleasantly visible from the building.

AMSAII PROPOSITIONS ON THE ORGANIZATION OF HOSPITALS FOR THE INSANE (1853)*

I. The general controlling power should be vested in a Board of Trustees or Managers, if a State institution, selected in such manner, as will be likely most effectually to protect it from all influences connected with political measures or political changes; if of a private corporation, by those properly authorized to vote.

II. The Board of Trustees should not exceed twelve in number, and be composed of individuals possessing the public confidence, distinguished for liberality, intelligence and active benevolence; above all political influence, and able and willing faithfully to attend to the duties of their station. Their tenure of office should be so arranged, that where changes are deemed desirable, the terms of not more than one-third of the whole number should expire in any one year.

III. The Board of Trustees should appoint the Physician, and on his nomination, and not otherwise, the Assistant Physician, Steward, and Matron. They should, as a Board, or by Committee, visit and examine every part of the institution, at frequent stated intervals, not less than semi-monthly, and at such other times as they may deem expedient, and exercise so careful a supervision over the expenditures and general operation of the Hospital, as to give to the community a proper degree of confidence in the correctness of its management.

IV. The Physician should be the Superintendent and Chief Executive Officer of the establishment. Besides being a well educated Physician, he should possess the mental, physical, and social qualities, to fit him for the post. He should serve during good behavior, reside on, or very near the premises, and his compensation should be so liberal, as to enable him to devote his whole time and energies to the welfare of the Hospital. He should nominate to the Board suitable persons to act as Assistant Physician, Steward and Matron; he should have the entire control of the medical, moral, and dietetic treatment of the patients, the unrestricted power of appointment

---

*Source: American Journal of Insanity, July 1853: 68–69.

and discharge of all persons engaged in their care, and should exercise a general supervision and direction of every department of the Institution.

V. The Assistant Physician, or Assistant Physicians, where more than one are required, should be graduates of medicine, of such character and qualifications as to be able to represent and to perform the ordinary duties of the Physician during his absence.

VI. The Steward, under the direction of the Superintending Physician, and by his order, should make all purchases for the Institution, keep the accounts, make engagements with, pay and discharge those employed about the establishment; have a supervision of the farm, garden and grounds, and perform such other duties as may be assigned to him.

VII. The Matron, under the direction of the Superintendent, should have a general supervision of the domestic arrangements of the House, and under the same direction, do what she can to promote the comfort and restoration of the patients.

VIII. In institutions containing more than 200 patients, a second Assistant Physician and an Apothecary should be employed, to the latter of whom, other duties, in the male wards, may be conveniently assigned.

IX. If a Chaplain is deemed desirable as a permanent officer, he should be selected by the Superintendent, and like all others engaged in the care of the patients, should be entirely under his direction.

X. In every Hospital for the Insane, there should be one Supervisor for each sex, exercising a general oversight of all the attendant and patients, and forming a medium of communication between them and the officers.

XI. In no Institution should the number of persons in immediate attendance on the patients be in a lower ratio than one attendant for every ten patients; and a much larger proportion of attendants will commonly be desirable.

XII. The fullest authority should be given to the Superintendent to take every precaution that can guard against fire or accident within an institution, and to secure this an efficient night-watch should always be provided.

XIII. The situation and circumstances of different institutions may require a considerable number of persons to be employed in various other positions, but in every Hospital, at least all those that have been referred to are deemed not only desirable, but absolutely necessary, to give all the advantages that may be hoped for from a liberal and enlightened treatment of the Insane.

XIV. All persons employed in the care of the Insane should be active, vigilant, cheerful, and in good health. They should be of a kind and benevolent disposition, be educated, and in all respects trust-worthy, and their compensation should be sufficiently liberal to secure the services of individuals of this description.

Minimum Standards for Mental Hospitals: American Psychiatric Association (1924)[*]

(1) The chief executive officer must be a well-qualified physician and experienced psychiatrist.

(2) All other persons employed at the institution ought to be subordinate to him and subject to removal by him if they fail to discharge their duties properly.

(3) The positions and the administration of the institution must be free from control by partisan politics.

(4) There must be an adequate medical staff of well-qualified physicians; the proportion to total patients to be not less than 1 to 150, and to the number of patients admitted annually not less than 1 to 40. There must also be adequate provision for dental work.

(5) There must be a staff of consulting specialists employed under such terms as will insure adequate service. A record of their visits must be kept.

(6) The medical staff must be organized, the services well defined and the clinical work under the direction of a staff leader.

(7) Regular staff conferences must be held not seldomer than once a week where the work of the physicians and the examination and treatment of the patients will be carefully reviewed. Minutes of the conferences must be recorded.

(8) The patients must be classified in accordance with their condition and most important requirements.

(9) The classification must include a reception and intensive treatment unit, and a unit for physical illnesses, and surgical cases of adequate capacity, equipment, and medical and nursing staff.

(10) Each medical service must be provided with an office and an examining room, containing sufficient conveniences and equipment for the work to be performed, and with such clerical services as may be required for the keeping of the medical and administrative records.

(11) There must be carefully kept clinical histories of all the patients, in proper files for ready reference.

(12) The hospital must be provided with adequate laboratories and an X-ray department properly equipped and manned, or provisions made for having such work as cannot be performed, attended to at other laboratories.

(13) There must be a working medical library and journal file.

(14) The treatment facilities and equipment must include:

   (a) A surgical operating room.

   (b) A dental department.

---

*Source: American Journal of Psychiatry, October 1924: 399–402.

(c) Hydrotherapy equipment including tubs for prolonged baths.

(d) Examination rooms for the specialties in medicine and surgery.

(e) Provision for occupation and training in occupation, physical exercise and reaction [sic; recreation] for all patients who are in condition to utilize it.

All the above to be adequately equipped and manned.

(14) [sic] There should be an out-patient clinic and social workers.

(15) There must be an adequate nursing force, not less than a proportion of 1 to 8, and in the intensive treatment and sick and surgical services not less than 1 to 4.

(16) The hospital must not be so grossly overcrowded as to prevent adequate classification and treatment.

(17) Mechanical restraint and seclusion must, if used at all, be under strict regulations and a system of control by the physicians, and limited to the most urgent conditions.

STANDARDS FOR PSYCHIATRIC HOSPITALS AND OUT-PATIENT CLINICS APPROVED BY THE AMERICAN PSYCHIATRIC ASSOCIATION (1945–46)[*]

The Committee on Psychiatric Standards and Policies of the American Psychiatric Association is cognizant of the fact that the attention of the entire nation has been focused upon the need for adequate preventive and curative mental health services for all the people, and that there is a definite demand for such hospital and out-patient services within the means of all classes of society.

To comply with such popular demand, The American Psychiatric Association . . . has approved the following standards and policies for all mental hospitals and out-patient clinics. The Council recognizes that such standards cannot be achieved within a short time, but it should be the goal of every hospital and clinic to establish them within ten years, thus qualifying as both a treatment and training center.

Standards for Psychiatric Hospitals

1. All hospitals should have a small unit or department which will take the place of the present receiving ward, where patients upon admission will remain a brief period (usually not to exceed two weeks) to be classified and housed according to their condition. This unit will require the services of a psychiatrist for every 30 patients under observation; a graduate nurse for every 4 patients and a trained attendant for every 6 patients under observation.

---

*Source: American Journal of Psychiatry, Sept. 1945: 264–69.

2. Approved hospitals should have a special unit or department for acutely mentally ill, where a patient will receive individual medical, psychiatric, nursing care and treatment, and individual services in the field of occupational, recreational and allied therapy. Intensive psychotherapy, in conjunction with physio-hydro-therapy, as well as modern organic therapy must be considered as indispensable (sic) in each case. The size of such a unit should accord with the admissions within a three- to six-months' period. This unit will have a small sub-unit for disturbed acutely ill individuals who will receive the same individual care and treatment.

All cases in the unit for acutely ill should be housed either in single rooms or in small dormitories. Such a unit will require a psychiatrist for every 30 patients; a graduate nurse for every 4 patients, a trained attendant for every 6 patients; a physio-hydro-therapist, an occupational-therapist, and a recreational therapist for every 30 patients requiring such treatment, and any other service indicated.

3. Hospitals should have a unit or department for a convalescing group where a patient will receive somewhat similar care, although not requiring as intensive treatment as in the unit for the acutely ill. The size of such unit will be determined by the number of home convalescing patients during a period of six months. Such a unit will require a psychiatrist for every 50 patients; a graduate nurse for every 10 patients; a trained attendant for every 7 patients; an occupational therapist for every 30 patients; a recreational therapist for every 50 patients, and any other service indicated.

4. Hospitals assuming responsibility for patients with a favorable prognosis but who require intensive prolonged treatment and care should have a unit or department for such patients. Such a re-educational service will require a psychiatrist for every 75 patients; a graduate nurse for every 25 patients; a trained attendant for every 8 patients; a physio-hydro-therapist, and occupational-therapist and a recreational therapist for every 75 patients, and any other service indicated. This unit will have a special sub-unit for chronic disturbed patients.

5. Hospitals receiving patients who require continued treatment should have a special unit or department. Such a unit will need a psychiatrist for every 200 patients; a graduate nurse for every 40 patients; a trained attendant for every 6 patients; a physio-hydro-therapist for every 200 patients; an occupational therapist for every 50 patients; a re-educational therapist for every 50 patients; a recreational therapist for every 100 patients, and any other service indicated.

6. Hospitals receiving senile and arteriosclerotic patients should have a special unit or department for such patients. Such service will require a psychiatrist for every 200 patients; a graduate nurse for every 50 patients; a trained attendant for every 8 patients; an occupational-recreational therapist for every 100 patients; and any other service indicated. This depart-

ment will also include a special infirmary section with a graduate nurse in charge.

7. Hospitals should have a special unit known as a medical and surgical department for patients who are actually physically ill, requiring either medical or surgical treatment. This unit will require well trained physicians . . . This unit should meet minimal standards of the American College of Physicians.

8. Mental hospitals receiving children under 16 years of age will require a special unit or department known as the children's unit . . . [Staffing standards stated.]

9. If a mental hospital receives alcoholics and/or other drug addicts, it should have a special unit or department for their care or treatment . . . [Staffing standards stated.]

10. Mental hospitals should have a special unit or department for tuberculous patients . . . [Staffing standards stated.]

No institution can be considered a modern hospital unless it has adequate facilities for all types of physical examinations and tests required by the American College of Surgeons, including well organized clinical and pathological laboratories under competent direction; a roentgenological department; and a medical library under supervision of the clinical director.

[Other standards include a superintendent who is a psychiatrist with administrative ability appointed on a nonpolitical basis; in hospitals of more than 1,000 patients, an assistant superintendent; a "very well trained and experienced psychiatrist" as clinical director "who will be the coordinator and stimulating head of the medical staff." He will organize instruction and rotation; seminars; and weekly (or more frequent) staff meetings. It is "desirable" that these all be "diplomates of the American Board of Psychiatry and Neurology." All staff members "should be encouraged to devote a certain number of hours per week to research or scientific study and investigation."

[A director of nursing with considerable education and experience must be in charge of all nursing, including attendants. Listed (and usually discussed) as desirable were:

- "a well organized department of clinical psychology;"
- a training school for nurses;
- "a larger corps of well trained psychiatric nursing instructors";
- one trained and qualified social worker per 100 admissions, under an experienced chief who has organized a department for "adequate pre-admission, admission and follow-up";
- a dental department;
- a department of pharmacy;

- a non-medical administration department;
- a medical record system under a qualified librarian;
- a library for the patients, directed by a librarian.

[Also included in the original were suggestions for a commitment law and standards for outpatient clinics.]

MINIMUM CONSTITUTIONAL STANDARDS
FOR ADEQUATE TREATMENT OF THE MENTALLY ILL
(UNITED STATES SUPREME COURT, *WYATT VERSUS STICKNEY* 1972)*

I. *Definitions*:

a. "Hospital"—Bryce and Search Hospitals.

b. "Patients"—all persons who are now confined and all persons who may in the future be confined at Bryce and Searcy Hospitals pursuant to an involuntary civil commitment procedure.

c. "Qualified Mental Health Professional"—

(1) a psychiatrist with three years of residency training in psychiatry;

(2) a psychologist with a doctoral degree from an accredited program;

(3) a social worker with a master's degree from an accredited program and two years of clinical experience under the supervision of a Qualified Mental Health Professional;

(4) a registered nurse with a graduate degree in psychiatric nursing and two years of clinical experience under the supervision of a Qualified Mental Health Professional.

d. "Non-Professional Staff Member"—an employee of the hospital, other than a Qualified Mental Health Professional, whose duties require contact with or supervision of patients.

II. *Humane Psychological and Physical Environment*

1. Patients have a right to privacy and dignity.

2. Patients have a right to the least restrictive conditions necessary to achieve the purposes of committment.

3. No person shall be deemed incompetent to manage his affairs, to contract, to hold professional or occupational or vehicle operator's licenses,

---

*Wyatt v. Stickney 344 F. Supp. 373 and 387 (M.D. Ala. 1972). For recent revisions, see "Recent Court Ruling in Alabama's Wyatt Case Modifies 20-Year-Old Patient Care Standards." *Hospital and Community Psychiatry* 43 (August 1992): 851–52.

to marry and to obtain a divorce, to register and vote, or to make a will *solely* by reason of his admission or commitment to the hospital.

4. Patients shall have the same rights to visitation and telephone communications as patients at other public hospitals, except to the extent that the Qualified Mental Health Professional responsible for formulation of a particular patient's treatment plan writes an order imposing special restrictions . . . Patients shall have an unrestricted right to visitation with attorneys and with private physicians and other health professionals.

5. Patients shall have an unrestricted right to send sealed mail. Patients shall have an unrestricted right to receive sealed mail from their attorneys, private physicians, and other mental health professionals, from courts, and government officials . . .

6. Patients have a right to be free from unnecessary or excessive medication. No medication shall be administered unless at the written order of a physician . . . Medication shall not be used as punishment, for the convenience of staff, as a substitute for program, or in quantities that interfere with the patient's treatment program.

7. Patients have a right to be free from physical restraint and isolation. Except for emergency situations, in which it is likely that patients could harm themselves or others and in which less restrictive means of restraint are not feasible, patients may be physically restrained or placed in isolation only on a Qualified Mental Health Professional's written order which explains the rationale for such action . . .

8. Patients shall have a right not to be subjected to experimental research without the express and informed consent of the patient . . .

9. Patients have a right not to be subjected to treatment procedures such as lobotomy, electro-convulsive treatment, aversive reinforcement conditioning or other unusual or hazardous treatment procedures without their express and informed consent after consultation with counsel or interested party of the patient's choice.

10. Patients have a right to receive prompt and adequate medical treatment for any physical ailment.

11. Patients have a right to wear their own clothes and to keep and use their own personal professions . . .

12. The hospital has an obligation to supply an adequate allowance of clothing to any patients who do not have suitable clothing of their own . . .

13. The hospital shall make provision for the laundering of patient clothing.

14. Patients have a right to regular physical exercise several times a week. Moreover, it shall be the duty of the hospital to provide facilities and equipment for such exercise.

15. Patients have a right to be out-doors at regular and frequent intervals, in the absence of medical considerations.

16. The right to religious worship shall be accorded to each patient who desires such opportunities . . .

17. The institution shall provide, with adequate supervision, suitable opportunities for the patient's interaction with members of the opposite sex.

18. The following rules shall govern patient labor . . .

19. *Physical Facilities*

A patient has a right to a humane psychological and physical environment within the hospital facilities. These facilities shall be designed to afford patients with comfort and safety, promote dignity, and ensure privacy. The facilities shall be designed to make a positive contribution to the efficient attainment of the treatment goals of the hospital.

A. *Resident Unit*

The number of patients in a multi-patient room shall not exceed six persons. There shall be allocated a minimum of 80 square feet of floor space per patient in a multi-patient room. Screens or curtains shall be provided to ensure privacy within the resident unit. Single rooms shall have a minimum of 100 square feet of floor space. Each patient will be furnished with a comfortable bed with adequate changes of linen, a closet or locker for his personal belongings, a chair, and a bedside table.

B. *Toilets and Lavatories*

There will be one toilet provided for each eight patients and one lavatory for each six patients. A lavatory will be provided with each toilet facility. The toilets will be installed in separate stalls to ensure privacy, will be clean and free of odor, and will be equipped with appropriate safety devices for the physically handicapped.

C. *Showers*

There will be one tub or shower for each 15 patients. If a central bathing area is provided, each shower area will be divided by curtains to ensure privacy . . .

D. *Day Room*

The minimum day room area shall be 40 square feet per patient. Day rooms will be attractive and adequately furnished . . . Areas used for corridor traffic cannot be counted as day room space; nor can a chapel with fixed pews be counted as a day room area.

E. *Dining Facilities*

The minimum dining room area shall be ten square feet per patient . . . and will be furnished with comfortable chairs and tables with hard, washable surfaces.

F. *Linen Servicing and Handling*

The hospital shall provide adequate facilities and equipment for handling clean and soiled bedding and other linen. There must be frequent changes of bedding and other linen, no less than every seven days to assure patient comfort.

G. *Housekeeping*

Regular housekeeping and maintenance procedures which will ensure that the hospital is maintained in a safe, clean, and attractive condition will be developed and implemented.

H. *Geriatric and Other Nonambulatory Mental Patients*

There must be special facilities for geriatric and other nonambulatory patients to assure their safety and comfort . . .

I. *Physical Plant*

(1) Pursuant to an established routine maintenance and repair program, the physical plant shall be kept in a continuous state of good repair and operation in accordance with the needs of the health, comfort, safety and well-being of the patients.

(2) Adequate heating, air conditioning and ventilation systems and equipment shall be afforded . . . the temperature in the hospital shall not exceed 83°F nor fall below 68°F.

(3) Thermostatically controlled hot water shall be provided in adequate quantities . . .

(4) Adequate refuse facilities will be provided . . . [to] prohibit transmission of disease and not create a nuisance or fire hazard or provide a breeding place for rodents and insects.

(5) The physical facilities must meet all fire and safety standards . . .

19A. The hospital shall meet all standards established by the state for general hospitals, insofar as they are relevant to psychiatric facilities.

20. *Nutritional Standards*

Patients, except for the non-mobile, shall eat or be fed in dining rooms. The diet for patients will provide at a minimum the Recommended Daily Dietary Allowances as developed by the National Academy of Sciences . . . The hospital will not spend less per patient for raw food . . . than the most recent per person costs of the Low Cost Food Plan for the Southern Region . . . Provisions shall be made for special therapeutic diets and for substitutes at the request of the patient, or his guardian or next of kin, in accordance with the religious requirements of any patient's faith. Denial of a nutritionally adequate diet shall not be used as punishment.

III. *Qualified Staff in Numbers Sufficient to Administer Adequate Treatment*

21. Each Qualified Mental Health Professional shall meet all licensing and certification requirements . . .

22 a. All Non Professional Staff Members who have not had prior clinical experience in a mental institution shall have a substantial orientation training.

22b. Staff members on all levels shall have regularly scheduled in-service training.

23. Each Non-Professional Staff Member shall be under the direct supervision of a Qualified Mental Health Professional.

24. *Staffing Ratios*

The hospital shall have the following minimum numbers of treatment personnel per 250 patients . . .

Classification Number of Employees

Unit Director	1
Psychiatrist (3 years' residency training in psychiatry)	2
MD (Registered physicians)	4
Nurses (RN)	12
Licensed Practical Nurses	6
Aide III	6
Aide II	16
Aide I	70
Hospital Orderly	10
Clerk Stenographer II	3
Clerk Typist II	3
Unit Administrator	1
Administrative Clerk	1
Psychologist (Ph.D.) (doctoral degree from accredited program)	1
Psychologist (M.A.)	1
Psychologist (B.S.)	2
Social Worker (MSW) (from accredited program)	2
Social Worker (B.A.)	5
Patient Activity Therapist (M.S.)	1
Patient Activity Aide	10
Mental Health Technician	10
Dental Hygienist	1
Chaplain	.5
Vocational Rehab. Counselor	1
Volunteer Services Worker	1
Mental Health Field Representative	1
Dietitian	1
Food Service Supervisor	1
Cook II	2
Cook I	3
Food Service Worker	15
Vehicle Driver	1
Housekeeper	10

Messenger	1
Maintenance Repairman	2

IV. *Individualized Treatment Plans*

25. Each patient shall have a comprehensive physical and mental examination and review of behavioral status within 48 hours after admission to the hospital.

26. Each patient shall have an individualized treatment plan. This plan shall be developed by appropriate Qualified Mental Health Professionals, including a psychiatrist, and implemented as soon as possible—in any event no later than five days after the patient's admission. Each individualized treatment plan shall contain:

  a. a statement of the nature of the specific problems and specific needs of the patient;

  b. a statement of the least restrictive treatment conditions necessary to achieve the purposes of commitment;

  c. a description of intermediate and long-range treatment goals, with a projected timetable for their attainment;

  d. a statement and rationale for the plan of treatment for achieving these intermediate and long-range goals;

  e. a specification of staff responsibility and a description of proposed staff involvement with the patient in order to attain these treatment goals;

  f. criteria for release to less restrictive treatment conditions, and criteria for discharge;

  g. a notation of any therapeutic tasks and labor to be performed by the patient in accordance with Standard 18.

27. As part of his treatment plan, each patient shall have an individualized post-hospitalization plan. This plan shall be developed by a Qualified Mental Health Professional as soon as practicable after the patient's admission to the hospital.

28. In the interests of continuity of care, whenever possible, one Qualified Mental Health Professional . . . shall be responsible for supervising the implementation of the treatment plan, integrating the various aspects of the treatment program and recording the patient's progress . . . [and] for ensuring that the patient is released, where appropriate, into a less restrictive form of treatment.

29. The treatment plan shall be continuously reviewed . . . and modified if necessary. Moreover, at least every 90 days, each patient shall receive a mental examination from, and his treatment plan shall be reviewed by, a Qualified Mental Health Professional other than the professional responsible for supervising the implementation of the plan.

30. In addition to treatment for mental disorders, patients . . . also are entitled to and shall receive appropriate treatment for physical illnesses such as tuberculosis . . .

31. Complete patient records shall be kept on the ward in which the patient is placed and shall be available to anyone properly authorized in writing by the patient. These records shall include [what the next 16 paragraphs detail].

32. In addition to complying with all the other standards herein, a hospital shall make special provisions for the treatment of patients who are children and young adults. These provisions shall include but are not limited to [education; a treatment plan that deals with development; teachers; recreation and play; and contact with family].

33. No later than 15 days after a patient is committed to the hospital, the superintendent . . . or his . . . agent shall examine the committed patient and shall determine whether the patient continues to require hospitalization and whether a treatment plan complying with Standard 26 has been implemented. If the patient no longer requires hospitalization in accordance with the standards for commitment, or if a treatment plan has not been implemented, he must be released immediately unless he agrees to continue with treatment on a voluntary basis.

34. The Mental Health Board and its agents have an affirmative duty to provide adequate transitional treatment and care for all patients released after a period of involuntary confinement . . .

V. *Miscellaneous*

35. Each patient and his family, guardian, or next friend shall promptly upon the patient's admission receive written notice, in language he understands, of all the above standards for adequate treatment. In addition a copy of all the above standards shall be posted in each ward.

CHAPTER TITLES, CONSOLIDATED STANDARDS MANUAL,
1981 JOINT COMMISSION ON ACCREDITATION OF HOSPITALS
(N.B.: THE ACTUAL STANDARDS FILL A BOOK OF 206 PAGES)*

Program Management

1. Governing Body
2. Chief Executive Officer
3. Professional Staff Organization
4. Written Plan for Professional Services and Staff Composition

---

*Joint Commission on Accreditation of Hospitals. *Consolidated Standards Manual for Child, Adolescent, and Adult Psychiatric, Alcoholism, and Drug Abuse Facilities.* 1981 Edition. Chicago: JCAH.

5. Personnel Policies and Procedures
6. Volunteer Services
7. Fiscal Management
8. Facility and Program Evaluation
9. Quality Assurance
10. Utilization Review
11. Patient Care Monitoring
12. Staff Growth and Development
13. Research
14. Patient Rights
15. Patient Records

Patient Management

16. Intake
17. Assessment
18. Treatment Plans

   Treatment Plans
   Progress Notes
   Treatment Plan Review
   Discharge Summary and Aftercare

19. Special Treatment Procedures

Patient Services

20. Anesthesia Services
21. Community Education Services
22. Consultation Services
23. Dental Services
24. Dietetic Services
25. Emergency Services
26. Outreach Services
27. Pastoral Services
28. Pathology Services
29. Pharmacy Services
30. Professional Library Services
31. Radiology Services
32. Referrals
33. Rehabilitation Services

   Activity Services
   Education Services
   Speech, Language, and Hearing Services
   Vocational Rehabilitation Services

Physical Plant Management

34. Building and Grounds Safety
35. Functional Safety and Sanitation
36. Therapeutic Environment
37. Housekeeping Services
38. Infection Control
39. Sterile Supplies and Equipment

WHAT DO GOOD PSYCHIATRIC HOSPITALS LOOK LIKE?
(FROM TORREY ET AL., *CARE OF THE SERIOUSLY MENTALLY ILL* 1990)

Hospital services for people with serious mental illness usually are delivered in state psychiatric hospitals or in psychiatric units of general hospitals. Similar medically oriented services to mentally ill people are sometimes provided in nursing homes. The major impediments to good services are the same in each setting: Services are often organized for the convenience of staff and management rather than to meet the needs of the patients. This is one of the hallmarks of "total institutions," and in this respect hospitals and nursing homes are similar to prisons, concentration camps, institutions for people with mental retardation, and public shelters for homeless people . . . Services inevitably become organized around the needs of the staff . . . A fundamental premise of good hospital services is, in the words of the NIMH model plan, that "services should be based on the needs of the client rather than the needs of the system or the needs of the providers."

Ideal Hospital Services

Quality of Staff

- Applicants for staff positions are screened to ensure that their credentials are valid, that they have no criminal history, and that there are no allegations of patient abuse or neglect in prior employment . . .
- initial training [and] intensive ongoing training . . .
- All professionals are fully trained and licensed . . .
- Job stability and salaries are adequate . . .
- Job advancement is determined by the quality of care delivered, not just by administrative skills . . .

Quantity of Staff

- It is not possible to recommend precise optimal staffing ratios . . . However, there should be a sufficient number of all professional and paraprofessional staff to ensure good care at all times.

- It should not be necessary to pull staff and assign them to unfamiliar wards because of staff shortages.
- It should not be necessary to require staff to work overtime or double shifts.
- Staffing patterns on weekends should allow for the same staff-to-patient ratios as on weekdays.

Quality of Treatment

- Each patient has an individual treatment plan . . . developed promptly upon admission . . . reviewed, evaluated, and updated in writing regularly, with the participation of the patient and the family.
- Psychopharmacology is skilled . . .
- Patients are regularly screened for tardive dyskinesia . . .
- Extensive initial diagnostic assessments are conducted . . . [as are] specialized tests . . . Patients' previous medical and service records are available . . .
- Complete, high-quality routine medical and dental care are provided . . .
- Patients are treated with dignity and respect . . .
- Patient education . . . is available.
- Total hours of seclusion and restraint are very low . . .
- The hospital has the capacity to accurately diagnose patients with multiple problems . . . Specialized programs are available . . .
- . . . Hospital and community staff confer and cooperate in planning treatment and discharge . . . to further improve continuity of care.
- Discharge planning begins the day of admission . . . No patient is discharged without advance notification to all those concerned, a plan that includes adequate housing and outpatient treatment, and a supply of medication . . .
- Patients' legal rights are protected by a patient advocate and access to legal assistance.
- . . . Hospital policies maximize the use of funds for the patient's use and needs.
- Allegations of patient abuse and neglect by staff are automatically investigated by a committee that includes individuals from outside the hospital.

Environment

- Each patient has his or her room for long hospital stays . . .
- Separate bathrooms are attached . . .
- Patients have personal belongings . . .
- Common living areas are comfortable and decorated . . .
- Patients dine in small eating units . . .
- A variety of meaningful daytime activities . . . are available.
- Special activities . . . are available . . .
- Patients have an adequate amount of their own clothing . . .
- All fire and building safety regulations . . . are met.

Use of Non-State-Operated (Community) Hospitals

- The public psychiatric system has guaranteed access to an adequate number of local inpatient psychiatric beds . . . throughout the state, for short-term treatment of individuals in an acute phase of their illness.
- All standards listed above . . . are met by the local inpatient facilities being used by the state as well as by the state psychiatric hospitals.

Bibliography

Abbott, Andrew. 1988. *The System of Professions*. Chicago: University of Chicago Press.

Allison, Paul D. 1984. *Event History Analysis*. Beverly Hills: Sage.

American Hospital Association. 1990. AHA *Guide to the Health Care Field*. Chicago: author.

Andrews, Judson B. 1869. "The Physiological Action and Therapeutic Uses of the 'Acidum Phosphoricum Dilutum.'" *American Journal of Insanity* 26: 113–29.

———. 1870. "Exophthalmic Goitre with Insanity." *American Journal of Insanity* 27: 1–13.

———. 1871. "The Physiological Action and Therapeutic Use of Chloral." *American Journal of Insanity* 28: 35–56.

———. 1883. "Case of Charles Stockley, Convicted of Murder. Plea— Temporary Insanity." *American Journal of Insanity* 40: 145–61.

———. 1886. "Urethan." *American Journal of Insanity* 43: 256–64.

———. 1888. "The Case of Peter Louis Otto—A Medico-Legal Study." *American Journal of Insanity* 45: 207–20.

———. 1880. "Insanity." Frederick A. Castle (ed.), *Wood's Household Practice of Medicine, Hygiene, and Surgery: A Practical Treatise for the Use of Families, Travelers, Seamen, Miners, and Others*. New York: William Wood and Company: 609–35.

———. 1891. "Traumatic Hysteria from Railroad Injury." *American Journal of Insanity* 48: 37–42.

———. 1893. "President's Address Before the American Medico-Psychological Association." *American Journal of Insanity* 50: 49–60.

Anonymous. 1848. "Institutions for the Insane in the United States." *American Journal of Insanity* 5: 53–62.

———. 1872. "State Provision for the Insane. Buffalo State Asylum— Its History and Description." *American Journal of Insanity* 29: 1–13.

———. 1882. *In Memoriam: James Platt White*. Buffalo: privately printed. (Original copy in the Medical Archives of SUNY at Buffalo.)

———. 1886a. Review of "How to Care for the Insane," by William G. Granger, M. D. *American Journal of Insanity* 43: 117–18.

———. 1886b. "The Commencement Exercises of the Training School for Attendants at the Buffalo Asylum." *American Journal of Insanity* 43: 120–26.

AR (N. B.: "AR" is used to indicate the Annual Report for the year indicated. See below, New York State, 1872–1985).

Ashley, Jo Ann. 1976. *Hospitals, Paternalism, and the Role of the Nurse*. New York: Teachers College Press.

Bachrach, Leona L. 1976. *Deinstitutionalization: An Analytical Review and Sociological Perspective*. Washinton: National Institute of Mental Health.

———. 1978. "A Conceptual Approach to Deinstitutionalization." *Hospital and Community Psychiatry* 29: 573–78.

———. 1986. "The Future of the State Mental Hospital." *Hospital and Community Psychiatry* 37: 467–74.

Banham, Reyner et al. 1981. *Buffalo Architecture: A Guide*. Cambridge: MIT Press.

Becker, Howard S. 1986. *Writing for Social Scientists*. Chicago: University of Chicago Press.

Belknap, Ivan. 1956. *Human Problems of a State Mental Hospital*. New York: McGraw-Hill.

Benson, J. Kenneth. 1977. "Organizations: A Dialectical View." *Adminstrative Science Quarterly* 22: 1–21.

Bland, Charles L. 1975. "Institutions of Charity in Jacksonian Erie County: 1829–1861." Unpublished paper, Department of History, State University of New York at Buffalo.

———. 1976 "Public Relief in Erie County: 1861–1896." Unpublished paper, Department of History, State University of New York at Buffalo.

BN (N. B. "BN" and "BEN" are used to indicate *Buffalo News* and *Buffalo Evening News*).

Bockoven, J. Sanbourne. 1956. "Moral Treatment in American Psychiatry." *Journal of Nervous and Mental Disease* 124: 167–94, 292–321.

Bowman, Lee G. and Terrence E. Deal. 1991. *Reframing Organizations*. San Francisco: Jossey-Bass.

Braverman, Harry. 1974. *Labor and Monopoly Capital: The Degradation of Work in the Twentieth Century*. New York: Monthly Review Press.

Brenner, M. Harvey. 1973. *Mental Illness and the Economy*. Cambridge: Harvard University Press.

Brown, Thomas E. 1985. "Foucault Plus Twenty: On Writing the History of Canadian Psychiatry in the 1980s." *Canadian Bulletin of Medical History* 2: 23–49.

Brussel, James A. 1954. "History of the New York State Department of Mental Hygiene." *New York State Journal of Medicine* 54: 822–26.

Bullough, Vern L. and Bonnie Bullough. 1978. *The Care of the Sick: The Emergence of Modern Nursing*. New York: Prodist.

Carroll, Glenn R. 1984. "Organizational Ecology." *Annual Review of Sociology* 10: 71–93.

———. 1987. *Publish and Perish: The Organizational Ecology of Newspaper Industries*. Greenwich, CT: JAI Press.

Catalano, Ralph A., David Dooley, and Robert L. Jackson. 1985. "Economic Antecedents of Help Seeking: Reformulation of Time Series Tests." *Journal of Health and Social Behavior* 26: 141–52.

Caudill, William. 1958. *The Psychiatric Hospital as a Small Society*. Cambridge: Harvard University Press.

Center for Mental Health Services. 1994a. "The Evolution and Expansion of Mental Health Care in the United States Between 1955 and 1990." Mental Health Statistical Note 210. Washington, DC: U.S. Department of Health and Human Services, Substance Abuse and Mental Health Services Administration.

———. 1994b. "Male-Female Admissions Differentials in State Mental Hospitals, 1880–1990." Mental Health Statistical Note 211. Washington, DC: US Department of Health and Human Services, Substance Abuse and Mental Health Services Administration.

Cohen, Barbara. 1981. "Buffalo Psychiatric Center. Architect: H. H. Richardson." Unpublished paper, State University of New York at Buffalo.

Cohen, Barbara J. and Marjorie McMahon. 1981. "Buffalo Psychiatric Center. Historical Data." Unpublished paper, State University of New York at Buffalo.

Cohen, Stanley and Andrew Scull. 1983. *Social Control and the State*. New York: St. Martin's Press.

Commission on Quality of Care (New York State). 1984. *A Review of Living Conditions in Nine New York State Psychiatric Centers, May 1984*. Albany: author.

————. 1985. *Patient Living Conditions at Buffalo Psychiatric Center*. Albany: author.

Cook, George. 1866. "Provision for the Insane Poor in the State of New York." *American Journal of Insanity* 23: 45–75.

Council of State Governments. 1950. *The Mental Health Programs of the Forty-Eight States*. Chicago: author.

Cowles, Edward. 1916. "Training School for Nurses and the First School in McLean Hospital." Henry M. Hurd (ed.), *The Institutional Care of the Insane in the United States and Canada*. Vol. I. Baltimore: The Johns Hopkins University Press: 289–300.

Dain, Norman. 1971. *Disordered Minds: The First Century of Eastern State Hospital in Williamsburg, Virginia 1766–1866*. Charlottesville: University Press of Virginia.

Delacroix, Jacques and Glenn R. Carroll. 1983. "Organizational Foundings: An Ecological Study of the Newspaper Industries of Argentina and Ireland." *Administrative Science Quarterly* 28: 274–91.

Deuther, Charles G. 1870. *The Life and Times of the Rt. Rev. John Timon, D. D.: First Roman Catholic Bishop of the Diocese of Buffalo*. Buffalo: the author.

Deutsch, Albert. 1949. *The Mentally Ill in America*. 2nd ed. New York: Columbia University Press.

————. 1948. *The Shame of the States*. New York: Harcourt, Brace.

DiMaggio, Paul J. and Walter W. Powell. 1983. "The Iron Cage Revisited: Institutional Isomorphism and Collective Rationality in Organizational Fields." *American Sociological Review* 48: 147–60.

Dix, Dorothea L. 1971. *On Behalf of the Insane Poor: Selected Reports*. New York: Arno Press and the New York Times.

Dorwart, Robert A. and Sherrie S. Epstein. 1993. *Privatization and Mental Health Care: A Fragile Balance*. Westport, CT: Auburn House.

Dowdall, George W. and Janet Lynne Golden. 1989. "Photographs as Data: An Analysis of Images from a Mental Hospital." *Qualitative Sociology* 12: 183–213.

Dowdall, George W., Rita J. Kirshstein, James R. Marshall, and Diane M. Pinchoff. 1982. "Mental Hospitalization and Economic Decline in Buffalo." Paper presented to the annual meeting of the Society for the Study of Social Problems, San Francisco.

Dowdall, George W., James R. Marshall, and Wayne A. Morra. 1990. "Economic Antecedents of Mental Hospitalization: A Nineteenth-Century Time-Series Test." *Journal of Health and Social Behavior* 31: 141–47.

Dowdall, George W. and Diane M. Pinchoff. 1994. "Evaluation Research and the Psychiatric Hospital: Blending Management and Inquiry in Clinical Sociology." *Clinical Sociology Review* 12: 176–89.

Dwyer, Ellen. 1987. *Homes for the Mad: Life Inside Two Nineteenth Century Asylums*. New Brunswick: Rutgers University Press.

———. 1988. "The Historiography of the Asylum in Great Britain and the United States." Pp. 110–60 in *Law and Mental Health: International Perspectives*, vol. 4, ed. David N. Weisstub. New York: Pergamon Press.

Earle, Pliny. 1887. *The Curability of Insanity: A Series of Studies*. Philadelphia: J. B. Lippincott Company.

Eisenhauer, Paul. 1984. "A Concrete Cure for Insanity: Professionalization and Asylum Architecture in nineteenth Century America." Paper presented to the Society for the Study of Social Problems, San Antonio.

Erie Alliance for the Mentally Ill. 1989. *The Mind Matters: A Practical Guide to Services for the Mentally Ill in Erie County*. 2nd edition. Snyder, NY: author.

Foucault, Michel. 1965. *Madness and Civilization: A History of Insanity in the Age of Reason*. New York: Random House.

Fowlkes, Martha R. 1975. "Business as Usual—at the State Mental Hospital." *Psychiatry* 38: 55–64.

Fox, D. M. and J. Terry. 1978. "Photography and the Self Image of American Physicians, 1880–1920." *Bulletin of the History of Medicine* 52: 425–57.

Frank, Richard G. and Mark S. Kamlet. 1985. "Direct Costs and Expenditures for Mental Health Care in the United States in 1980." *Hospital and Community Psychiatry* 36: 165–68.

Frank, Richard G. and Mark S. Kamlet. 1986. "Quality, Quantity, and Total Expenditures on Publicly Provided Goods: The Case of Public Mental Hospitals." *Journal of Public Economics* 29: 295–316.

Franklin, Jack L., Brenda Solovitz, Mark Mason, Jimmie R. Clemmons, and

Gary E. Miller. 1987. "An Evaluation of Case Management." *American Journal of Public Health* 77: 674–78.

Gallagher, Eugene B. 1987. "Editorial: Half-Filled Pages in Mental Health Research." *Journal of Health and Social Behavior* 28: vi-vii.

Geertz, C. 1973. *The Interpretation of Cultures*. New York: Basic Books.

Gerber, David A. 1989. *The Making of an American Pluralism: Buffalo, New York, 1825–1860*. Urbana: University of Illinois Press.

Ginsberg, S. T. 1974. "A Brief History and Current Status of Accreditation of Psychiatric Facilities." *Hospital & Community Psychiatry* 25: 90–92.

Goffman, Erving. 1961. *Asylums*. Garden City: Anchor.

Golden, Janet and Eric C. Schneider. 1982. "Custody and Control: the Rhode Island State Hospital for Mental Diseases, 1870–1970." *Rhode Island History* 41: 113–25.

Goldman, Howard H., Neal H. Adams, and Carl A. Taube. 1983. "Deinstitutionalization: The Data Demythologized." *Hospital and Community Psychiatry* 34: 129–34.

Goldman, Howard H., Carl A. Taube, Darrel A. Regier, and Michael Witkin. 1983. "The Multiple Functions of the State Mental Hospital." *American Journal of Psychiatry* 140: 296–300.

Goldman, Howard H. and Joseph P. Morrissey. 1985. "The Alchemy of Mental Health Policy: Homelessness and the Fourth Cycle of Reform." *American Journal of Public Health* 75: 727–31.

Goldman, Mark. 1983. *High Hopes: The Rise and Decline of Buffalo, New York*. Albany: State University of New York Press.

Goldstein, Michael S. 1979. "The Sociology of Mental Health and Illness." *Annual Review of Sociology* 5: 381–409.

Granger, William D. 1886. *How to Care for the Insane. A Manual for Attendants in Insane Asylums*. New York and London: G. P. Putnam's Sons.

———. 1894. "Memoir of Judson Boardman Andrews, M. D." *Transactions New York State Medical Association* 11: 646–53.

———. 1916. "First Training School for Attendants at the Buffalo State Hospital (Asylum), 1883–1886." Henry M. Hurd (ed.), *The Institutional Care of the Insane in the United States and Canada*. Vol. I. Baltimore: The Johns Hopkins Press: 301–309.

Grimes, John Maurice. 1934. *Institutional Care of Mental Patients in the United States*. Chicago: author.

Grob, Gerald N. 1966. *The State and the Mentally Ill: A History of the Worcester State Hospital in Massachusetts, 1830–1920*. Chapel Hill: The University of North Carolina Press.

———. 1973. *Mental Institutions in America: Social Policy to 1875*. New York: The Free Press.

———. 1979. "Rediscovering Asylums: the Unhistorical History of the Mental Hospital." Morris J. Vogel and Charles E. Rosenberg (eds.), *The Therapeutic Revolution: Essays in the Social History of American Medicine*. Philadelphia: University of Pennsylvania Press: 135–57.

———. 1979b. "Reflections on the History of Social Policy in America." *Reviews in American History*: 293–306.

———. 1980. "Abuse in American Mental Hospitals in Historical Perspective: Myth and Reality." *International Journal of Law and Psychiatry* 3: 295–310.

———. 1981. "Public Policy-Making and Social Policy." *Policy Studies Annual Review*: 703–30.

———. 1983. *Mental Illness and American Society, 1875–1940*. Princeton: Princeton University Press.

———. 1985. "The Origins of American Psychiatric Epidemiology." *American Journal of Public Health* 75: 229–36.

———. 1991. *From Asylum to Community: Mental Health Policy in Modern America*. Princeton: Princeton University Press.

Gronfein, William. 1985. "Incentives and Intentions in Mental Health Policy: a Comparison of the Medicaid and Community Mental Health Programs." *Journal of Health and Social Behavior* 26 (September): 192–206.

———. 1992. "Goffman's *Asylums* and the Social Control of the Mentally Ill." *Perspectives on Social Problems* 4: 129–53.

Gruenberg, Ernest M. and Janet Archer. 1979. "Abandonement of Responsibility for the Seriously Mentally Ill." *Milbank Memorial Fund Quarterly/Health and Society* 57: 485–506.

Hadley, Trevor R., Dennis P. Culhane, Frederick J. Snyder, and Theodore C. Lutterman. 1992. "Expenditure and Revenue Patterns of State Mental Health Agencies." *Administration and Policy in Mental Health* 19: 213–33.

Hadley, Trevor R. and Martin C. McGurrin. 1988. "Accreditation, Certification, and the Quality of Care in State Hospitals." *Hospital and Community Psychiatry* 39: 739–42.

Halliday, Terrence C., Michael J. Powell, and Mark W. Granfors. 1987. "Minimalist Organizations: Vital Events in State Bar Associations, 1870–1930." *American Sociological Review* 52 (August): 456–71.

Hamilton, Samuel W. and Mary E. Corcoran. n. d. [1942] "A Survey of the Buffalo State Hospital." Unpublished typescript, Director's Office, Buffalo Psychiatric Center.

Hamilton, Samuel W., Grover A. Kempf, Grace C. Scholz, and Eve G. Caswell. 1941. *A Study of the Public Mental Hospitals of the United States: 1937–1939*. Supplement No. 164 to the Public Health Reports. Washington: U. S. Public Health Service.

Hannan, Michael T. and John Freeman. 1989. *Organizational Ecology*. Cambridge: Harvard University Press.

Harring, Sidney L. 1983. *Policing A Class Society*. New Brunswick: Rutgers University Press.

Hauser, Robert M. 1982. "Occupational Status in the Nineteenth and Twentieth Centuries." *Historical Methods* 15: 111–26.

Hershberg, Theodore and Robert Dockhorn. 1976. "Occupational Classification." *Historical Methods Newsletter* 9: 59–98.

Hill, Henry Wayland (ed.). 1923. *Municipality of Buffalo, New York: A History*. 4 vols. New York: Lewis Historical Publishing Co.

Hilgartner, Stephen and Charles L. Bosk. 1988. "The Rise and Fall of Social Problems: A Public Arenas Model." *American Journal of Sociology* 94: 53–78.

Hitchcock, Henry-Russell. 1966. *The Architecture of H. H. Richardson and His Times*. Revised edition. Cambridge: The M. I. T. Press.

Hudson, Christopher G. 1990. "The Performance of State Community Mental Health Systems: A Path Model." *Social Service Review* 64: 94–120.

Hurd, Henry M. (ed.). 1914. *The Institutional Care of the Insane in the United States and Canada*. 4 vols. Baltimore: The Johns Hopkins Press.

Isaac, Larry W. and Larry J. Griffin. 1989. "Ahistoricism in Time-Series Analyses of Historical Process: Critique, Redirection, and Illustrations from U. S. Labor History." *American Historical Review* 54: 873–90.

Jarvis, Edward. 1855. *Insanity and Idiocy in Massachusetts: Report of the Commission on Lunacy, 1855*. With a critical introduction by Gerald N. Grob. Cambridge: Harvard University Press. [1955]

Joint Commission on Mental Illness and Health. 1961. *Action for Mental Health*. New York: Basic.

Johnson, Ann Braden. 1990. *Out of Bedlam: The Truth About Deinstitutionalization*. New York: Basic.

Katz, Michael B. 1978. "Origins of the Institutional State." *Marxist Perspectives* 1: 6–22.

———. 1983. *Poverty and Policy in American History*. New York: Academic Press.

———. 1984. "Poorhouses and the Origins of the Public Old Age Home." *Milbank Memorial Fund Quarterly/Health and Society* 62: 110–40.

———. 1986. *In the Shadow of the Poorhouse*. New York: Basic Books.

Katz, Michael B., Michael J. Doucet, and Mark J. Stern. 1982. *The Social Organization of Early Industrial Capitalism*. Cambridge: Harvard University Press.

Kiesler, Charles A. and Amy E. Sibulkin. 1987. *Mental Hospitalization: Myths and Facts About a National Crisis*. Newbury Park, CA: Sage.

Knoke, David. 1982. "The Spread of Municipal Reform: Temporal, Spatial, and Social Dynamics." *American Journal of Sociology* 87 (May): 1314–39.

Kowsky, Francis R. 1980a. "The William Dorsheimer House: a Reflection of French Suburban Architecture in the Early Work of H. H. Richardson." *The Art Bulletin* 62: 134–47.

———. 1980b. *Buffalo Projects: H. H. Richardson*. Buffalo: Buffalo State College Foundation.

———. 1980c. *The Architecture of Frederick Clarke Withers and the Progress of the Gothic Revival in America after 1850*. Middletown, Conn.: Wesleyan University Press.

La Fond, John Q. and Mary L. Durham. 1992. *Back to the Asylum*. New York: Oxford.

Lerman, Paul. 1982. *Deinstitutionalization and the Welfare State*. New Brunswick: Rutgers.

Levine, Murray. 1980. *From State Hospital to Psychiatric Center*. Lexington: D. C. Heath.

Lipton, Alan A. and Franklin S. Simon. 1985. "Psychiatric Diagnosis in a State Hospital: Manhattan State Revisited." *Hospital and Community Psychiatry* 36: 368–73.

Lutterman, Theodore C., Noel A. Mazade, Cecil R. Wurster, and Robert W. Glover. 1988. "Expenditures and Revenues of State Mental Health Agencies, 1981–1985." *Hospital and Community Psychiatry* 39: 758–62.

March, James G. 1981. "Footnotes to Organizational Change." *Administrative Science Quarterly* 26: 563–77.

Marshall, James R. and George W. Dowdall. 1982. "Employment and Mental Hospitalization: the Case of Buffalo, New York, 1914–1955." *Social Forces* 60: 843–53.

Marshall, James R. and Donna P. Funch. 1979. "Mental Illness and the Economy: A Critique and Partial Replication." *Journal of Health and Social Behavior* 20: 282–89.

McGovern, Constance M. 1985. *Masters of Madness.* Hanover: University Press of New England.

Mechanic, David. 1980. *Mental Health and Social Policy.* 2nd ed. Englewood Cliffs, N. J.: Prentice-Hall.

———. 1986. "The Challenge of Chronic Mental Illness: A Retrospective and Prospective View." *Hospital and Community Psychiatry* 37: 891–896.

Meyer, John W. and W. Richard Scott. 1983. *Organizational Environments: Ritual and Rationality.* Beverly Hills: Sage.

Meyer, Marshall W. and Lynne G. Zucker. 1989. *Permanently Failing Organizations.* Newbury Park, CA: Sage.

Miller, Robert D. 1981. "Beyond the Old State Hospital: New Opportunities Ahead." *Hospital and Community Psychiatry* 32: 27–31.

Mitchell, S. Weir. 1894. "Address Before the Fiftieth Annual Meeting of the American Medico-Psychological Association, held in Philadelphia, May 16th, 1894." *The Journal of Nervous and Mental Disease* 21 (July): 413–37.

Morgan, David R. and Michael W. Hirlinger. 1989. "Socioeconomic Dimensions of the American States: An Update." *Social Science Quarterly* 70: 184–96.

Morrissey, Joseph P. 1989. "The Changing Role of the Public Mental Hospital." David A. Rochefort (ed.), *Handbook on Mental Health Policy in the United States.* New York: Greenwood Press: 311–38.

Morrissey, Joseph P. and Howard H. Goldman. 1984. "Cycles of Reform in the Care of the Chronically Mentally Ill." *Hospital and Community Psychiatry* 35: 785–93.

Morrissey, Joseph P., Howard H. Goldman, and Lorraine V. Klerman. 1980. *The Enduring Asylum: Cycles of Institutional Reform at Worcester State Hospital*. New York: Grune and Stratton.

National Institute of Mental Health. 1983. *Mental Health, United States 1983*. Washington: U. S. Department of Health and Human Services.

————. 1986. *State and County Mental Hospitals—United States and Each State, 1986*. Washington: U. S. Government Printing Office.

————. 1988. "List of State and County Mental Hospitals, 1987–88." Unpublished data. Rockville, MD: NIMH.

New York State. 1872–1984. *Annual Report of the Buffalo State Asylum for the Insane*. Albany: State of New York. (title, author, and publisher vary.)

New York State Office of Mental Health. 1992. *Preliminary Report to the Governor and the Legislature on the Future of State Psychiatric Inpatient Care for Adults, Including Individual Facility Capital Plans for the Western Region*. Albany: author.

New York State Office of Mental Health. 1993a. *Statewide Chartbook of Mental Health Information, 1992*. Albany: author.

Ochsner, Jeffrey Karl. 1982. *H. H. Richardson: Complete Architectural Works*. Cambridge: The MIT Press.

O'Gorman, James F. 1974. *H. H. Richardson and His Office: A Centennial of His Move to Boston*. Cambridge: Department of Printing and Graphic Arts, Harvard College Library and David R. Godine.

Ouchi, William G. and Alan L. Wilkins. 1985. "Organizational Culture." *Annual Review of Sociology* 11: 457–83.

Ozarin, Lucy. 1989. "State Hospitals as Acute Care Facilities." *Hospital and Community Psychiatry* 40: 5.

Paul, Sister Mary. 1984. "Contributions of the Daughters of Charity to Health Care, 1800–1980." Unpublished typescript, Sisters of Charity Hospital, Buffalo, New York.

Pavalko, Eliza K. 1989. "State Timing of Policy Adoption: Workmen's Compensation in the United States, 1909–1929." *American Journal of Sociology* 95: 592–615.

Pinchoff, Diane M., and Mahmud Mirza. 1982. "The Changing Role of the State Hospital Director: Restructuring the Top Management Team." *Administration in Mental Health* 10: 92–103.

Potter, William Warren. 1895. "Special Article. 1845—Then and Now— 1895. Fifty Years of Medical Journalism in Buffalo." *Buffalo Medical Journal* 35: 65–113.

Powell, Walter W. and Paul J. DiMaggio. 1991. *The New Institutionalism in Organizational Analysis*. Chicago: University of Chicago Press.

Ratcliff, Kathryn Strother. 1980. "On Marshall and Funch's Critique of 'Mental Illness and the Economy.'" *Journal of Health and Social Behavior* 21: 389–91.

Rochefort, David (ed.). 1989. *Handbook on Mental Health Policy in the United States*. New York: Greenwood Press.

Rosenberg, Charles E. 1962. *The Cholera Years: The United States in 1832, 1849, and 1866*. Chicago: The University of Chicago Press.

———. 1968. *The Trial of the Assassin Guiteau: Psychiatry and Law in the Guilded Age*. Chicago: The University of Chicago Press.

———. 1981. "Inward Vision and Outward Glance: the Shaping of the American Hospital, 1880–1914." David J. Rothman and Stanton Wheeler (eds.), *Social History and Social Policy*. New York: Academic Press: 19–55.

———. 1987. *The Care of Strangers: The Rise of America's Hospital System*. New York: Basic Books.

Rothstein, William G. 1972. *American Physicians in the Nineteenth Century*. Baltimore: The Johns Hopkins University Press.

Rothman, David J. 1971. *The Discovery of the Asylum: Social Order and Disorder in the New Republic*. Boston: Little, Brown.

———. 1980. *Conscience and Convenience: The Asylum and Its Alternatives in Progressive America*. Boston: Little, Brown.

Schinaar, A. P., A. B. Rothbard, D. Yin, and T. Lutterman. 1992. "Public Choice and Organizational Determinants of State Mental Health Expenditure Patterns." *Administration and Policy in Mental Health* 19: 235–50.

Scull, Andrew T. 1977. *Decarceration: Community Treatment and the Deviant: A Radical View*. Englewood Cliffs, N.J.: Prentice-Hall.

———. 1979. *Museums of Madness: The Social Organization of Insanity in nineteenth Century England*. New York: St. Martin's Press.

———. 1981. "Humanitarianism or Control? Some Observations on the Historiography of Anglo-American Psychiatry." *Rice University Studies* 67: 21–41.

———. 1984. "Afterword: 1983." *Decarceration*. 2nd edition. New Brunswick, NJ: Rutgers University Press: 161–89.

———. 1989. *Social Order/Mental Disorder: Anglo-American Psychiatry in Historical Perspective*. Berkeley and Los Angeles: University of California Press.

Sheehan, Susan. 1982. *Is There No Place on Earth for Me?* Boston: Houghton Mifflin.

———. 1995. "The Last Days of Sylvia Frumkin." *The New Yorker* Feb. 20 and 27, 1995: 200–11.

Singh, Jitendra and Charles J. Lumsden. 1990. "Theory and Research in Organizational Ecology." *Annual Review of Sociology* 16: 161–95.

Smith, Christopher J. and Robert Hanham. 1981. "Deinstitutionalization of the Mentally Ill: a Time Path Analysis of the American States, 1955–1975." *Social Science and Medicine* 15D: 361–78.

Smith, H. Perry (ed.). 1884. *History of the City of Buffalo and Erie County, with Illustrations and Biographical Sketches of Some of its Prominent Men and Pioneers*. Syracuse: D. Mason & Co.

Spaulding, John M. 1986. "The Canton Asylum for Insane Indians: An Example of Institutional Neglect." *Hospital and Community Psychiatry* 37: 1007–11.

Staples, William G. 1991. *Castles of Our Conscience*. New Brunswick: Rutgers.

Starr, Paul. 1982. *The Social Transformation of American Medicine*. New York: Basic Books.

State Board of Charities. 1883–1888. *Annual Report*. Albany: New York State.

State Commission in Lunacy. 1892. *Third Annual Report*. Albany: New York State.

Stern, Mark Jay. 1979. *The Demography of Capitalism: Industry, Class, and Fertility in Erie County, New York, 1855–1915*. Unpublished doctoral dissertation, York University.

Stevens, Rosemary. 1989. *In Sickness and In Wealth: American Hospitals in the Twentieth Century*. New York: Basic Books.

Stinchcombe, Arthur. 1965. "Social Structure and Organizations." James G. March (ed.), *Handbook of Organizations*. Chicago: Rand McNally: 142–93.

Stryjewski, Joseph. 1979. "A Retrospective Study of the Incare Census of the Buffalo Psychiatric Center from April 1974 to March 1978." Unpublished paper, Buffalo Psychiatric Center.

Sutton, John R. 1988. *Stubborn Children: Controlling Delinquency in the United States, 1640–1981*. Berkeley: University of California Press.

Talbott, John A. 1978. *The Death of the Asylum: A Critical Study of State Hospital Management, Services, and Care*. New York: Grune and Stratton.

———. 1979. "Deinstitutionalization: Avoiding the Disasters of the Past." *Hospital and Community Psychiatry* 30: 621–24.

———. 1985. "The Fate of the Public Psychiatric System." *Hospital and Community Psychiatry* 36: 46–50.

Taube, Carl A., David Mechanic, and Ann A. Hohmann. 1989. *The Future of Mental Health Services Research*. Rockville, MD: National Institute of Mental Health.

Timon, John. 1862. *Missions in Western New York, and Church History of the Diocese of Buffalo, by the Bishop of Buffalo*. Buffalo: Catholic Sentinel Press.

Tolbert, Pamela S. and Lynne G. Zucker. 1983. "Institutional Sources of Change in the Formal Structure of Organizations: the Diffusion of Civil Service Reform, 1880–1935." *Administrative Science Quarterly* 28 (March): 22–39.

Tomes, Nancy. 1978. " 'Little World of Our Own': the Pennsylvania Hospital Training School for Nurses, 1895–1907." *Journal of the History of Medicine and Allied Sciences* 33: 507–30.

———. 1981. "A Generous Confidence: Thomas Story Kirkbride's Philosphy of Asylum Construction and Management." Andrew Scull (ed.), *Madhouses, Mad-Doctors, and Madmen*. Philadelphia: University of Pennsylvania Press: 121–43.

———. 1984. *A Generous Confidence*. New York: Cambridge Univerity Press.

Toner, J. M. 1873. "Statistics of Regular Medical Associations and Hospitals of the United States." *Transactions of the American Medical Association* 24: 314–33.

Torrey, E. Fuller. 1988. *Nowhere to Go*. New York: Harper & Row.

Torrey, E. Fuller, Sidney M. Wolfe, and Laurie M. Flynn. 1988. *Care of the Seriously Mentally Ill: A Rating of State Programs*. 2nd edition. Washington, D.C.: Public Citizen Health Research Group and the National Alliance for the Mentally Ill.

Torrey, E. Fuller, Karen Erdman, Sidney M. Wolfe, and Laurie M. Flynn. 1990. *Care of the Seriously Mentally Ill: A Rating of State Programs*. 3rd edition. Washington, D. C.: Public Citizen Health Research Group and the National Alliance for the Mentally Ill.

Treiman, Donald. 1976a. *Occupational Prestige in Comparative Perspective.* New York: Academic Press.

———. 1976b. "A Standard Occupational Prestige Scale for Use with Historical Data." *Journal of Interdisciplinary History* 7: 283–304.

Tyor, Peter L. and Jamil S. Zainaldin. 1979. "Asylum and Society: An Approach to Institutional Change." *Journal of Social History* 13: 23–48.

Utica State Asylum. 1843–1980. *Annual Report.* Albany: New York State.

Vogel, Morris J. 1980. *The Invention of the Modern Hospital: Boston, 1870–1930.* Chicago: The University of Chicago Press.

Ward, Mary Jane. 1946. *The Snake Pit.* New York: Random House.

Weick, Karl E. 1976. "Educational Organizations as Loosely Coupled Systems." *Administrative Science Quarterly* 21: 1–19.

Willard, Sylvester D. 1865. *Report on the Condition of the Insane Poor in the County Poor Houses of New York.* Albany: Chas. Van Benthuysen, Printer.

Wise, P. M. 1896. *A Text-book for Training Schools for Nurses, Including Physiology and Hygiene and the Principles and Practice of Nursing.* 2 vols. New York and London: G. P. Putnam's Sons.

Wright, Frank L. 1947. *Out of Sight, Out of Mind.* Philadelphia: National Mental Health Foundation.

Young, Ruth C. 1988. "Is Population Ecology a Useful Paradigm for the Study of Organizations?" *American Journal of Sociology* 94 (July): 1–24.

———. 1989. "Reply to Freeman and Hannan and Brittain and Wholey." *American Journal of Sociology* 95: 445–46.

Zucker, Lynne G. 1987. "Institutional Theories of Organization." *Annual Review of Sociology* 13: 443–64.

———. 1988. *Institutional Patterns and Organizations: Culture and Environment.* Cambridge: Ballinger.

———. 1989. "Combining Institutional Theory and Population Ecology: No Legitimacy, No History. (Comment on Carroll-Hannan.)" *American Sociological Review* 54: 542–45.

Index